The Best Olympics Ever?

SUNY series, Sport, Culture, and Social Relations
C.L. Cole and Michael A. Messner, editors

Alan M. Klein, *Little Big Men: Bodybuilding Subculture and Gender Construction*

Todd, W. Crosset, *Outsiders in the Clubhouse: The World of Women's Professional Golf*

Wanda Ellen Wakefield, *Playing to Win: Sports and the American Military, 1898–1945*

Laurel R. Davis, *The Swimsuit Issue and Sport: Hegemonic Masculinity in Sports Illustrated*

Jim McKay, *Managing Gender: Affirmative Action and Organizational Power in Australian, Canadian, and New Zealand Sport*

Juan-Miguel Fernandez-Balboa (ed.), *Critical Postmodernism in Human Movement, Physical Education, and Sport*

Genevieve Rail (ed.), *Sport and Postmodern Times*

Shona M. Thompson, *Mother's Taxi: Sport and Women's Labor*

Nancy Theberge, *Higher Goals: Women's Ice Hockey and the Politics of Gender*

Helen Jefferson Lenskyj, *Inside the Olympic Industry: Power, Politics, and Activism*

C. Richard King and Charles Fruehling Springwood (eds.), *Beyond the Cheers: Race as Spectacle in College Sport*

David Andrews (ed.), *Michael Jordan, Inc.: Corporate Sport, Media Culture, and Late Modern America*

Margaret Gatz, Michael A. Messner, and Sandra J. Ball-Rokeach (eds.), *Paradoxes of Youth and Sport*

Helen Jefferson Lenskyj, *The Best Olympics Ever? Social Impacts of Sydney 2000*

The Best Olympics Ever?

Social Impacts of Sydney 2000

Helen Jefferson Lenskyj

STATE UNIVERSITY OF NEW YORK PRESS

Published by
State University of New York Press, Albany

For information, address State University of New York Press,
90 State Street, Suite 700, Albany, NY 12207

Production by Judith Block
Marketing by Patrick Durocher

Library of Congress Cataloging-in-Publication Data

Lenskyj, Helen Jefferson.
     The best Olympics ever? : social impacts of Sydney 2000 / Helen Jefferson
Lenskyj.
         p. cm. — (SUNY series, sport, culture, and social relations)
     Includes bibliographical references (p.) and index.
     ISBN 0-7914-5473-8 (alk. paper) — ISBN 0-7914-5474-6 (pbk. : alk. paper)
         1. Olympic Games (27th : 2000 : Sydney, N.S.W.) 2. Olympics—Social
aspects—Australia—History. 3. Olympics—Economic aspects—Australia—History.
I. Title. II. SUNY series on sport, culture, and social relations.

GV722 2000 .L46 2002
796.48—dc21   2001055121

10 9 8 7 6 5 4 3 2 1

Contents

—*ᕦᕤ*—

Acknowledgments

rencied

I would like to thank all the community leaders and activists in Sydney who generously gave their time and energy to help me complete this book. Without their invaluable input, the book would simply not have been written. I also wish to acknowledge the University of New South Wales Center for Olympic Studies, where I spent over four months as a visiting scholar. Its director, Prof. Richard Cashman, and coordinator, Tony Hughes, were most supportive and gracious hosts, and the center provided me with a welcoming academic home while I was in Sydney completing the research for this book.

Once again, friends and colleagues at the University of Toronto, the University of New South Wales, the University of Technology Sydney, and elsewhere have been most supportive and helpful, as, of course, has my home department, Sociology and Equity Studies in Education, at the Ontario Institute for Studies in Education of the University of Toronto.

Prof. Jim McKay, of the University of Queensland, and the anononymous reviewers provided constructive criticism and helpful feedback on the first draft of this book, and I am grateful for their serious engagement with my work.

Thanks to State University of New York Press acquisitions editors Ron Helfrich and Dale Cotton, to Sport, Culture, and Social Relations series editors C. L. Cole and Michael A. Messner, production editor Judith Block, marketing manager Patrick Durocher, and copyeditor Marilyn Silverman. Thank you to Liz Green for her invaluable help with research and proofreading, and Jeanie Stewart for indexing assistance.

Finally, I would like to thank my partner and my children, without whose love and support this would not have been possible.

Abbreviations and Websites

—◦◦◦—

Aboriginal and Torres Strait Islander Commission (ATSIC) <www.atsic.gov.au>
Anti-Olympic Alliance (AOA) <www.cat.org.au/aoa/news.html>
Associated Press (AP)
Australian Broadcasting Commission (ABC) <www.abc.net.au>
Australian Bureau of Statistics (ABS) <www.abs.gov.au>
Australian Capital Territory (ACT)
Australian Defence Force (ADF)
Australian Federal Police (AFP) <www.afp.gov.au>
Australian Greens <www.greens.org.au>
Australian Institute of Health and Welfare (AIHW)
Australian Labor Party (ALP)
Australian Olympic Committee (AOC)
Australian Security Intelligence Organization (ASIO) <www.asio.gov.au>
Australian Society for Sport History (ASSH)
Australian Tourist Commission (ATC) <www.atc.net.au>
Bankstown Bushland Society (BBS)
Bondi Olympic Watch (BOW)
Cable News Network (CNN)
Campaign Against Corporate Tyranny with Unity and Solidarity (CACTUS)
Canadian Association for the Advancement of Women and Sport (CAAWS)
Canadian Broadcasting Corporation (CBC)
Central business district (CBD)
Committee for the Elimination of Racial Discrimination (CERD)
Daily Telegraph <www.dailytelegraph.news.com.au>
Darling Harbor Authority (DHA)
Darug Tribal Aboriginal Corporation (DTAC)
Department of Foreign Affairs and Trade (DFAT) <www.dfat.gov.au>
Entertainment and Sports Programming Network (ESPN)
Environmental Protection Agency (EPA)
Federal Olympic Security Intelligence Center (FOSIC)
Federation Internationale de Volleyball (FIVB)
Goods and Services Tax (GST)
Green Games Watch 2000 (GGW2000)
Green Left Weekly <www.greenleft.org.au>
Greenpeace Australia <www.greenpeace.org.au>
The Guardian (U. K.) <www.guardianunlimited.co.uk>
Homebush Bay Environmental Reference Group (HomBERG)

Homeless Persons' Information Center (HPIC)
Human Rights and Equal Opportunity Commission (HREOC)
Indigenous Social Justice Association (ISJA)
International Olympic Committee (IOC) <www.olympic.org>
Liquor, Hospitality and Miscellaneous Workers Union (LHMU) <lhmu.org.au/union/>
Local government area (LGA)
Main Press Center (MPC)
Melbourne Indymedia <www.s11.org>
Member of the Legislative Assembly (MLA)
National Broadcasting Company (NBC)
National Indigenous Advisory Committee (NIAC)
New South Wales (NSW)
New South Wales Council of Social Services (NCOSS) <www.ncoss.org.au>
New South Wales Government <www.nsw.gov.au>
New York Times <www.nytimes.com>
Northern Territory (NT)
Not in my backyard (NIMBY)
Olympic Coordination Authority (OCA) <www.oca.nsw.gov.au>
Olympic Impact Coalition (OIC)
People Ingeniously Subverting the Sydney Olympic Farce Forever (PISSOFF)
Public Interest Advocacy Center (PIAC)
Public Service Association (PSA) <www.psa.labor.net.au>
Redfern Legal Center (RLC)
Resident action group (RAG)
Salt Lake Olympic Committee (SLOC)
School Administration and Support Staff (SASS)
Social Impact Advisory Committee (SIAC)
State Environment Planning Policy (SEPP)
Statement of Environmental Effects (SEE)
Student Representative Council, UTS (SRC)
Sunday Times (UK) <www.sunday-times.co.uk>
Sydney Alternative Media Center (SAMC) <www.samcentre.org>
Sydney Harbor Foreshore Authority (SHFA)
Sydney Housing Action Collective (SHAC) <www.shac.net>
Sydney Independent Media Center (IMC) <www.sydney.indymedia.org>
Sydney Morning Herald (Herald) <www.smh.com.au>
Sydney Organizing Committee for the Olympic Games (SOCOG)
    <www.sydney.olympic.org>
Sydney Paralympic Organizing Committee (SPOC)
Technical and Further Education (TAFE)
Textile, Clothing and Footwear Union of Australia (TCFUA)
Toronto Star <www.thestar.com>
United States Olympic Committee (USOC)
University of NSW (UNSW) <www.unsw.edu.au>
University of Technology Sydney (UTS) <www.uts.edu.au>
University of Western Ontario (UWO)
Victoria University of Technology (VUT)
Village Voice <www.villagevoice.com>
Waverly Council <www.waverly.nsw.gov.au>
Western Australia (WA)
World Economic Forum (WEF)

Note: all information on NSW and Australian legislation was obtained from the
Australian Law Information website <www.austlii.edu.au>

Introduction

—∞∞∞—

When Spanish-speaking International Olympic Committee (IOC) president Juan Antonio Samaranch announced in 1993 that Sydney (which he pronounced with three syllables as Syd-en-ee) had won the right to host the 2000 Summer Games, his statement went down in Australian journalism history as the favorite way to begin an article on the Sydney Olympics. Seven years later, journalists, along with Olympic organizers and most Australians, awaited Samaranch's second magic utterance: that Sydney 2000 was the "best Olympics ever". They were not disappointed.

It is safe to predict that the vast majority of trade books and articles, along with many academic publications, will follow the "best ever" model, and that there will be no dearth of sources that praise the successes of Sydney 2000. I do not deny that there were positive outcomes, but it is not the purpose of this book to examine them in detail. My goal is to disclose what the Sydney 2000 Olympic industry suppressed: the real Olympic costs and impacts, the forgotten victims of Olympic-related housing and homelessness crises, the unrecognized and undermined efforts of community organizations, the Olympic industry's co-optation of universities, Sydney 2000's "symbolic reconciliation" efforts in light of over two hundred years of Indigenous people's suffering, and other key social issues related to Sydney's Olympic preparations. While the event itself is the topic of chapter 9, most of the discussion focuses on the period leading up to September 2000.

In taking this political approach, I make no claim that the book is comprehensive or balanced, or that it employs a traditional scholarly approach. Rather, it is an attempt to examine social inequities generated or exacerbated by Sydney's Olympic preparations from the perspective of disadvantaged people whose voices would not otherwise be heard. In terms

An earlier version of part of this chapter, titled "The More Things Change: Women, Sport, and the Olympic Industry, 1900–2000," appeared in *Fireweed* 71/72, 2000, pp. 78–83.

of data collection, I relied more on independent individuals and groups than on state or Olympic industry sources, although a comprehensive sample of official documentation is examined (see the appendix). My analysis is grounded in basic principles of participatory democracy: that citizens have the right to participate in decisions that affect their futures, and that *conscientization* and collective community action constitute effective routes to empowerment (Alinsky, 1971; Freire, 1973).

As early as 1976, the French sport critic Jean-Marie Brohm identified the threats posed by the "capitalist sports industry," exemplified by the Olympic Games, and called for "anti-Olympic propaganda and agitation on the basis of the principles of proletarian internationalism . . . to expose the machinations of bourgeois states against the oppressed classes and peoples" (Brohm, 1978 [English translation], 174). Many of Brohm's predictions were borne out in the 1976 Montreal Olympics, as critical analyses such as Nick Auf der Maur's (1976) demonstrated. However, it was not until the late 1980s that international anti-Olympic organizing began to have some measurable impact, as I have shown in my earlier book on the topic (Lenskyj, 2000). On a related front, British investigative journalists Vyv Simson and Andrew Jennings coauthored the first major exposé of Olympic bidding processes, *The Lords of the Rings,* in 1993, followed by Jennings's *The New Lords of the Rings* in 1996 and *The Great Olympic Swindle* in 2000; the first two books were often dismissed as journalistic hyperbole until the 1999 disclosures of improprieties in the Salt Lake City bid process amply demonstrated the validity of their claims.

Extensive research on the Olympics and other hallmark events has shown that, even when they are staged in democratic countries, the usual practices of public consultation and involvement in decisions regarding urban planning and development, environmental and social impact assessments, tenants' rights, police powers and public behavior, and freedom of speech and public assembly are often jeopardized (see, e.g., Cox, 1998; Lenskyj, 2000; Wamsley & Heine, 1996; Whitson & Macintosh, 1996). As Brent Ritchie and Michael Hall (2000, 8) summarized the problem, "In focusing on one narrow set of commercial, economic and political interests in the pursuit of major sporting events such as the Olympics, other community and social interests, particularly those of inner-city residents, are increasingly neglected." Therefore, by giving community and social interests a central place in the analysis, I intend to address the imbalance created by the powerful Olympic industry.

Background to the Research

I was born in Sydney in 1943 and lived there until 1966, when I moved to Toronto. I remain an Australian by citizenship and by self-identification, a fact that guided me in writing this book. While I was living in Sydney in 2000—and attending meetings of Olympic watchdog groups, interviewing community leaders, and listening to Olympic industry rhetoric on all fronts—I had mixed feelings. I hoped that everything would go smoothly in September 2000, especially for my friends and colleagues who were planning a variety of protest actions. On the other hand, I had serious concerns, since evidence from community groups, police sources, and the mass media suggested that the probability of violent police action directed at protesters, especially Indigenous protesters, was high.

As events unfolded, it became clear that I had underestimated the power of the Olympic industry to engage the mass media and government departments, in order to achieve its goal of a superficially problem-free Olympics. In the months before the Games, community groups across a broad political spectrum faced the challenge of forming effective coalitions on Olympic-related issues. At the same time, their efforts were seriously undermined from the outside by various agencies of the state. Unfortunately, by September 14, it was clear that the promised mass rally on the opening day would not take place. And, for sixteen days, international television viewers saw only the "best ever" Olympic facade, rather than the real story of Sydney 2000.

In many respects, this book constitutes a continuation of my first Olympic book, *Inside the Olympic Industry: Power, Politics and Activism* (Lenskyj, 2000). Although each book stands alone, they make better sense read sequentially. Because of the need to have minimal overlap between the two books, the detailed examination of Homebush Bay environmental issues, found in my first book, is not repeated here. A detailed discussion of the methodology may be found in the appendix.

Olympic Critiques and Consequences

When I began working in the field of sport sociology in 1980, my initial focus was on women, sport, and sexuality. I subsequently specialized in research on systemic discrimination, the chilly climate, and sexual and homophobic harassment experienced by women, particularly lesbians, in sport and recreation contexts. Despite the often controversial nature of this research, I rarely encountered as much resistance and hostility from professional and academic colleagues as I have in the last few years as a result of my critiques of the Olympic industry. I am not, of course, alone in experiencing its far-reaching powers, as the following example will illustrate.

In October 1999, a Canadian Broadcasting Corporation (CBC) television researcher invited me to be a panelist at a community forum on the Toronto 2008 Olympic bid. The other invited participants included prominent Olympic critics: Andrew Jennings, author of *The New Lords of the*

Rings (1996); Michael Shapcott, one of the founders of the Bread Not Circuses Coalition, a Toronto Olympic watchdog organization; David Hulchanski, a University of Toronto professor and internationally known expert on housing and homelessness; and Michael Walker, a Toronto councillor. David Crombie, chair, and/or John Bitove, CEO of the Toronto bid committee, were also participants.

In January 2000, the researcher contacted me again, this time with an invitation to take a front row seat at the forum on January 11. I replied that I had been invited to join the panel, not the audience. When I asked for the new list of panelists, his reply made it clear that all the high-profile critics, except for Walker, had been dropped. Most significantly, Shapcott, Hulchanski, and I had all been downgraded to members of the audience, and Jennings had disappeared. When I asked whether it was the case that the Toronto bid committee leaders (Crombie and Bitove) had refused to take part if Shapcott, Hulchanski, and Lenskyj were on the stage, the researcher admitted that this was true. He also told another Bread Not Circuses member, Jan Borowy, that it would have been "impossible to mount a forum with Lenskyj or Hulchanski sitting on the panel" and said he felt "set up" because the Toronto bid was "dictating" who would participate.

The Chilly Climate for Olympic Critics

It is important to understand the forces that are generating the chilly climate experienced by Olympic critics in university-based sport studies and Olympic studies, as well as in women's sport circles. It is clear that some Olympic scholars are merely sycophants of the Olympic industry, and gain financial, material, and symbolic privileges by maintaining an uncritical stance. The rewards include (often subsidized) international travel, research grants, publications, a high media profile, and, most significantly, honorary membership in the "Olympic Family"—a status that brings its own unique rewards and accolades. For their part, some academics are motivated less by personal gain than by the need to generate funds for the university-based centers for Olympic studies established in Australia, Canada, Europe, and elsewhere in the 1980s and 1990s. Regardless of the rationale, financial arrangements between universities, Olympic sponsors, and national Olympic committees pose a threat to free and open debate and critique of the Olympic industry, as I will demonstrate in chapter 6.

A recent Australian example illustrates some of the benefits of "Olympic Family" membership. In the 1980s, David Fidler, a Darwin television news broadcaster, had created a false identity as an Olympian, claiming that he had been a member of the Australian swim team at the 1968 Olympics in Mexico City. For fifteen years, Fidler had traded on that myth to boost his television career. But apparently, for an Australian media personality, posing as an Olympic athlete is a much more serious offense than making blatantly racist statements on air. Unlike notorious Sydney "shock-jock" Ron Casey, who was given a second chance at good behavior before being forced to quit his job in May 2000 because of his racist on-air statements, Fidler had to resign as soon as his mythical "Olympian" identity was exposed earlier that year (Temple, 2000).

Women's Sport and Olympic Critique: Not a Good Mix

The chilly climate for Olympic critics within women's sport circles—both academic and professional—can largely be explained by the predominance of liberal feminist perspectives in that context. As has been the pattern in other areas of feminist movements—both its first wave at the beginning of this century and its second wave at the end—feminist sport activists tend to be divided, in broad terms, into liberals and radicals. Liberal feminist approaches, which have dominated women's sport advocacy and research in Australia, Canada, the United States, and the UK, usually defined gender equality in terms of girls' and women's access to the same or equivalent sporting opportunities as boys and men. The liberal agenda called for the removal of policy and legislative barriers that prevented (White, middle-class) girls and women from enjoying the same sporting opportunities as their male counterparts; in short, liberal feminists wanted to reform rather than transform existing social structures.

For women holding this liberal political position, increased female participation, particularly in competitive sport, represented a major step forward, and there is no doubt that liberal feminist initiatives produced a number of important gains, particularly over the last thirty years when many of the remaining barriers to female participation, at least in Western countries, were finally removed. However, given the tendency to theorize inequality primarily in terms of gender, liberal approaches paid insufficient attention to the links between sexism, racism, classism, and homophobia in sport, and as a result the gains were not equally distributed throughout the female population (Lenskyj, 1992).

In the first three decades of the twentieth century, the liberal approach manifested itself locally in the move toward more interschool and intercollegiate sporting competition for girls and women, and internationally, in efforts to have more female athletes and more women's events at multisport spectacles such as the (British) Commonwealth Games and the Olympic Games. By the end of the twentieth century, the Olympics had become one of the major forces dictating the organization of female sport domestically as well as internationally. The possibility that the male model of sport, exemplified by Olympic competition, needed reforming—or even transforming—was rarely contemplated. It is valid to argue, of course, that since feminism is about choices, girls and women who simply desire equal access to the same sporting opportunities as boys and men deserve that right, and should not be called upon to be pioneers in transforming existing sporting practices. Nevertheless, simple equality should not be confused with either equity or social justice.

In liberal women's sport contexts today, the mythical allure of the Olympics and Olympians shapes the political agenda in both symbolic and material ways. Despite the stated goals of promoting recreational sporting opportunities for girls and women of all ages and ability levels, many women's sport advocacy organizations continue to give Olympic sport and Olympic sportswomen top billing. As is the pattern in mainstream society, the Olympic credentials of women in sport leadership positions within these organizations are routinely flaunted, with little apparent attention given to the chilling effect this practice might have on "rank-and-file" members with neither Olympic experience nor Olympic aspirations. In one of the early planning meetings of Women's Sport International, for example, much of the discussion centered on the need to eliminate (female) gender testing from the Olympics. The argument that this issue affected only a tiny minority of women internationally and did not deserve such a high priority in an organization purportedly concerned with the broader goal of promoting mass female sporting participation was not seriously addressed.

In the year of the Sydney Olympics, stories of Olympic sportswomen dominated women's sport media in Australia, Canada, and the United States, thereby reflecting the long-standing popular wisdom that female Olympians are optimal "role models" for girls and women of all ages, abilities, and backgrounds. Not only mainstream magazines but also those published by women's sport advocacy groups demonstrated the same preoccupation with Olympic sport, as story after story reflected the assumption that there was an unbroken line between community recreation and Olympic competition, and that Olympic sportswomen provided an unproblematic example for all girls and women to follow.

Uncritical reliance on the "role model" approach seems to imply that the major barrier to female sporting participation is lack of imagination and inspiration: in other words, "it's all in our heads." Girls and women simply need to see concrete evidence of female athleticism—preferably a "role model" who is similar to themselves and who has achieved her "Olympic dream"—in order to realize that they, too, can succeed in sport, according to this way of thinking. Alarmingly reminiscent of Nike's Just Do It slogan, this approach ignores the systemic barriers facing girls and women, as manifested in their everyday experiences of racism, sexism, classism, and homophobia.

There is extensive research evidence from a number of countries demonstrating that girls and women tend to value the social side of sport—the fun and friendship—more than their male counterparts, who are more likely to put winning and beating their opponents at the top of their list of priorities. This does not mean that female athletes don't want to win, or that male athletes don't enjoy the camaraderie, but rather that there are some gender-related patterns of priorities, even at the level of high performance sport (Lenskyj, 1994). However, programs that attempted to promote friendship and cultural exchange among Olympic athletes have not been hugely successful, largely because of nationalistic fervor and the preoccupation with winning. It was well-known that professional athletes—the American basketball team, for example—rejected the athletes' village in favor of more luxurious accommodations during recent Olympics, and as September 2000 approached, there were stories in the Sydney and Toronto media about several other Olympic competitors who chose not to stay in the village. Former Olympic athletes have spoken of coach and peer pressure to avoid mingling with athletes from other countries; some have even been ridiculed for visiting art galleries or reading local newspapers while on tour. For their part, coaches would no doubt argue that they had to control athletes' training regimes and free time in order to ensure peak performance.

It is not difficult to understand why young Olympic athletes choose not to rock the boat. On the one hand, their status brings with it considerable symbolic privilege, and in the case of professional athletes, financial and material benefits as well. On the other hand, it is difficult for most athletes to challenge coaches' and administrators' power over their lives. In light of these realities, why pretend that Olympic sport is about anything other than winning? In April 2000, retired Australian Olympic swimmer Nicole Stevenson was quoted in the *Sydney Morning Herald* in an article on the athletes' village: "Unfortunately, some of the younger athletes are so amazed by how big and how wonderful it [the Village] is, they lose sight that they are there for one reason—to compete" (Stevenson quoted in Bernoth, 2000). One might ask about the cultural celebrations and exchanges, the contribution to international understanding, the festival of world youth, the camaraderie of the Olympic village, and all the other intangible benefits that are the staples of "Olympic spirit" rhetoric.

Recent developments in women's volleyball further demonstrate the pitfalls of "playing the game" by men's rules. The International Volleyball Federation decreed that female (but not male) players had to wear skimpy form-fitting bodysuits or face a fine of $US3,000. Some teams from richer countries paid the fines (and expressed their outrage), while women from the have-not teams such as Cuba's had to wear the revealing uniforms. Clothing requirements for women in international beach volleyball competition similarly exploit female bodies to sell the sport, and in the case of the temporary Olympic beach volleyball stadium on Sydney's famous Bondi Beach, this sport exploited the natural environment as well (see chapter 8).

With liberal approaches to gender equality holding sway in women's sport advocacy circles, radical and socialist analyses that call for an end to professionalized, commercialized, and elite sporting systems gain little exposure in women's sport discourse. Similarly, a radical feminist scholar who attempts to expose the seamy underside of the Olympic industry—especially its racist, colonialist, classist, and elitist practices—is unlikely to be popular. After all, her liberal feminist counterparts are directing all their efforts toward getting more Olympic sports and events for women, more balanced media coverage of female athletes, and more women in coaching, administration, and sport media, rather than deconstructing the "Olympic dream" and "Olympic spirit" rhetoric and calling for the complete dismantling of the Olympic industry, as I did in *Inside the Olympic Industry* (Lenskyj, 2000*)*.

The Staying Power of "Olympic Spirit" Rhetoric in Sydney

As I have argued before (Lenskyj, 2000), pseudoreligious metaphors such as Olympic spirit, Olympic family, Olympic movement, and Olympism have long been used to shore up the myths of "the pure Olympic athlete" and "pure Olympic sport"—ahistorical and decontextualized concepts that obscure the everyday business, political, and sporting practices that comprise the Olympic industry. This kind of discourse also serves to lift the Olympics out of the realm of more mundane hallmark events such as world fairs, and more ordinary urban megaprojects such as waterfront redevelopments and theme parks. Just as critical sport scholars in Canada and the United States in the 1970s renamed the fitness movement the fitness *industry* when it became evident that profit-making was its key defining feature, some sport scholars and many community critics in Australia, Canada, the United States, and Europe now apply the term *industry* to the Olympics. Obviously more complex than a mere sixteen-day sporting event, the Olympics are systematically organized to maximize private sector investment, to generate multi-billion-dollar television revenues, and to capitalize on the competition between transnational corporations for exclusive Olympic sponsorship status.

Jean-Marie Brohm exposed these practices in his essay, "The Olympic Games and the Imperialist Accumulation of Capital" where he described the development of the "capitalist sports industry" (Brohm, 1978 [English translation]). More recently, as David Whitson and Donald Macintosh (1996, 292) argued, much of the discourse surrounding the Olympics and other international sporting events "sounds like a celebration of globalism and indeed of global capitalism."

The Olympic metaphors that I listed above hide the fact that the organization and hosting of the Games is an industry, and not a lifestyle, an extended family, or a religious cult. Sydney Olympic organizers relied on "Olympic spirit" discourse to diffuse public outrage on the numerous occasions when Olympic officials failed to live up to the lofty standards touted in the pseudoreligious rhetoric. Olympic industry advocates routinely used the fallback position: "people will forget ... when the Olympics begin." In the case of Sydney, the list of readily "forgettable" problems included IOC scandal and corruption, the marching band issue, the ticket issue, and Kevan Gosper's torch relay debacle. This rhetoric conceptualized "the public" as easily duped by the Olympic circus, and, admittedly, this probably held true for many people. By July 2000, however, there was some public disenchantment, with an opinion poll reporting that 19 percent of Sydney residents had negative sentiments about the Olympics, and that 14 percent—half a million residents—were planning to leave the city during the Games (Half a million, 2000).

The Context: A Reformed International Olympic Committee?

Olympic scholars Douglas Booth and John MacAloon are among those who have identified the shortcomings of the reform process within the IOC (Booth, 2000; MacAloon, 2001). The *patriarchal kinship structure,* as Booth termed it, remained firmly in place under IOC president Samaranch's control, and the twelve-member executive board had more power than before, particularly with regard to the eight-year reelection process and the expulsion of "uncooperative" members. The fifteen new athlete-members had been elected by peers, without any background checks; some were alleged to have been involved in doping (using performance-enhancing drugs) (MacAloon, 2001).

The additional fifteen new members who were international federation presidents were in a conflict-of-interest situation: promoting their own sport versus the broader goals of "Olympism." Despite the new rule banning IOC members' visits to bid cities, presidents could visit in their federation roles. Moreover, some presidents had a history of "blackmailing" bid committees to get the best deal—venues, competition schedules, and accommodations—for their sport, and these practices promoted cronyism, "white elephant" (expensive and redundant) venues, unauthorized perks, and gigantism (too many Olympic sports and events) (MacAloon, 2001). In this context, many of the shortcomings evident in Sydney 2000 preparations can be seen as evidence of the continuing IOC problems of lack of transparency and accountability, and "Olympic family" arrogance and sense of entitlement.

"He Just Doesn't Get It": The Olympic Torch Fiasco

An incident involving an Australian IOC member, vice president and (at that time) presidential hopeful, Kevan Gosper, demonstrated to many Australians that reform was superficial, to say the least. A young Greek-Australian, Yianna Souleles, had been selected by her school's teaching staff, following arrangements made by the local parish priest and the Greek Olympic committee, to run the first leg of the torch relay after the torch was lit on Mt. Olympus. The media followed these events with great interest, just as they did the subsequent incident involving Gosper and his daughter. According to most media reports, Gosper was approached by Greek Olympic committee members who asked him to let his daughter Sophie replace Yianna, because, with her blond hair and blue eyes, the former allegedly looked more like "a typical Australian girl." (The fact that a significant proportion of the population was born outside the country, and, together with Australia's Indigenous population, was more likely to have black hair and brown eyes, apparently escaped the Greek committee's attention). It was also likely that the Greek committee wanted to ingratiate itself with Gosper, because of the ongoing problems with preparations for the 2004 Olympics in Athens (McKay, Hutchins, & Mikosza, 2000).

Gosper promptly accepted the invitation on behalf of his daughter, and later defended his decision on the grounds that he felt in his heart that it was appropriate for Sophie, the daughter of an "Olympian," to carry the torch first. Yianna was downgraded to a later leg of the relay on Greek soil, a change that she accepted with grace and equanimity. The same could not be said for Gosper, whose arrogance in the face of almost universal censure for his poor judgment convinced many Australians that Olympic reforms were inadequate: Gosper just "didn't get it" (McKay, Hutchins, & Mikosza 2000; see also Headon, 2000).

The timing of these events was significant. By mid-1999, the IOC bribery scandal was largely under control, thanks to the efforts of expert spin doctors Hill and Knowlton, an international public relations firm based in New York that had been retained to improve the IOC's tarnished image. Then in October 1999, Sydney Olympic organizers became embroiled in the ticketing fiasco, after it was revealed that premium tickets to popular events had been offered through high-priced packages to members of private clubs, while the general public was led to believe that tickets were in short supply. Shortly after, there was public outrage over plans to use predominantly American marching bands during the opening ceremony. Finally, by mid-2000, with the torch relay about to begin in Greece, people inside and outside the Olympic industry predicted that all the problems of the past would be forgotten as Olympic euphoria caught hold among all Australians. Gosper changed all that, at least for a few weeks.

The Best Olympics Ever?

This book begins with an analysis of the key role played by the national and international mass media in presenting procorporate and pro-Olympic industry messages, and generally trivializing the concerns of Olympic watchdog organizations. The *Sydney Morning Herald*'s important whistle-blowing initiatives and more balanced reporting of Olympic-related protest and social impact issues are examined in light of the controversial distribution of Olympic "properties" between the two major newspaper corporations in the country.

Chapters 2 and 3 set out the full context of Sydney's Olympic preparations and anti-Olympic activism. Chapter 2 examines legislation enacted in the 1990s during government and Olympic industry attempts to enhance police power, control public behavior, and criminalize disadvantage. Chapter 3 focuses on a key political issue in Australia at this time: reconciliation between Black and White Australia. Chapters 4 and 5 present an analysis of housing and homelessness problems that were exacerbated by Sydney 2000, followed by a discussion of other related social issues, hidden impacts, and Olympic "legacy" questions. Chapter 6 represents an exposé of the full extent of university complicity in the Olympic industry.

In chapters 7, 8, and 9, I take an ethnographic approach in order to examine local and global resistance to the Olympic industry, with the Bondi Beach volleyball stadium controversy representing a classic example of the power of the Olympic industry over local communities, and the subsequent threat to democracy posed by the hosting of the Olympic Games. Actual events in September 2000 are the focus of chapter 9, with an emphasis on the packaging of "Aboriginality" in the opening and closing ceremonies, antiglobalization protests, and anti-Olympic and Indigenous activists' tireless efforts to draw world attention to reconciliation.

1

The Mass Media

Olympic Industry Boosters and Critics

—⟩⟨⟩⟨⟩⟨—

As is the situation in most Western countries, Australia's mass media reflect and reinforce the role of sport as a key component of popular culture. It would be hard to imagine an Australian newspaper or news broadcast that did not include extensive coverage of sporting events. The Sydney 2000 slogan Share the Spirit exemplified this view of sport as an unqualified good. First of all, it suggested the "spirit of Australia": the liberal myth of upward social mobility through hard work, egalitarianism, and anti-elitism, and a national identity cemented by largely uncritical support for all competitive sporting endeavors. Secondly, the slogan evoked the "Olympic spirit": the pursuit of sporting excellence.

The Australian media played an indispensable role in shaping public opinion concerning Olympic sport in general and the Sydney 2000 Olympic bid and preparations in particular. And, as 2000 approached, the international media joined in these efforts to boost public support for all things Olympic. The Olympic product was, of course, eminently marketable, and it was relatively easy for the Olympic industry to use the mass media to maintain its relentless promotion of the Sydney 2000 project not only as a "magic moment" in Australian history, but also as a "once-in-a-lifetime" opportunity to boost the economy through tourism, employment, and private sector investment.

Following the discussion of Australian media ownership and the distribution of Olympic properties, this chapter will examine media treatment of Olympic-related issues in the first half of 1996—the crucial period

An earlier version of part of this chapter, titled "Sydney 2000: Olympic Sport and the Australian Media," appeared in the *Journal of Australian Studies* 62, 1999, pp. 76–83.

leading up to the Atlanta Games and the halfway mark in Sydney's Olympic preparations—in order to show the state of play at that particular historical point. This chapter will also examine the changing role of the media in the late 1990s, following the International Olympic Committee (IOC) bribery scandal.

The focus will be on the print media, with particular attention to the coverage provided by the *Sydney Morning Herald* (hereafter the *Herald*) throughout the 1990s. I analyzed the *Herald*'s Olympic coverage every day of publication over the following periods: January-June 1996, April-May 1997, and April-May 1998; from November 1998 to February 2001, I systematically monitored the *Herald*'s website <smh.com.au>.

MEDIA OWNERSHIP: THE GIANTS

The ownership structure of the Australian media industry became increasingly concentrated in the 1980s and 1990s (Turner & Cunningham, 1997). By 2000, Rupert Murdoch's News Limited owned six capital city newspapers and one national newspaper *(The Australian)*, representing 67 percent of total newspaper circulation in the country, while John Fairfax, publisher of the *Herald, The Age* (Melbourne), *Australian Financial Review,* and *Business Review Weekly,* controlled 22 percent (Australia's media giants, 2000). Not too surprisingly, with Murdoch's empire expanding, power struggles at the top were often reflected in the pages of Fairfax's papers.

A *Green Left Weekly* article (Healy, 2000) captured the problems flowing from the "marketplace of ideas"—which, under capitalism, transformed ideas into commodities to be bought and sold by the mass media. Neatly summarizing the divide between the two major print media corporations, Sean Healy explained how "down-market" and "popular" News Limited publications, such as Sydney's *Daily Telegraph,* aimed at the stereotypical Australian-born, White, suburban, working-class family man, serving up "a standard fare of blaring sensationalism, crime stories, sport and gambling . . . tough on crime and dole bludgers [welfare bums], anti-union, crudely nationalist and covertly racist." Bryan Dawe, of the popular television satire, *The Games,* probably had a News Limited publication in mind when he described a particular tabloid as "a light-hearted mixture of racism and pornography." Fairfax's "up-market" papers such as the *Herald* played to different prejudices—those of "the wealthy, well-educated, inner-city professional"—and, as the "liberal establishment media," displayed a clear probusiness bias (Healy, 2000, 17).

In the Australian context, long-standing antigovernment sentiment, hostility to unions, and opposition to Indigenous land claims—in other words, racism—all helped to create fertile ground for procorporate media messages that were the key components of the propaganda model developed by Noam Chomsky and Edward Herman (Chomsky, 1988; Herman & Chomsky, 1988). This approach conceptualized the mass media as a key force in ideological struggles, an effective means of "manufacturing consent," and a powerful tool for corporate elites. For their part, consumers could resist corporate propaganda by deconstructing its hidden messages and developing alternative, community-based media sources. In the Sydney Olympic context, electronic communication (e-mail and the Internet) was particularly well suited to this kind of resistance (see chapter 7).

Sydney Media as Bid Boosters

In the mid-1990s, the *Herald's* coverage of issues related to Sydney 2000's budget, administration, and construction was dominated by pro-Olympic journalist Glenda Korporaal, who also happened to be the coauthor of Sydney bid chief Rod McGeoch's book, *The Bid*, in 1994, and Australian IOC vice president Kevan Gosper's book, *An Olympic Life*, in 2000 (McGeoch & Korporaal, 1994; Gosper & Korporaal, 2000). McGeoch/Korporaal's explicit business orientation continued to influence the *Herald's* coverage in 1996, especially in relation to volatile issues such as government versus private funding and environmental protection. In a 1998 controversy involving allegations that McGeoch was exploiting his Olympic connections for personal profit, Korporaal's *Herald* article (1998) included an acknowledgment that she was coauthor of *The Bid*.

By 2000, Korporaal had switched allegiances by joining the staff of News Limited's *Daily Telegraph*. At this time, however, Korporaal's byline failed to signal to readers that she was coauthor of a book by a second powerful Olympic industry figure—Gosper—and that she might have been in a conflict-of-interest situation. Australian journalists who were members of the Media, Entertainment, and Arts Alliance committed themselves to follow the Journalists' Code of Ethics (2000), which specifically directed them to disclose conflicts of interest and not to allow "advertising or other commercial considerations" to influence their accuracy, fairness, or independence.

Chomsky's propaganda model noted the importance of "necessary illusions": the ways in which the mass media occasionally engaged in self-criticism in order to convey editorial independence. In the Australian context, newspaper editorials, letters to the editor, television documentaries such as *Media Watch,* and political satires such as *Good News Week* all supported the illusion that the media functioned as their own monitors and critics. Unlike views expressed in the independent media, however, dissenting voices and debates were carefully contained in the mainstream media.

Despite the *Herald*'s positioning as the most liberal of the Sydney newspapers, in the mid-1990s it had at least two regular columnists, including sports reporter Jeff Wells, whose views regularly came under attack in letters to the editor amid allegations of sexism and racism. In a similar illusion of debate and balance, Australia's best-selling sports magazine, *Inside Sport,* (in)famous for its regular ten-page centerfold pictorials of women in bikinis, had as regular contributors two respected sport scholars, Colin Tatz and Douglas Booth, who presented radically dissenting views on controversial issues, including racism and drugs in sport (Lenskyj, 1998). In fact, Tatz's article on White Australians' racist treatment of Aboriginal people, both inside and outside sport, was one of the few to name the hypocrisy of the Sydney 2000 bid supporters who focused on China's human rights abuses and ignored Australia's own shameful record (Tatz, 1995a)

SELLING OLYMPIC PROPERTIES

In 1997, it was announced that, for the first time in Olympic history, Sydney 2000 would have two newspaper sponsors: Fairfax and News Limited. In keeping with the IOC charter's requirement to maximize Olympic news coverage and audiences, Olympic minister Michael Knight assured the Australian media at the time that "All Olympic events are open to be covered by all news media, so there's no exclusivity in terms of editorial. . . ." (Knight quoted in Coultan & Evans, 1999).

Sharing Olympic sponsor status made the two media giants key Olympic players on two major and potentially conflicting fronts: the coverage of Olympic news stories, and the marketing and promotion of what were termed *SOCOG properties.* The goodies were divided up as follows: the torch relay and the ticket sales to News Limited, and volunteer recruitment, the arts festival, and the school newspaper to Fairfax. These arrangements served the interests of the Sydney Organizing Committee for the Olympic Games (SOCOG) very well, by covering both the upmarket and downmarket readership sectors, and by maximizing the number of Olympic stories on any given day. Even squabbles between the two newspaper companies put the Olympic industry on the front page, and it was in the interest of neither to resort to a "sour grapes" position by ignoring an Olympic story.

Although it was understood that the newspapers' sponsorship rights were for marketing and promotional purposes only, and not for giving a particular company an exclusive news story, it soon became clear that there was a fine distinction between the two dimensions. In March 1999, the Australian Press Council and the Media Entertainment and Arts Alliance expressed concerns about these arrangements, whereby the two News Limited papers received information about the torch and ticketing programs before other media—a situation that allegedly resembled "checkbook journalism" (Korporaal & Evans, 1999). At that time, the particular controversy concerned News Limited's announcement of the Olympic torch design, a story that Knight claimed was an Olympic promotion, and not a news item. Fairfax's director of group publishing, Robert Whitehead, revealed that his company had declined to enter into an agreement similar to News Limited's: "We refuse to buy editorial exclusives. The notion is anathema to a free press. Fairfax papers are the only ones now able to provide balanced, objective Games coverage" (Whitehead quoted in Coultan & Evans, 1999).

Discussing these issues on an Australian Broadcasting Commission (ABC) radio program, a journalist for News Limited's *Australian* assured listeners that, regardless of one paper's ownership of a particular SOCOG property, Olympic organizers had no influence over the editorial "slant" that a news story took (King, 1998). Of course, it would be hard to imagine that a newspaper company, having spent millions of dollars on exclusive rights to promote the torch relay, would then permit its journalists to criticize that particular "Olympic property" by drawing attention to the Anglo-Celtic overrepresentation in the list of escort runners' names that appeared in the *Daily Telegraph*'s February 28, 2000 supplement, "Tickets to History."

The division of media marketing rights did not prevent Fairfax or News Limited from capitalizing on Olympic news at every opportunity. As was the case during the bid process, they used their "value-in-kind" contributions to good effect, by regularly offering special supplements, glossy posters, souvenir programs, and so forth, to mark various points on the Olympic dateline: 1,000 days to go, 500 days to go. On June 7, 2000, for example, the *Herald* published a eight-page section, "100 Days to Go," which also appeared as a special supplement to the *New Zealand Herald, the West Australian, The Age (Melbourne), USA Today*, as well as in the *Herald*'s Sydney rival, the *Daily Telegraph*.

In a classic ambush marketing (illegal use of Olympic words and symbols) coup, Qantas—which was *not* the official Olympic airline—managed to occupy one quarter of the *Herald*'s supplement, with a full page Qantas ad and a full page ad for the One World airline alliance, which included Qantas. International recognition of this airline proved a major challenge for Ansett, a less recognized airline that was the official Olympic carrier. For example, as late as September 2000, after Ansett's ad campaign had been running for years, the *Guardian*'s (U.K.) Sydney-based Olympic reporter Patrick Barkham asserted that Qantas was an Olympic sponsor (Barkham, 2000b).

Over three years before the Games began, the *Herald* started publishing a half-page weekly feature titled *Insight*, which presented "official information" from SOCOG. The section focused on promoting souvenir sales and auctions of Olympic "collectables," as well as advertising test events, profiling Olympic athletes and sports, and recruiting volunteers and paid workers.

Some of the early versions of *Insight* were sprinkled with inspirational thoughts from Olympics' founding father, Pierre de Coubertin. On June 21, 1997 (p. 15), for example, it carried his pronouncement that "Humanity must take from the heritage of the past all the force it can use to build the future. Olympism is one of those forces." Printed in the adjacent column was a news item on the probable selection of Bondi Beach for Olympic beach volleyball competition—a particularly ironic juxtaposition in view of subsequent developments that proved that "all the force" of the Olympic industry was indeed powerful—more powerful than the widespread community opposition to the Bondi Beach stadium, as shown in chapter 8.

By 2000, the half-page had expanded to a weekly three- or four-page section called *Spirit 2000*. The cover routinely carried a "feel-good" story, and the *Herald*'s Olympic editor Matthew Moore and others presented more critical Olympic coverage on an inside page, where stories about the venues and the sporting events also appeared. Overall, as Moore argued, this weekly section was largely devoted to celebrating Olympic athletes and sport, a fact that some critics of the *Herald*'s investigative journalism tended to ignore.

On November 19, 1999, with three hundred days to go, the *Herald* launched its SYDNEYGAMES newsletter, available electronically upon request anywhere in the world. The newsletter included most of the content of the weekly *Spirit 2000* section, as well as the top Olympic news stories of the day, and, by mid-2000, was posted four or five times per week.

OLYMPIC COVERAGE IN 1996: HALFWAY TO 2000

The *Herald*'s coverage of power struggles between the Australian Olympic Committee (AOC), SOCOG, and the New South Wales (NSW) government in 1996 provided clear evidence of support for corporate interests. In the original terms of the Olympic bid, the NSW government was to provide over $1b for Olympic construction and to make good any losses, and the AOC was to receive 90 percent of any SOCOG profits to fund Australia's Olympic athlete program. Both the NSW government and the AOC had veto power over SOCOG budget. In March 1996, with higher than expected television revenues, Michael Knight sought a change in the agreement so that the NSW government could gain a share of any profit over the estimated $26m—which in March was upgraded to $210m if other budgeted costs were kept in line.[1]

---

[1]Figures are given in Australian dollars unless otherwise specified. Before and during the Sydney 2000 Olympics, the Australian dollar was valued at between 55 and 65 cents U.S.

According to *Herald* reporter Glenda Korporaal, John Coates, the AOC, and the IOC were correct in wanting to "avoid Games revenues being used to pay for long-term facilities for the State" (Korporaal, 1996a, 32), a contradictory statement in view of the way in which the legacy of Olympic facilities is routinely held up as a major benefit to the host city, state, and country. Korporaal went on to criticize Knight for "throwing the spotlight" on the AOC's control of 90 percent of the profit and for "aiding the public perception that the State Government is generously shouldering the financial burden." An AOC official, less subtly, complained that the government was trying to portray the AOC as "money-hungry bastards" (Korporaal, 1996a; Korporaal & Vass, 1996). It is worth noting that AOC assets were at that time valued at $23m, including a $7.3m investment in a Queensland casino (Korporaal, 1996c). One might reasonably argue that Knight, as an elected representative, was only doing his job by trying to gain a bigger share of profits for taxpayers, but it clearly disrupted the corporate agenda to mention the government's considerable financial involvement—approximately one third of the budget at that time— in the same breath as the AOC profit. (By 2000, the NSW treasurer reported that the government's contribution had increased to one-half.)

Strategically placed adjacent to Korporaal's piece was an article on Atlanta's tight budget, absence of government funding, and the expectation of zero profit for its organizing committee (Turner, 1996). In a follow-up story a few days later, yet another article on Atlanta's financial problems reported how added security for the 1996 Games was expected to cost the American taxpayer an extra $1b (Games dollars, 1996). Presumably, the reader was expected to admire Sydney's superior financial planning and to be grateful that Australian taxpayers would have any share of the profit. On the profit issue, the AOC ultimately agreed to give up the power of veto on SOCOG matters in exchange for a guaranteed $100m of profits, thus forgoing the earlier 90 percent profit figure. Korporaal praised John Coates's business sense in going for the guaranteed sum rather than the unknown percentage (Korporaal, 1996b).

But the issue was not laid to rest. *Herald* headlines two months later were proclaiming "Sydney $375m Olympic Blow-out" and "Public Funds for Games up by $400m" (Humphries, 1996a; Vass, 1996). Failure of anticipated private sector funding ($65m) for several major facilities was blamed, and unexpected costs in environmental cleanup to the Homebush Bay site were also cited—a fairly predictable blame-shifting to the troublesome environmentalist lobby. Knight was quoted as defending the additional $400m in public funding as taxpayers' investment in the future. By July 1996, the government estimate stated that the Olympic Village would cost at least $300m less than the original projection, thus significantly decreasing the cost to taxpayers (Humphries, 1996b; Korporaal, 1996d).

Lest the corporate sector be offended by the implication that it was shirking its responsibility, an article under the same "Olympic blow-out" banner explained that the NSW Registered Clubs Association, which was expected to fund the $23.2m Olympic velodrome, had been suffering from a "misunderstanding" about its right to use Olympic symbols for marketing purposes (Wright, 1996). Above this report, the *Herald* strategically placed an article on IOC rules concerning the promotion of Sydney 2000 in Atlanta, and drew attention to the Atlanta Organizing Committee's "unusually aggressive tactics" designed to protect sponsors and licensees from illegal use of Olympic words and symbols (known as "ambush marketing") (Clark, 1996). What was not mentioned in the *Herald*'s coverage was the fact that, one year earlier, in March 1995, the Australian Senate Legal and Constitutional References Committee had heard submissions that called for equally "aggressive tactics" in order to protect the IOC's and AOC's copyright and trade monopolies over Olympic properties.

Green Games or Empty Promises?

One of the much vaunted features of the Sydney 2000 Olympic Bid was the promise of a Green Games, with Olympic facilities designed according to environmentally sustainable development (ESD) principles. Early in 1996, Olympic environmental planning came under attack from a Sydney physics professor, who claimed that lack of design integration between the projects at the Homebush Olympic site had jeopardized the proposed solar-thermal energy plant and diluted the commitment to a Green Games. This was followed by scathing criticism of the design plan by a landscape architecture professor. The *Herald* devoted extensive coverage to the "expert" critiques and a headline titled "Games Vision 'Boring Mediocrity' " spanned six columns at the top of the page, even though the story was only two columns wide. The article only briefly summarized the Olympic Coordination Authority's (OCA) denials of all these allegations (Beale, 1996; Byrne, 1996). The adjacent article, although covered by the same banner headline, reported on the winners of the Royal Australian Institute of Architects Gold Medal Awards—a transparent attempt to link the winning firm of Denton, Corker, and Marshall to the Olympic project. This group of experts was lavishly praised for their achievements, and much was made of their unique strengths in large commercial projects (Susskind, 1996a).

Two weeks later in the *Herald,* architects again attacked the government for focusing "too narrowly" on price in their tendering of the design work for Olympic buildings. One of the complaints came from the same firm of Denton, Corker, and Marshall, who stated that their (presumably superior) standards of work did not allow for cost-cutting, and that there-fore they had not been in contention for the tender—a criticism that portrayed the government as bargain-hunters who had missed the oppor-tunity to use the country's top design team. This time, the *Herald* reported the government architect's response in more detail, explaining that the preference for NSW firms was aimed at boosting the local building indus-try and architecture profession (Susskind, 1996b). Overall, however, more favorable attention was paid to the critics than to the government's legiti-mate concerns with cost.

As might be expected, media treatment of environmentalists was not uniformly positive. It occasionally served the antigovernment agenda to give them air time—especially if the environmentalist was a university-based "expert" rather than a grassroots activist—but it more often served the corporate agenda to blame them for problems with the Olympic bud-get and timetable. For example, in a heated attack on environmentalists (as well as human rights advocates, union leaders and others), an article in the business section of News Limited's *Australian* provided an unfet-tered forum for a "leading construction industry heavyweight" to lash out at all of the so-called pressure groups whose interventions, he alleged, would delay progress at the Olympic construction site. According to this Olympic project management director, environmental issues could be taken too far, with the result that the enterprise becomes "uncommercial." He concluded by warning that unpredictable delays cost money and asking sarcastically, "Who knows if there is someone worried about immigration or the fact that perhaps there are not enough female workers on the site?" (Allen, 1996, B3).

Dominated by the views of one member of the corporate sector, this article would leave readers with the impression that environmental and human rights concerns were alien to the Sydney Olympic project, even though at the time of the bid preparation, supporters boasted of Australia's superior human rights record (in contrast to China's) and Greenpeace endorsement of (part of) the Sydney 2000 design. There were, in fact, several environmental health issues associated with Olympic construction, apart from the obvious problems associated with remediating the Homebush Bay Olympic site, which at this time were still mostly unknown to the media and the public (see Lenskyj, 2000, chapter 8). Air, water, and noise pollution were significant problems in the Sydney metropolitan area, with commercial aviation and heavy industry in and around the region largely responsible for the problem. Early in 1996, the *Herald* presented a series of articles on pollution, while aircraft noise, which was the subject of a commission of inquiry, was reported on an almost daily basis. A higher incidence of respiratory problems had been reported in the western sub-urbs, where most Olympic events were to take place. It was therefore particularly hypocritical that, in his self-congratulatory account of the bid, McGeoch attempted to discredit the Beijing bid on these same grounds: that is, that air pollution and dust storms in the Beijing area produced "a strong risk of sinus and bronchial problems as athletes were trying to perform at their physical peak" (McGeoch & Korporaal, 1994, 226).

The details about Beijing came from a research report that McGeoch had commissioned to uncover, and to present, in as unfavorable a light as possible, all of the problems with the Beijing bid. It was McGeoch's proposed strategy for releasing the document, rather than the document itself, which was more disturbing. Intent on mounting a public relations campaign that could not be "sourced back to the Sydney bid," he enlisted the services of a London public relations expert (to whom he referred as his "private weapon"). The plan was to fund a human rights group in London to speak out about China issues and then to publish a book based on the research report—with none of this to be linked to the Sydney bid. The NSW government got wind of the campaign, which they correctly perceived as a threat to Australia-China relations, and McGeoch was forced to abandon the plan. It was clear that he was more concerned about "the millions of dollars in corporate money riding on [the bid's] performance" than about the ethics of the situation or the implications for international relations (McGeoch & Korporaal, 1994, 233). Although little was made of this scheme when the book was first released in 1994, it was examined in detail five years later, as the IOC scandal unfolded, in a special *Herald* report titled "Breaking China" (Ryle & Hughes, 1999).

Drugs: Demonizing "Other" Countries' Athletes

The predictable pattern in Australian media reports on the use of performance-enhancing drugs in Olympic sport was strongly evident in the period leading up to the 1996 Games. The uncovering of "drug cheats" from Communist countries and big sporting powers such as the United States was hailed as a step forward in the struggle for "clean" international sporting competition, and the culprits were presumed guilty until proven otherwise. Chinese female swimmers and their famous muscular physiques were a favorite target, and the establishment of a "rebel world swimming association" to counter the international swimming federation's alleged inactivity on the Chinese "problem" was sympathetically reported (Hutcheon, 1996; Magnay, 1996a).

However, when Australian athletes tested positive for banned substances, the media tended to treat them as innocent victims. At a 1995 international competition, swimmer Samantha Riley was found to have taken a prohibited prescription headache drug, and, while Scott Volkers, the coach who provided it, was banned for four years (subsequently reduced to six months), Riley escaped with only a strong warning. (Volkers's ban conveniently ended a few days before the team left for Atlanta.) Both pleaded ignorance that the drug contained a banned substance. A July 1996 report on drug testing in the *Weekend Australian* revisited the "ignorance" and "innocents abroad" defenses with sympathetic references to Riley, and warnings that the ingredients in medications purchased overseas might differ from an Australian product with the same name (Jenkins, 1996).

When track athlete Dean Capobianco tested positive to the steroid Stanazolol during pre-Olympic competition in the Netherlands in May 1996, Australian sport officials managed to keep the issue out of the media until July 16. Media response was immediate: on July 17 and 18, the *Herald* had two front page stories, a front page opinion piece, an editorial, and two pages of background articles. These included an unsympathetic chronicle of his performance since 1988, peppered with phrases like "immature race," "lucky to be selected," "a dreadful heat," "sluggish," and "bad form"—a not-so subtle message that he wasn't a medal contender anyway (Dates of dignity and despair, 1996). On the sympathetic side, other articles reported on the "sabotage defense" and interviews with his lawyer, his coach and, finally, his mother—all protesting his innocence.

Jeff Wells's opinion piece, tellingly titled "Capo falls to white man's burden," appeared on the front page rather than in Wells's usual place in the sport section (Wells, 1996). The caption referred to Capobianco's perceived potential as the world's fastest White man in the 400m race; Wells implied that he had disappointed (presumably White) Australians by getting caught. The "fastest man" title took on further significance in light of ongoing debates about the particular running event that would determine that status.

One *Herald* article made much of the "official gag" and the "legal stranglehold" whereby the AOC and John Coates prohibited the Australian team from talking to the press about Capobianco on threat of expulsion from the Games. Near the end, the article finally explained that the AOC Athletes' Agreement, already signed by all team members, forbade talk about any matter apart from their own performance (Magnay & Blake, 1996). However, the *Herald* failed to report that Coates had ignored infringements of the agreement by Australian swimmer Nicole Stevenson just one week earlier, when she had aired her views on the drug habits of the Chinese women swimmers (Magnay, 1996c). It is also relevant that Samantha Riley's press conference—which, according to the *Herald's* editorial, was Australia's response to Chinese sport officials' underhand attempts to "exploit" the Riley incident—had been held one day before the Capobianco controversy became public (Testing, 1996).

Faced with a "decidedly sympathetic" international press, Riley had duly avoided answering questions about drugs and had focused on her own performance and prospects (Magnay, 1996d). Finally, maintaining the illusion of self-criticism, *Herald* reporter Patrick Smith discussed how Australia risked being labeled either *hypocritical* or *naive* by criticizing drug cheats in other countries while suffering the embarrassment of positive tests for two of its own athletes, Riley and Capobianco (Smith, 1996). In 1996, however, this kind of commentary was rarely found in the Australian mass media.

THE *SYDNEY MORNING HERALD* AS OLYMPIC CRITIC

The editorial sector of the *Herald* prided itself on having developed a culture of editorial independence, codified in the late 1980s in a seven-point charter; current Olympic editor Matthew Moore, formerly head of the staff union and a political reporter, had been active in the campaign to establish this autonomy. There were, of course, continual battles with management, owners, and shareholders, but, by the mid-1990s, *Herald* journalists generally experienced no managerial opposition to legitimate news stories that were critical of the government and Olympic organizers, as long as they were accurate and balanced.

This is not to suggest that there was no criticism or unhappiness on the part of Olympic organizers, as the experiences of the *Herald*'s environment editor, Murray Hogarth, demonstrated. He had first uncovered evidence of environmental contamination at the Homebush Bay Olympic site while he was preparing an ABC-TV *Four Corners* documentary in 1995. Starting work as a *Herald* journalist in 1996, he continued to investigate these issues, with the environmental groups Greenpeace Australia and Green Games Watch 2000 serving as important resources. His subsequent *Herald* articles revealed how Olympic and government officials had kept the dioxin contamination problem under wraps since 1992 in order not to harm the Olympic bid (see Lenskyj, 2000; chapter 8).

The Environment Protection Authority's investigations vindicated Hogarth by showing that Olympic organizers had indeed breached the regulations—but not before he had borne the brunt of Olympic boosters' "extreme displeasure" along with the predictable *unpatriotic* and *unAustralian* labels. One former ministerial adviser threatened Hogarth with lawsuits and discreditation, calling him "the last toxic site on the list to be cleaned up" (Hogarth, 1998, 102).

Overall, Hogarth viewed the *Herald*'s early 1990s boosterism of the Olympic bid and preparations as atypical, and the tougher approach to Olympic issues after 1998 as indicative of its usual uncompromising editorial approach. He acknowledged that management may have been uncomfortable dealing with the conflict between the paper's critical content and its role as an Olympic sponsor, but reported that he had experienced "no suggestion of pressure" not to run his stories (Hogarth, 1999). Moore agreed that, while there was extensive debate, there was no managerial pressure to stop writing critical stories (Moore, 2000d).

Of course, from Olympic organizers' point of view, critiques in Fairfax newspapers were to some extent "balanced" by News Limited's generally blind support for all things Olympic. Not only were Sydney's *Daily Telegraph* and Melbourne's *Herald-Sun* excellent sources of Olympic boosterism, but some of their columnists—Piers Ackerman, for example—could be relied upon to produce anti-Greenpeace diatribes whenever that group was poised to disclose a new environmental problem. In fact, some activists had reason to believe that the IOC's international spin doctors, Hill and Knowlton, may have been responsible for this pattern (Luscombe, 1999).

In the late 1990s, in the wake of the international Olympic bribery scandals, Sydney Olympic organizers generated their own new controversies over ticket sales, the marching band, and Kevan Gosper's torch relay blunder. In light of these events, one might reasonably expect that Olympic journalists would start identifying the *patterns* of secrecy, arrogance, and sense of entitlement on the part of Australian members of the "Olympic family," and to situate those patterns and values in the bigger context of the transnational Olympic industry. In practice, the mass media were much more likely to attack individuals than to examine the system that normalized dishonesty at all levels: from the IOC, national Olympic committees, and bid and organizing committees, to the so-called values of Olympic sport itself, which might be characterized as winning at all costs by whatever means necessary. "You don't win a silver medal, you lose gold"—the advertisement that Nike ran during the 1996 Games—summarized what was, for many, the most salient value of Olympic sporting competition.

Admittedly, some Australian Olympic reporters had limited experience in the area, and lacked the time as well as the background knowledge to be able to write about the big social issues underlying the Olympics, or to draw the links between individuals and the system. Moreover, as Moore explained, a news story needed to reflect the concerns of readers, who were generally more interested in the impact the Olympics would have on their cities and their lives than in the broader philosophical and ideological questions (Moore, 2000d). From an international perspective, a Swedish Broadcasting Corporation radio journalist, who had been sent to Australia two years before the Games, reported that there was limited interest on the part of his Stockholm bosses in broader social issues such as homelessness in the Olympic city (Dennis, 2000).

With Atlanta 1996 and Sydney 2000 representing the first two consecutive Olympics to share a common language, as well as the more advanced state of information technology in the late 1990s, Sydney journalists were in a better position to compare these two international events than their counterparts in other Olympic host cities in the 1980s and 1990s. Yet there was not widespread media interest in making these comparisons, except in the few instances where Sydney reporters tried to tap long-standing anti-American sentiments by identifying what they viewed as the shortcomings of the 1996 Atlanta Olympics as examples that Sydney should not follow.

Challenging Olympic Industry Secrecy: The FOI Route

In the early 1990s, with widespread support for the bid, and later for the Olympics, it appeared that most journalists and politicians simply accepted the alleged need for a high level of secrecy and confidentiality regarding the endorsement and host city contracts. Every company bidding for a Sydney 2000 contract had to sign a confidentiality agreement regarding every aspect of the process, and the NSW cabinet imposed a ban on Freedom of Information (FOI) requests for Olympic documents.

There were, however, several *Herald* journalists with well-developed investigative journalism skills, and in the late 1990s, their contributions helped to unveil a number of important Olympic industry secrets concerning Sydney 2000. In 1998, Moore decided to investigate Atlanta's 1996 Olympic contracts. Finding that there was a relatively high level of access to these documents, and that neither the American public nor American society seemed to have suffered any ill effects, he made more than ten FOI applications to Sydney's Olympic organizers to see if he could match this level of availability of information. It was soon clear that he could not do so, and, rather than appealing the FOI denials through the court—a route that occasionally produced a positive outcome for the *Herald*—he focused on the absurdity of the situation as his story. It was illuminating to discover that, in a country with a reputation for secrecy, the USA's FOI provisions were more generous than Australia's, a difference that Sydney's Olympic officials attributed to Australia's different traditions and mechanisms for ensuring fairness (M. Moore, 1998b).

On January 14, 1999, the auditor-general's *Performance Audit Review* of the June 1998 Olympic budget estimates was finally tabled in Parliament. The preface explained that the delays had been caused by the "unnecessary secrecy" surrounding Sydney 2000 preparations, most notably FOI exemptions of documents "central to the understanding of the State's obligations," and government agencies' criticism of the auditor-general's draft report for disclosing allegedly "commercially sensitive information." Tellingly, these agencies complained that they would have to answer "a large number of queries from the public" if detailed revenue and expense estimates were released. Yes, the auditor-general responded, "It is true that accountability has costs. It is also true that avoiding accountability has potentially much larger costs" (Performance Audit Review, 1999, preface). Focusing on the secrecy issue, Moore reported that, in late 1998, the auditor-general had strongly criticized the OCA for denying the *Herald*'s FOI application for access to the criteria used in selecting successful tenders, and had claimed that OCA was breaching public sector guidelines, including those set down by the Independent Commission Against Corruption (M. Moore, 1999a).

Three Sydney 2000 documents—the host city contract, the endorsement, and amendments—were eventually made public early in 1999, a few months after Moore's story and the release of the audit report, and, not coincidentally, at the height of the IOC bribery scandal. Interestingly, although Moore found through his earlier inquiries that the IOC had no objections to releasing this kind of information, Sydney Olympic organizers claimed that it did (M. Moore, 1998a). For its part, SOCOG simply stated, in a February 10 press release (SOCOG, 1999b), that the board had approved the release of the contract "now that all parties had given approval"—a mere six years after the event. No mention was made of FOI appeals or media pressure. Just one month later, the *Herald* was reporting on SOCOG's latest creative strategy to maintain a "state of secrecy": by claiming that its financial documents belonged to its (private) internal auditors, SOCOG ensured exemption from FOI provisions, which only applied to government bodies. The move was criticized by the auditor-general and the NSW ombudsman, both of whom noted that government agencies were increasingly "contracting out" of FOI laws by using private firms—involving close to $2m worth of business in NSW alone (Clark, 1999).

Other information on Olympic-related decisions—for example, the losing bids for the stadium, village, railway station, and Superdome—were not released. As Moore argued, hundreds of millions of dollars were involved in decisions that the government made in complete secrecy, in much the same way as publicly funded infrastructure projects such as the Eastern Distributor (expressway) were approved. Taxpayers were expected to accept all of these decisions on faith, whereas Moore believed that a public consultation process might have produced cheaper and more practical proposals. An April 1998 *Herald* editorial had expressed the same concerns, concluding, "There is a significant problem of transparency and accountability with the entire tendering process of the Sydney Olympics" (Politics and the Olympics, 1998).

It was clearly in the public interest for Olympic organizers first, to engage in a transparent decision-making process, and, second, to facilitate media coverage of that process. However, with agendas and decisions of all board and committee meetings regarded as confidential, public interest was ill-served, and Moore was justly critical of SOCOG and OCA policies that prevented journalists from doing their jobs properly. In Moore's experience, the minister would often leave a board meeting, issue a press release and announcement, and postpone revealing the full details to some future date when the board deemed it appropriate to do so. By March 2000, formal press conferences were replaced with "background briefings" where no television cameras or radio microphones were allowed (Peatling, 2000a). Such practices no doubt contributed to public and media skepticism.

Despite this level of secrecy, *Herald* journalists—Matthew Moore, Michael Evans, and Jacqueline Magnay, in particular—were able to keep some of the key financial and social impact issues on the front pages, and to ensure that readers heard from community leaders as well as Olympic industry officials. SOCOG's Social Impact Advisory Committee (SIAC) included a number of community representatives who, in their other roles, were leaders of social service organizations: for example, Gary Moore, director of the NSW Council of Social Services (NCOSS), and the Reverend Harry Herbert, director of the Board for Social Responsibility of the NSW Uniting Church. SOCOG obviously could not stop people like Moore and Herbert, or Aboriginal leaders Lowitja O'Donoghue and Charlie Perkins of SOCOG's National Indigenous Advisory Committee, from talking to the media, and their views were regularly reported.

Another Olympic Scandal: Tickets for the Rich

The right to promote and sell Olympic tickets was purchased by News Limited, and this companies' papers included ticket application booklets from May 30, 1999 on. The *Herald* subsequently reported that News Limited owner Rupert Murdoch had initially stopped SOCOG's plans to use newsagents, Olympic retail outlets, and the Internet as additional distributors of the order forms, and a *Herald* editorial pointed to the ways in which News Limited's monopoly unduly mystified the already complicated ticket-ordering process, as well as exacerbating SOCOG's ongoing problems of lack of transparency (Games time, 1999; Magnay & Moore, 1999).

In mid-1999, toward the end of the first cycle of ticket sales, SOCOG created the false impression that tickets were in short supply, even to the point of claiming that some events were almost sold out. Moore was skeptical of SOCOG's figures; in the case of baseball, for example, it was claimed that 96 percent of tickets were already sold—when even the 1996 Olympics, held in a baseball city and country, had not matched these sales.

The *Herald* filed an FOI request in early October 1999, seeking the release of information on the numbers of tickets sold to the public on a session-by-session basis during the first round of sales. Knight claimed that, although he favored releasing the information, the other thirteen SOCOG board members did not, and the request was denied (Humphries & Jacobsen, 1999). A few days later, Knight was reported to have rejected calls for increased public scrutiny of SOCOG's board meetings, including publication of agendas and minutes. Despite the Salt Lake City precedent following the bribery investigations of 1998-1999, when most organizing committee meetings, as well as agendas, minutes, and reports, were open to the public, Knight resorted to the "commercial in confidence" argument, claiming that SOCOG board could not deal with private commercial matters if its meetings were public (M. Moore, 1999g).

On the ticket question, Moore subsequently published a controversial story about SOCOG's premium ticket option. Members of Sydney's exclusive social club, Tattersall's, had been offered between 300 and 400 guaranteed seats to the most popular events, without having to enter the public ballot system that had been advertised as the only method of securing such seats. Fortuitously, as Moore explained, the story appeared on the day that Knight and Hollway were appearing before a parliamentary hearing, with the result that SOCOG was finally forced to reveal the full details of the premium ticket scheme and to comply with FOI requests for a breakdown of ticket availability for every sport (M. Moore, 1999h, see chapter 5).

Herald journalists continued to experience problems with the dual sponsorship system, which converted news stories into products over which one newspaper company had exclusive marketing rights (Magnay & Moore, 1999). For example, on February 29, 2000, the *Herald* provided readers with details of the prices and availability of lower-priced Olympic Opportunity tickets, but only in its late edition because, as Moore explained, Fairfax had to "pinch it [the information] from the News Ltd *Telegraph*" (M. Moore, 2000a). In this particular instance, it was clearly in the public interest to maximize news coverage concerning affordable tickets to Olympic events, but commercial arrangements between the two major newspaper companies served Olympic industry interests first and foremost.

PRIVILEGING TELEVISION RIGHTS HOLDERS

Just as Olympic sport sets international standards and defines international sporting practices through sport federations and national Olympic committees, television largely dictates the actual staging of the Olympics. There was no dearth of examples from the Sydney Olympics:

- NBC's insistence on Bondi Beach as the best television venue for beach volleyball (see chapter 8)

- NBC's request that the overhead power lines and forty-eight electrical towers at Homebush Bay be removed and the cables put underground,

in order to improve television images; the NSW government contributed $20m toward what Knight first called "a luxury we can't afford"
(O'Rourke, 2000)

- the positioning of the running track at the Olympic stadium resulting
  in winds that seriously impeded athletes' performances, simply because television cameras needed a shadow-free main area, not facing
  the afternoon sun (Magnay, 1996b)

- NBC's decision to protect its $1.2b purchase of television rights by
  delaying all telecasts until evening prime time (since most of the
  network's viewing audience lived in a time zone twelve to fifteen hours
  behind Sydney time)

- the IOC's policy banning moving images or audio coverage via the Internet

The *Olympic Arrangements Act 2000* gave OCA ultimate authority
regarding commercial broadcasting, telecasting, recording, or filming Olympic events or activities within or outside an Olympic venue or facility, or
an Olympic live site. Approval was granted if OCA was satisfied that the
process would not "adversely affect the organization or conduct . . . of
commercial arrangements related to the Olympic Games." (S.68(4)). A
fine of up to $250,000 could be imposed for unauthorized activities of this
kind. A "person authorized by OCA" could, after giving direction to stop
the activity, confiscate the equipment used for unauthorized filming. Mag-
netometer screening of all those admitted to Olympic venues, together
with state-of-the-art camera surveillance systems, would detect hidden
equipment and unauthorized filming.

The regulation was clearly intended to prohibit non-rights-holders from
broadcasting from public areas of Olympic Park, although Olympic organizers also claimed that it was in the interests of security and public safety
to minimize the number of video news crews in the area (Evans, 2000f).
Major international broadcasters, including Cable News Network (CNN),
Reuters, Associated Press (AP), Entertainment and Sports Programming
(ESPN), Network and Fox, threatened legal action under international
trade agreements that prohibited such restrictions. Although SOCOG's
special arrangements with sponsors such as NBC were exempt from the
NSW Trade Practices Act, Australia, as a signatory to the World Trade
Organization, was still subject to international trade provisions.

In its August 2000 briefing paper, *Liberty in the Olympic City,* the
Public Interest Advocacy Center (PIAC) claimed that proposed restrictions
on other media gave Olympic rights-holders unprecedented advantages,
while at the same time posing an unreasonable restriction on freedom of
speech and on Australians' capacity to benefit from the Games (PIAC,
2000b). Like other critics, PIAC maintained that the Games' media policy
should maximize free-to-air coverage, a particular concern in light of

recent moves to extend rights to cable television companies so that more comprehensive Games coverage would be available for viewers willing to pay the additional cable costs.

Indeed, the Olympic Charter rule 59 required the organizing committee to implement "all necessary steps" in order "to ensure the fullest news coverage by the different media and the widest possible audience for the Olympic Games" (IOC, 1997, 75). Moreover, the IOC itself had the power to establish access rules for members of non-rights-holding radio and television organizations. Therefore, not too surprisingly, the IOC pressured SOCOG to modify its plan. SOCOG finally agreed to issue eight daily permits to be distributed among the one hundred forty non-rights-holders, and an additional eight daily permits for Australian television stations; a balloting system would determine which companies would be granted access on any given day. Live broadcasts from the Olympic site could only cover nonsport topics, and actual sport coverage was limited to two minutes, three times per day. At previous Olympics, non-rights-holders had been allowed to report from public areas for three minutes, three times per day.

The final arrangements apparently satisfied the IOC, whose August 3 press release announced its projections of record-breaking reach, coverage, and viewership for the Sydney Olympics. Nearly half of the international broadcasters were increasing their coverage over that of the 1996 Olympics, with the most significant increases—181 percent to 292 percent—for Australia, Canada, South Africa, China, Greece, and the United States. Finally, the news release reiterated its free-to-air policy (IOC, 2000b). In hindsight, however, it was clear that NBC suffered when the host city lay in a time zone fifteen hours ahead of American eastern time.

DANGEROUS VISITORS: NONACCREDITED MEDIA

In a less publicized aspect of the credentialing process, Sydney Olympic organizers made a serious attempt to avoid what they saw as Atlanta's failure to "manage" the nonaccredited media. Popular wisdom, particularly in SOCOG and OCA circles, held that these journalists would arrive in Sydney determined to uncover controversial background stories, and Atlanta's fate was seen as an example of an undesirable level of international "scrutiny" (*Performance Audit Review,* 1999). It was important, from the Olympic and tourism industry perspectives, to exercise some control over these roving reporters, and Tourism NSW proposed the novel solution of providing the expected 15,000 unaccredited print media with their own facility, the Sydney Media Center (SMC), in Sydney's central business district at Darling Harbor. IOC regulations only required a media center for the 6,000 accredited print media, who were located at the Main

Press Center (MPC) at Olympic Park, and for the 12,000 accredited broadcast media and technicians working in the Sydney Olympic Broadcasting Organization.

In tourist trade jargon, it was important to assist these journalists "to find and file stories that are consistent with the destination positioning that Australia seeks to achieve. . . ." (Chalip, 2000, 3). This particular selling job was, in fact, a long-term project, having had its beginnings in 1989 during the early stages of the bid, with the Australian Tourist Commission's (ATC) wooing of international journalists through the Visiting Journalists' Program. Its aim was to produce "favorable publicity on Australia as a tourist destination," and between 1998 and 2000, over 3,000 media writers and broadcasters were invited to Australia under the program, and almost $2.3b worth of publicity was generated (ATC, 2000).

The NSW Department of State and Regional Development, Tourism NSW, the ATC, and the Department of Foreign Affairs and Trade directed $4m toward the SMC, which was estimated to cost $8.2m; private funding provided the balance. The Sydney Harbor Foreshore Authority owned the property, which was slated for redevelopment after the Games "for residential, business and recreational purposes"—no doubt in keeping with its upscale neighbor, the Darling Harbor redevelopment. The goal of the SMC, according to the information in the Commonwealth Government's media kit distributed in 2000, was "to inform media about Australia's achievements, attractions, business and investment opportunities, tourism, lifestyle, arts and culture" and to "position" the country's image as "a high tech, multicultural and sophisticated trading partner and exciting tourist destination." On the same theme, lessons in "selling Australia and Sydney as tourist destinations" were, according to one source, a component of Sydney's Olympic volunteer training program—presumably yet another attempt to reinforce the Olympic mantra that the host city would reap long-lasting tourism benefits (M. Evans, 1999d). And, outside of Sydney, Australian towns and cities hosting pre-Olympic training also hoped to capitalize on the tourist potential by encouraging international athletes to become "ambassadors" for them (Chalip, 2000). (In another example of the Olympic industry's opportunistic use of athletes, the Media Institute instructed Canadian national swim team members on ways to promote the Toronto 2008 bid to the media while they were in Sydney for the Olympics (MacNeill, 2000).

The Sydney Media Center's (SMC) facilities included a media conference room, internet access, a resource center, workstations, and hospitality facilities. It was open to any journalists who could demonstrate their affiliation with a media outlet. Members of Sydney's Independent Media Center (IMC), an alternative Olympic news source, investigated accessibility to the SMC a few months before the Games. Finding that it only required a journalist's ID, they proceeded to make laminated passes for themselves as IMC volunteer staff, and by the end of August, one member had succeeded in gaining entry.

Milton Cockburn, SOCOG's general manager media, was critical of the ever-expanding numbers of Olympic sports, venues, athletes, and media, a trend which, he predicted, would price them out of the reach of most cities. He called for a cap on the number of media personnel, in particular. With 16,800 press and broadcast accreditations, he estimated that the cost of hosting the media in Sydney would exceed $100m—a "huge subsidy" provided by SOCOG and the NSW government. He did acknowledge, however, that with 44 percent of SOCOG's revenue derived from television rights, broadcasters did "at least pay their way" (Cockburn, 2000, 21). The fact that services to the Olympic family and national Olympic committees carried a $60m price tag according to the 1998 *Performance Audit Review*, was not addressed.

Cockburn went on to claim that the media had lost interest in the host city contract, which was made public in 1999, when they realized that the accredited media were "the real beneficiaries"—presumably because they were provided with press centers, free transport, free seats, and so forth. To imply that journalists were ignorant of IOC requirements for the accredited media until the release of the Sydney 2000 host city contract was not entirely accurate. With an Olympic Games held somewhere in the world every two years, few journalists would be unaware of the general practices—and perks, such as they were—associated with covering the big event. Moreover, the *Herald* did in fact publish an article on the $58m costs of hosting the media (Macey, 1999)

THE FINE ART OF MEDIA BEAT-UPS

As already discussed in this chapter, the Australian mass media, for the most part, shared a procorporate agenda. Nowhere was this more obvious than in their coverage of the antiglobalization protests held at the World Economic Forum (WEF) meetings in Melbourne on September 11–13, 2000 (S11)—the same week that the Sydney Olympics began. (A full account of these events and their implications for Sydney 2000 protests is presented in chapter 9.)

Protesters' allegations of police violence—readily substantiated by television footage—resulted in a formal investigation by the Victorian Office of the Ombudsman. As part of the evidence for this inquiry, Dr. Bernard Barrett, former state historian for the Victorian government, prepared a comprehensive and incisive analysis of the police baton charge and the news media, titled "Beating Up" (Barrett, 2000). The term refers to the process by which the news media, often in collaboration with politicians, police, or other state authorities, present selective and biased coverage in order to generate scare stories or to fuel moral panic about volatile issues such as violence, drugs, youth, and immigration. There is some debate over the extent to which beat-ups are simply created by journalists struggling to produce new copy every day because that is their job, rather than by some underlying propaganda model of the mass media, as Chomsky and Herman would explain it (Lumby, 2000). Of course, copy is readily available to the "struggling journalist" who contacts politicians, police departments, or government offices—all of which have adequate funding and personnel to deal with media relations—whereas grassroots community groups operating on shoestring budgets lack these resources.

In the print media, a significant component of the beat-up process is the headline, which is designed to command readers' attention by means of exaggeration, distortion, and omission. Since mainstream journalists rarely compose their own headlines, there may be major differences between the title of the article and its contents, but, regardless of its accuracy, the impact of the headline remains significant.

S11: An Olympic Test Event

In the case of the WEF protests, owners of Australian media corporations were among the WEF membership, and both Fairfax and News Limited newspapers were implicated in the beat-up. For three months before the event, most newspaper accounts were building up an expectation that the protest would be violent; in fact, as Barrett argued, the corporate media took on the role of "counterprotesters." Predictably, readers were reminded of "violent" protests against the World Trade Organization's Seattle meeting in November 1999. S11 protest conveners, despite their stated goal of nonviolent tactics and their training workshops on nonviolent protest, were largely ignored in the mainstream press, where journalists tended to rely on input from the police public relations office and the pro-WEF views of people associated with privately funded think tanks.

S11's call to Shut Down the World Economic Forum was often interpreted as a "aggressive" slogan and a possible precursor to violence. Even a journalist from the ABC, a network often criticized by the right for its allegedly proleft bias, raised the question of violence in an interview with NSW Member of the Legislative Assembly (MLA) and Green Party representative Lee Rhiannon, who pointed out that, in the case of Seattle, violence came from police authorities. She explained that the S11 slogan was not violent, but rather a message to WEF delegates to stop their "exclusive elitist meeting" and their attacks on human rights around the world, and to respect Australia's democratic process and traditions by talking with Australians about issues that affected their lives (Rhiannon, 2000b).

Trumping all the other sources of anti-S11 propaganda was one of the world's largest public relations companies, Hill and Knowlton—the same spin doctors hired by the IOC in 1999 to clean up its image after the bribery scandals. Shortly before the September event, Hill and Knowlton offered its Australian clients "WEF-related crisis management services . . . focusing on corporate reputations and employees' safety in the light of S11 aims and the Seattle experience," according to an *Australian Financial Review* (*AFR*) story (cited by Barrett, 2000, 3). As another *AFR* story (Potter, 2000) described the situation, Hill and Knowlton were "keen to drum up business with doom-laden dossiers." Barrett reported that some of the subsequent newspaper stories on the protests looked as if "they had been cut and pasted from handouts" issued by the WEF, Hill and Knowlton, the police media office, and procorporate think tanks (Barrett, 2000, 15).

Hill and Knowlton's background brief on S11 activities—a "highly confidential" document—was sent to its Australian clients (and, helpfully, leaked to Crosswinds website in early September). The brief correctly pointed out that protesters were fully aware of the fact that "nearly all the world's media outlets will have a presence in Australia seeking 'preview' stories in the lead up to the Olympics" and that a sufficiently "dramatic" protest would present "a great opportunity to make a significant global impact." Although it noted on the first page that the "civil disobedience" campaign had already started with a "peaceful demonstration" outside McDonald's Adelaide headquarters, it proceeded to document S11's links with "anarchy" websites including an anarchist bookshop and the Melbourne IMC.

The IMC example relied on a somewhat circular argument since one of the first functions of melbourne.indymedia.org, when it became active on August 1, 2000, was to cover S11 protests, which became the focus of most postings for the next few months (and, as organizers noted, the focus of most hate mail against protesters, as well). S11, according to the Hill and Knowlton brief, had "tangible" links with "affinity groups" including the Seattle protest organizers—a "finding" that should have come as no surprise to anyone. "It can be assumed," their clients were warned, "that S11 has downloaded the resources from another anarchist website . . . which were alleged to be used in Seattle." Moreover, the brief claimed, "S11's reach has extended far beyond the shores of Australia" and it was therefore "possible" that overseas protesters would travel to Melbourne (Hill and Knowlton, 2000).

Clearly, by belaboring the links with anarchists in general and with Seattle's anarchist protesters in particular, the brief sought to discredit all

S11 groups, and to generate even more concern among Hill and Knowlton clients, who had already been exposed to the news media beat-up and the general expectation of violence. Although the brief noted the fact that S11 was appealing to "the complete gamut" of protest groups, and provided a list of these groups, it repeatedly emphasized the anarchy connection. Clearly, "anarchists" sounded so much more threatening than animal rights advocates or artists (also included in the list), as well as fitting the news media's *ratbag* and *rag-tag* labels very nicely. In fact, anarchists were only one of a wide range of organizations involved in the Seattle protest, the S11 coalition, and Sydney's Anti-Olympic Alliance (AOA). (A full account of the S11 and AOA protests is presented in chapters 8 and 9.)

Another *AFR* article, despite its unpromising title "Instant anarchy" (Potter, 2000), provided one of the most accurate and unbiased mainstream media accounts of the S11 organization—and one that activists circulated as one of the few positive examples of its kind. In what appeared to be genuine admiration for the expertise of the "committed young computer geeks" who set up the S11 website, Potter confronted stereotypes of activists: "there wasn't a facial piercing, a spiked or matted hair or a calf-high Doc Maartens boot between them."

In contrast, a "beat-up" article on S11 protest by Uli Schmetzer in the *Chicago Tribune* (reprinted in the *Seattle Times*) on September 13 contained so many glaring inaccuracies, as well as the usual distortions, that Sydney protest group members sought legal advice and a retraction. The article claimed that the IMC was directly responsible for coordinating S11 demonstrations, which, it alleged, had produced such "sobering" results as the harassment of Western Australia's premier Richard Court, damage to his car, injuries to five police officers, and WEF delegates trapped in the building. In reality, neither the Sydney nor the Melbourne IMC coordinated S11 protests. Moreover, Barrett pointed out, such articles routinely failed to mention that Court and another politician refused to follow police directives *not* to use private cars as transport because of protesters' blockades of the building's entrances.

Typical of the mainstream media's dismissive treatment of S11 protesters, many journalists equated "global corporations" with "globalization," and went on to claim that the latter was responsible for the e-mail communication, websites, and video equipment on which demonstrators relied to organize their protest. As Barrett explained, by failing to distinguish between "corporations" and "technology," such accounts misrepresented antiglobalization protesters' "real, stated issue" which was the problem of "non-elected, unaccountable global corporations dictating the domestic policies of sovereign nations" (Barrett, 2000, 8).

Anti-Olympic Protest: A Second Beat-up

There was evidence of a similar media beat-up—although on a somewhat smaller scale—in the Sydney press in the months leading up to the Olympics, with predictions of violent protest and confrontations with police appearing on a regular basis. The groundwork had been laid by events in Melbourne, which police and authorities used as a warning to Sydney protesters that a repeat performance would not be tolerated.

A March 2000 *Herald* story, for example, quoted the views of Sydney police inspector David Darcy on protest groups' plans not to apply for police permits to march. He alleged that, regardless of their intentions, silence was "a form of violence," and that violent outcomes might result from unauthorized protests (Darcy quoted in Bacon, 2000). In July, another *Herald* article warned, "Protest groups prepare to head for Sydney, via Melbourne and Seattle" (Connolly, 2000). "Extremists and anarchists" from the United States and the UK were expected to arrive in Australia, according to this report, and a police source was quoted as saying, "Nobody really knows how they will react or what they are capable of." To get answers to these profound questions, Australian police had consulted their Seattle counterparts. As Genevieve Derwent (2000) pointed out in the University of Technology Sydney student newspaper *Vertigo,* Connolly's choice of words throughout the article planted the idea of the inevitability of police violence and the "extremist" and unpredictable nature of the protesters. Equally important, some were allegedly from Seattle, and these "outsiders" were presumably more likely to commit "unAustralian" acts. Indigenous Social Justice Association leader Ray Jackson sent a rebuttal to the *Herald* regarding Connolly's allegations, but the letter was never published, in Jackson's view, because of SOCOG's tight control over the mainstream media (Jackson, 2001, 6).

A month before the Games began, a *Herald* story announced, "Anarchist protest plan revealed." The first three paragraphs reported on a scare story from the previous day's *Sunday Times* (London), and then went on to issue a not-so-veiled warning to anarchists by reiterating the NSW Police Service's zero tolerance position on "violent or unlawful activity" (Clennell, 2000). Titled "Trouble Brewing: Police Fear a Repeat of London's J18 Riots Could Disrupt Olympic Events," and subtitled "British Anarchists Plot to Disrupt the Sydney Games," Paul Ham's article from Murdoch's *Sunday Times* was the source of mostly false allegations that appeared repeatedly in both Murdoch and Fairfax papers—in Australian media beat-ups:

> Surveillance of websites and e-mails has uncovered plans to block entry
> to the Olympic stadium, disrupt competition with sit-ins and ambush the

wives of corporate bosses attending the games. McDonalds, Coca-Cola and other Olympic sponsors have been warned that they may be targeted for attack. (Ham, 2000)

Ham went on to state that both the WEF and the Olympics had "attracted interest from members of British anarchist cells" responsible for the June 18 anticapitalism "riots," and that "Australian cells *are believed* to be coordinating" WEF and anti-Olympic protests (emphasis added). Grassroots groups including ProtestNet, Feminist Avengers, and Ruckus were named as examples of militant "cells" and Ruckus was identified as a group that trained its members in "direct action"—although the fact that it appeared on the S11 website's links under the heading "Non-violent direct action" was conveniently overlooked.

The article proceeded to point out that Friends of the Earth and other "legitimate organizations" (presumably in contrast to illegitimate "anarchist cells") also opposed Olympic-related legislation that prohibited public protest. Although he then quoted an S11 representative who clearly stated that their group was planning *nonviolent* action, there was no doubt that, like the Australian media sources that Barrett examined, the article deliberately emphasized the potential for violence, and helped to create the public expectation that these groups were intent on violent protests.

The article concluded with the soon-to-be-famous quote, attributed to a spokesman (sic) from the office of the NSW director of public prosecutions, in defense of Olympic legislation: "A lot of overseas people are going to be causing all sorts of problems. . . . We're preparing just in case. You've got to keep the buggers under control" (Ham, 2000).

Later in August, a *Herald* article listed four Olympic security issues: cyber hackers, Aboriginal protest at Olympic Park and at the central business district (CBD), Anti-Olympic Alliance (AOA) threats "to block the entrance to the Olympic Stadium" before the opening ceremony, and the closure of at least twenty-six rural police stations during the Games (O'Rourke, 2000). At least two of these alleged "threats"—the cyber vandalism and the AOA protest—had no basis in fact; the only supporting evidence to be found was in earlier media beat-ups.

Apart from the sinister aspects of the media and police attempts to generate public expectations of violent protests, the "surveillance of websites and e-mails" was almost laughable. No activist would assume for a moment that e-mail was a secure method of communication, and websites are by definition accessible to anyone with a computer hookup. In fact, AOA members began including greetings to members of the NSW police who were monitoring their e-mail communication, and by September, Inspector David Darcy, the police officer responsible for community liaison, was posting his own messages to the Sydney IMC website. Police infiltration of anti-Olympic groups was a surer route to gathering "intelligence" on protest plans, but, based on my own experience in these groups, and my ongoing research, all the evidence pointed toward nonviolent protest.

Friendly Fire: Progressive Media Beat-ups

From the other side of the fence, a different media phenomenon was also in evidence in late August and early September, just before the Olympics began. Since this was a period when I was interviewed extensively by American and UK journalists from both mainstream and alternative media, in my roles as author of a forthcoming book critical of the Olympic industry, a recent participant in the AOA in Sydney, and a member of the anti-Olympic Bread Not Circuses coalition in Toronto, I became a part of that media process (see Lenskyj, 2000). Two examples will demonstrate how well-intentioned and progressive journalists, probably inadvertently, contributed to a form of media beat-up on the topic of anti-Olympic protest, while at the same time exemplifying a progressive approach to investigative journalism that was rarely found in Olympic-related stories.

In a lengthy interview with Nick DeMause of the alternative New York newsmagazine, the *Village Voice,* I explained what I believed would be the police response to the planned protests by Aboriginal groups and by the AOA. By that stage, I had completed the research for chapter 2 of this book, which reviews Olympic-related law-and-order legislation and enhanced police powers over public protest, and for chapter 3, which examines Indigenous issues. In both cases, I provided recent examples of police statements and police behavior that reinforced fears that nonviolent protesters—at that time, anticipated at about thirty thousand—would be violently suppressed by the police. In addition to my participation in AOA during the first half of the year, I was regularly in e-mail communication with Aboriginal and AOA activists after I left Sydney. It was in this context, after having provided a lengthy background explanation, that I made the statement, "I expect there will be violence, there may even be fatalities" (cited in DeMause, 2000).

Ironically, it was this statement that *Village Voice* editors chose to highlight at the top of DeMause's story, "Gold Medals, Iron Fist." The story opened with the equally alarming quote from the law-and-order side: "You've got to keep the buggers under control." If Victorian critic Dr. Bernard Barrett had read this account, he might have included it as an example of a media beat-up because of the apparently unsubstantiated predictions of violence. However, Indigenous Social Justice Association leader Ray Jackson, one of several activists whom DeMause interviewed and cited, described the planned protest in this way:

> We continue to stress that our actions will be peaceful. We do not want any physical force used by us or against us. But SOCOG has said no way, no one will cross over the Homebush Bay line. So there will be violence. The violence will not be perpetrated by us. But we certainly hold the right to defend ourselves. And how that pans out, we don't know. (Jackson quoted by DeMause, 2000)

The second example came from the progressive British newspaper, *The Guardian*. I had several telephone interviews with Sean Dodson, who subsequently coauthored a July 19 story on anti-Olympic protest with Patrick Barkham (2000). Titled "Protesters Limber Up for Olympics: cyber threat to opening of Sydney Games"—its headline was almost as alarmist as some of those that contributed to the S11 beat-up. Protesters' alleged plans to sabotage the Olympic website, previously reported in the British press, were repeated, and the article claimed that the Internet—specifically, the Sydney IMC—would be used to help organize "unauthorized" anti-Olympic demonstrations.

Neither of these claims was entirely accurate. The main purpose of the IMC was to provide alternative coverage of the Olympics and of anti-Olympic protest (which IMC organizers correctly predicted would be largely ignored by the mainstream press). It was not established for hacking purposes, and, although it occasionally advertised forthcoming events, that function was usually performed by the Active Sydney website activesydney.org.au. (For an in-depth discussion of the IMC, see chapter 7.) On the issue of protest, the *Guardian* article quoted Ray Jackson, who again pointed out that Aboriginal protesters' actions were dependent on what Olympic security forces did to prevent them from entering the Olympic site to set up a camp. In short, although careful reading would reveal the full context, there were enough minor errors to reinforce predictions of unlawful actions and violent confrontations between police and protesters.

CONCLUSION

In the early 1990s, the Olympic industry had relatively uncritical support from a generally docile Australian mass media, whose procorporate messages served Olympic organizers' interests well. The IOC bribery scandal that became public at the end of 1998 marked a new and troubling era for Sydney 2000 organizers, as serious investigative journalists began to uncover a variety of new, home-grown Olympic controversies. This is not to suggest that the mass media began giving more balanced coverage to Olympic protest groups; on the contrary, media beat-ups targeting S11 in Melbourne and anti-Olympic protest in Sydney served police, government, and Olympic organizers' interests most effectively. However, the Olympic industry did not emerge entirely unscathed, and the extent to which these crises threatened its hegemony will be examined in chapters 7, 8, and 9.

2

Police, Protest, and Olympic Legislation

"You've Got to Keep the Buggers under Control"

———≈≈≈———

Government and police authorities relied heavily on scare-mongering about international terrorism to justify the huge budgets, the enhanced police and security officers' powers, and the overzealous surveillance efforts that have characterized Olympic security preparations since the terrorist attacks at the 1972 Munich Olympics. At the same time, Olympic organizers faced the challenge posed by any hallmark event: to police the venues intensively but unobtrusively in order to preserve the required festive atmosphere. Law enforcement officers from state and federal levels, as well as military and intelligence personnel, were all heavily involved in Australia's Olympic security efforts, at considerable cost to the public purse.

TERRORISM: AMATEUR OR PROFESSIONAL?

In 1997, one of the authors of Australia's overall antiterrorism plan, Alan Thompson of the Australian Defence Academy in Canberra, acknowledged that there had been a fall in the rate of international terrorism in the 1990s, and, more recently, the attorney general and minister for defence (2000) also claimed that there was "no specific threat of terrorism against the Sydney 2000 Games." (At the time, these statements were valid.) Thompson did draw attention, however, to the security threat allegedly posed by another source—individuals or small groups with no history of involvement in terrorism or politically motivated violence—which he termed *amateur terrorism*. He cited the 1996 annual report of the Australian Security Intelligence Organization (ASIO), which claimed that domestic debates and protests, prompted, for example, by the French nuclear testing in the South Pacific, the proposed gun control legislation, and the federal elections, resulted in an increase in the number of threat assessments involving "amateur terrorists" that were carried out by ASIO (Thompson, 1996, 1997).

ASIO's official Olympic role was to collect, assess, and communicate information on possible sources of threat to the other federal and state agencies responsible for Olympic security (Sadleir, 1996). In 1997, ASIO, together with state police intelligence units, began monitoring individuals and groups believed to pose a threat to public order during the Olympics. ASIO had conducted 46 Olympic-related threat assessments, out of a total of 346, in 1998–1999; by 2000, it reported that 25 percent of its 885 threat assessments were related to the Olympics (ASIO, 2000). A Victorian police commissioner even admitted to the surveillance of "innocuous groups" as a pre-Olympic security measure because of the alleged tendency for extremists to hide in "moderate organizations," but at that time the NSW police minister denied that such groups were being infiltrated. The finding that police requests for phone taps in NSW from June 1992 to June 1993 exceeded the comparable figure for all of the United States, a pattern that continued throughout the 1990s, suggested a history of overzealous intelligence efforts (Boon-Kuo, 1998).

Olympic Security: A United Effort

The Olympic Coordination Authority (OCA) had primary responsibility for the construction of Olympic facilities and the provision of adequate security systems throughout. All venues were designed to maximize crime prevention, with particular attention to surveillance and access control. The main stadium, completed in 1999, had state-of-the-art video surveillance systems that covered every seat, as well as aisles, entrances, and underground tunnels, and were powerful enough to allow security guards to view such details as the accreditation cards worn by officials, journalists, and athletes. Thousands of surveillance cameras were installed in all Olympic venues, and areas outside their line of sight were equipped with alarm systems activated by motion, heat, or sound (Magnay, 1999).

With Sydney's Olympic bid promising the highest level of "effective, friendly, and unobtrusive" security for all Olympic visitors and tourists, Sydney Olympic organizers began security planning many years before the Games. The bomb explosion during the 1996 Olympics prompted them to redouble their efforts, with "the Atlanta experience" now appearing in Olympic discourse as the example that Sydney should not emulate. In 1997–1998, the security division of the Sydney Organizing Committee for the Olympic Games (SOCOG) developed a comprehensive electronic protection program and began to investigate the capacity of the Australian private security industry to provide supplementary staff for the Olympics. An Olympic Security Working Committee was established, with representation from NSW Police Service, SOCOG, OCA, and the Commonwealth Attorney General's department.

Protecting Visiting Dignitaries' Dignity

At the federal level, ASIO developed the Federal Olympic Security Intelligence Center (FOSIC) in 1999. Staffed by the Australian Federal Police (AFP) and officers from all Australian government security agencies, the center operated twenty-four hours a day during the Olympics. The AFP was also responsible for training and equipping two hundred "close protection officers" for visiting "Internationally Protected Persons" (heads of state and diplomats) and VIPs (key Olympic family members), and for the areas of strategic criminal intelligence and criminal activity committed against Commonwealth interests (AFP, 2000). By March 2000, the Australian Commonwealth Government had contributed $53m toward Olympic-related national security and border controls, including $23m on equipment to detect biological and chemical hazards, out of a total of $548m that it had directed toward the staging of the Games (2000 Games Media Unit, 2000).

The AFP's dignitary protection function had been revised a few years earlier following the Sydney visit of the chairman of the National People's Congress of China, in order to incorporate a new aspect of "dignity protection"—specifically, protection from "harassment" by local protesters. Members of the Chinese delegation had expressed their displeasure when people waved placards as the chairman passed by the Sydney Botanic Gardens. Police subsequently arrested the protesters under what civil liberties advocates saw as a fabricated application of the Royal Botanic Gardens Trust Act (Anderson, 2000). For their part, the AFP position was that Australia needed to be aware of foreign visitors' different "sensitivities" while at the same time adhering to Australians' basic right to lawful, peaceful assembly (Whiddett, 1996). It was clear by 2000, however, that these basic rights were in jeopardy.

The Australian Defence Force's (ADF) participation in Olympic security involved about 4,000 military personnel, whose Olympic-related duties included searches of venues and vehicles, bomb searches, and bomb disposal. A March 16, 2000 press release from the attorney general's and defense minister's offices pointed out that this number was almost equivalent to Australia's first military contingent to support UN peace-keeping efforts in East Timor—a claim that could well be interpreted as security "overkill" in the case of the Olympics and indisputable evidence to support claims that NSW would be in a *de facto* state of emergency for the six-week duration of the Olympics and Paralympics (Anderson, 2000). The training of "counterterrorism units," which included mock storming of jumbo jets and police-military searches of motor vehicles, began in early

1999. In May 2000, a three-day counterterrorist exercise involving the army's Special Air Service incurred $100,000 in damages to the Blacktown softball stadium, an expense defended by NSW Police Commissioner Peter Ryan in the cause of "realism" (Connolly & Kennedy, 2000). By August 2000, military forces were on 24-hour alert, focusing on 115 places in the city identified as potential terrorist targets.

ADF equipment available for Olympic-related use included armored vehicles and Black Hawk helicopters, to be used for security tasks and general support. In the months leading up to the Olympics, nighttime helicopter exercises regularly succeeded in keeping thousands of western suburbs and inner-city residents awake. In May 2000, three military helicopters were being deployed for "the real thing," as they hovered over the headland at Bondi Beach during the antistadium protests, in a transparent display of police and military muscle against about 150 unarmed men, women, and children engaged in nonviolent protest (see chapter 8).

In an unprecedented and disturbing move, the United States and Israel planned to send their own military and security personnel to operate unilaterally in Australia for the purpose of responding to "terrorist" attacks and protecting their teams (Head, 2000).

High-Level Security in Sydney

The Olympic Security Command Center was set up by the NSW Police at SOCOG headquarters in order to coordinate Olympic security, with the police service, under Ryan, taking ultimate responsibility for core security matters at competition venues, the Olympic villages, and the airports. No NSW police officers were permitted to take leave during the Olympics and Paralympics (the parallel multisport event for athletes with disabilities), and additional personnel from country areas were recruited to supplement their numbers. At the same time, the minister for police guaranteed that community safety levels and minimum staffing levels would be maintained in every region and local area command in the state. Some stations, however, had been closed down in 1999 and 2000, while two Sydney councils—Hurstville and Sutherland—began employing their own special constables, and three others, including the Olympic corridor suburb of Auburn, were reported to be considering doing so (Clennell, 1999). In June 2000, it was announced that civil servants from police headquarters would help with nonoperational duties in rural stations during the Olympics, together with 50 retired police officers who had responded to a call for extra staff (Doherty, 2000). These trends demonstrated that, like other infrastructure spending, the Olympics were demanding the lion's share of the police budget and personnel while regional NSW suffered the consequences.

Olympic security plans initially called for 4,500 out of the 13,600 NSW police officers, at a cost of $174m. This number was later increased to 4,875, following concerns about the poor response to the private security officer recruitment drive. Five hundred police were required just to protect the athletes' village, while approximately 3,500 contract security personnel were to be deployed at the venues and villages, and 230 specially trained dogs were to patrol venues and customs areas to detect explosives. An additional 3,500 security personnel were generated by the Olympic Volunteers in Policing program, which recruited men and women from the Rural Fire Service, the State Emergency Service, and the Surf Life Saving Association—three voluntary organizations with statewide branches. The Rural Fire Service volunteers were to conduct magnetometer searches and bag inspections at venue access points, and to perform marshaling duties at events and accommodation sites. Securing playing fields, closing roads, and monitoring local access were tasks to be undertaken by State Emergency Service volunteers. A comprehensive system of accreditation for all employees entering Olympic sites was implemented in January 2000, with background checks required before accreditation passes were issued. Volunteers were also subject to the probity checks, as were all SOCOG and OCA paid employees.

Ostensibly in the interests of security, public exclusion zones within Sydney Harbor and no-fly zones over outdoor Olympic venues were to be established and patroled. However, in light of sponsors' and television networks' demands that attempts at ambush marketing (advertising by competitors of the official Olympic sponsors) or unlicensed filming be suppressed, it is clear that the policing of these zones served commercial as well as security interests. Indeed, a 1999 *Herald* story revealed that volunteer law students would be used to search spectators for "illegal" items such as flags, or banners with political or commercial messages (Hornery, 1999). Not only were such actions arguably an infringement of human rights, but the cynical deployment of law students as (ambush marketing) law enforcement officers for the Olympic industry was also cause for concern. And by 2000, all these restrictions were clearly spelled out in the *Olympic Arrangements Act* discussed later in this chapter.

Fast-track Security Training

Chubb Security, Australia's largest security company, played a major role in security at Olympic venues, villages, and administrative sites. Its responsibilities included delivering a four–five month training program, to be completed by June 2000, and recruiting staff from other states to work during the Olympics. Most interstate staff coming to Sydney would reside with Sydney-based Chubb Security employees, in a program incongruously called "Adopt-a-guard" (Chubb Security, 1999).

By March 2000, the recruitment and training of the sixty-five thousand (paid) Olympic labor force was in the hands of the Olympic Labor Network, comprising eight private agencies. Security personnel recruitment and training was the responsibility of Workforce International. A special training program of the Department of Employment, Education, Training, and Youth Affairs, called the GROW program, focused on training disadvantaged people to fill Olympic jobs, including hospitality and security, as well as preparing them for post-Games employment. Finally, the Department of Technical and Further Education (TAFE) undertook the general volunteer training that was required for unpaid staff.

According to information presented to the Social Impact Advisory Committee by OCA in June 2000, Aboriginal people were among those "successfully targeted" by the government's GROW program (PIAC, 2000b). There were, however, some negative ramifications of this initiative. Indigenous Social Justice Association (ISJA) leader, Ray Jackson, documenting a March 6 meeting with SOCOG security personnel about the proposed Aboriginal protest, reported that "it was stated that they, SOCOG Security, had attempted to hire 'every Black security group in Australia.' " Jackson went on to predict, cynically, that Black security forces (Maori, Pacific Islander, African, and perhaps Indigenous) would be deployed in the vanguard in order to generate the spectacle of "Blacks beating the shit out of Blacks" (Jackson, 2000a, 9).

At the time of the Olympics, a full security license in NSW required at least 10 days' training and covered 12 basic competencies, with licensees trained as bodyguards, bouncers, and crowd controllers. The GROW program was longer, at 150 hours. Legislation enacted in 1999, the *Security Industry (Olympics and Paralympic Games) Act* s.5(2), provided for a shortcut in training: a special Olympic security license, effective from August 1 to November 30, 2000 and limited to "patrolling, protecting, watching or guarding property, and using security equipment" at Homebush Bay and other Olympic venues and facilities. According to the *SunHerald*'s exclusive official guide to Games jobs, *Work the Dream,* published on March 12, 2000, Workforce International was offering special Olympic security guard training and traineeships as well as employment opportunities for licensed security personnel. By May, their government-subsidized 6-day training program, at a cost of $200 per person, had only attracted 800 out of the 2,000 trainees required for the program, with the result that Workforce extended its recruitment drive to rural areas—although it did not reimburse transport or accommodation costs (Jacobsen, 2000b).

Chubb Security contributed a set of security guidelines to the 1999 manual titled *Business as Usual* produced by the Sydney 2000 Olympic Commerce Center, an initiative of the NSW Chamber of Commerce. The security recommendations for businesses ranged from requiring photo identification for all staff to installing closed circuit television. In another section of the manual, companies were advised to create secure reception areas, to monitor illegal parking, to develop bomb threat procedures, and in the central business district (CBD), to prepare staff for possible surges of visitors seeking shelter from rain or heat. Somewhat surprisingly, guidelines for dealing with protesters at that time—mid-1999—were relatively lenient. It was suggested that businesses should designate a place for protesters to gather, and should prepare staff for the possibility that buildings in the CBD would attract protest demonstrations simply because of their location (Chubb Security, 1999). By 2000, however, such provisions were proving unnecessary, since anti-Olympic demonstrations in the CBD and adjacent harbor foreshore areas were effectively banned.

SOCOG headquarters in Ultimo, within the CBD, were carefully guarded by Chubb Security long before the Games began. Not surprisingly, the sidewalk outside this building was often the site of organized anti-Olympic protests in 2000. Somewhat different expressions of dissatisfaction with Olympic organizers were in evidence in May 2000, when the decision of Australian IOC member Kevan Gosper to allow his daughter to run in the torch relay was evoking widespread outrage among Australians. SOCOG security had to be increased to cope with a number of disgruntled visitors who approached the front desk demanding to see someone in authority because they (incorrectly) assumed that SOCOG bore ultimate responsibility for the Gosper fiasco.

NSW POLICE: A CHECKERED HISTORY

The 1994 establishment of a Royal Commission, under the leadership of the Honorable J. Wood, to investigate "the nature and extent of corruption within the Police Service, particularly of an entrenched or systemic kind," marked a turning point in the NSW Police Service, which criminologist David Dixon (1999) aptly characterized as having "a culture of corruption." In addition to the highly publicized problems of police involvement in pedophilia, which produced two additional volumes of the Royal Commission's final report, Judge Wood documented a pattern of mistreatment of suspects, unlawful searches and interrogations, planting of evidence, fabrication of confessions and institutionalized perjury, involving nearly three hundred officers, only a minority of whom were removed or prosecuted (Anderson, 2000; Dixon, 1999).

The commission's findings produced a serious crisis in police legitimacy and a pressing need to restore public confidence in the force. These challenges were largely resolved by the introduction of a "clean outsider" in the person of the new police commissioner, Peter Ryan, who was given a $400,000 salary, an additional $400m on top of the existing police budget, and free rein—with the understanding that he would eradicate all corruption. Ryan was reported to have told his officers to concentrate on "getting crime down" and to "leave the reform process" to him (quoted in Dixon, 1999). There was never any corporate admission of wrongdoing, or any public apology, even though, as Dixon pointed out, "some humility about the breach of trust" might have been appropriate (Anderson, 2000; Dixon, 1999, 157).

Notwithstanding the reform rhetoric, most critics argued that the police service had not yet earned public trust and needed continued external scrutiny. Although findings of improper activities of the Special Branch threatened its continued existence, the Royal Commission and the NSW government deferred investigation of what was now called the "Protective Security Group" until after the Olympics because of its important role in Olympic security.

Post-Royal Commission boosts to the NSW Police budget included provision for new service revolvers—.22 semiautomatic Glock pistols—at a cost of $11m, a pay increase of 22 percent, and 100 new police positions. Capsicum (pepper) spray was introduced in 1998, along with training programs in crowd and riot control. Copwatch groups in NSW and Victoria campaigned against the use of capsicum spray, citing the demonstrated link to over 60 deaths in the United States, and the particular danger it posed to people with heart and respiratory diseases, and to pregnant women. Furthermore, they claimed that it wouldn't stop police shootings because it was only effective at close range. Evidence from Canada, the United States and Queensland since 1995 showed that police used the spray against the same populations they had targeted before: protesters, people with physical or mental disabilities, Indigenous people, trade unionists, and others (Copwatch, 1998).

Technological and other new equipment purchased by NSW Police in preparation for the Olympics totaled $34.7m. Significant advances in technology were in evidence, including offender database catalogues, digital photographs, and infrared surveillance cameras in public locations (Boon-Kuo, 1998). In the months before the Olympics, warnings circulated among activists regarding these surveillance cameras, which filmed them as they put up posters in the CBD; cameras were not always monitored at the time, but the film was stored so that "troublemakers" could be identified, if necessary, at a later date.

OLYMPIC LAWS: LEGAL RIGHTS VS. HUMAN RIGHTS

As early as 1994, a Public Interest Advocacy Center (PIAC) report identified the potential threat to human rights and civil liberties before and during the Games. In a submission to the NSW government's preliminary social impact assessment, PIAC emphasized the fact that Olympic security plans should not simply cater to Olympic visitors, but must take into account the civil liberties of Sydney residents, especially the poor and homeless, sex trade workers, people with disabilities, and sexual and racial/ethnic minorities. Its six recommendations to the NSW government, SOCOG, and Sydney City Council identified the policy and structural changes needed to protect human rights, minimize negative social impacts, and ensure genuine community consultation (PIAC, 1994). By 2000, however, there was minimal evidence that any of these paths had been followed. On the contrary, as human rights advocates argued, Olympic-related legislation was in contravention of United Nations provisions for freedom of movement and protection from arbitrary arrest, and the NSW (Labor) government, for its part, had failed to implement any policies that would effectively mitigate against these negative impacts.

As Louise Boon-Kuo (1998) found in her incisive analysis of police powers and the Olympics, parliamentary debate in the period between the 1993 awarding of the Games and 1998 did not show that politicians were making any links between the Olympics and the need for law and order, despite the popularity of law-and-order platforms. Similarly, the mainstream media were not calling for a crackdown on crime or enhanced police powers because of the Olympics. As Boon-Kuo argued, the marketing of Sydney as an Olympic city relied on an image of stability and widespread community support, a goal that would not be achieved by publicly acknowledging the need for specific law-and-order legislation to bring dissidents into line before the big event. On the contrary, it served bid interests very well to contrast Sydney as an open, tolerant city with Beijing and its history of suppression (McGeoch & Korporaal, 1994). By 1999, however, police leaders were publicly indicating that they were concerned about protest during the Olympics, and the overpolicing of public space began to reflect this emerging trend.

David Dixon (1999, 165–166) demonstrated how much of the legislation of the late 1990s simply provided legal conditions for long-standing street policing practices, a particular cause for concern in light of the Royal Commission recommendation calling for a fundamental review of police powers, rather than the pattern of allowing the police to set the legislative agenda. Public spaces became the target of state legislation well before the Olympics, as did areas identified by police as crime hotspots, and locales frequented by working-class, visible minority, and Aboriginal youth.

The *Crimes Legislation (Police and Public Safety) Act,* introduced in June 1998, permitted police to conduct an electronic or pat search of a person, their bags, or personal effects, in a public place, if the officer had "reasonable" grounds to suspect that the person had a dangerous implement. The officer could also take into account the fact that the person was in a location with a high incidence of violent crime (known as an "operational area" or "crime hot spot." Although police already had "move on" powers, based on 1937 *Traffic Regulations,* regarding persons loitering in a public street and thereby causing "an inconvenience" to others, the 1998 amendment further empowered police to move on a person believed to be obstructing another person or traffic, harassing or intimidating another person, or causing fear in "a person of reasonable firmness."

The *Police and Public Safety Act* included some safeguards. It required police officers to identify themselves, to give reason for their direction, and to issue a second direction and a second warning before charging the person with an offense (and a fine of up to $220). Moreover, it specifically restricted police "move on" powers in the case of industrial action or peaceful protest, and the operation of the act was to be monitored by the NSW ombudsman. Even with these provisions, there was early evidence of the arbitrary use of police powers to harass homeless people, youth, Aborigines, and sex trade workers (PIAC, 2000a). The first ombudsman's report, released in July 2000, documented the extent of police abuse of "move on" powers: half of the targeted individuals were under seventeen years of age, 85 percent were male, and 22 percent were Aboriginal or Torres Strait Islander (PIAC, 2000b).

The *Children (Protection and Parental Responsibility) Act* (1997) was passed despite widespread criticism from many sources, including the UN. Intended to hold parents responsible for supervising offending children, it provided additional search powers in specified operational areas when the person was believed to be sixteen years of age or under. In terms of move on and detention powers, the police could remove a child believed to be lacking adult supervision, or one suspected of living in or habitually frequenting a public place. The naming of crime hot spots—which were often entire local government areas such as Orange, Ballina, and Moree in rural NSW—facilitated routine, random knife searches on groups of young people simply because they were in a particular public space. Equally disturbing, the act's "antigang" provisions were aimed indiscriminately at all groups of young people, with no recognition that most gatherings did not pose an actual threat. Responding to government attacks on young people's rights and recognizing that "*legal rights* created by governments may not live up to basic *human rights* recognized by the international community (emphasis in original)," the Youth Justice Coalition and the University of Technology Sydney (UTS) Community Law and Research Center published a guide on Youth Street Rights in 1998 (UTS, 1998).

Speaking in Parliament in May 2000, Green MLA Ian Cohen provided evidence of the discriminatory application of the *Protection and Parental Responsibility Act.* In the country town of Moree, for example, a community group in 1999 reported that the act had been used on ninety-five occasions in less than one year, with ninety-one of the young people involved being Aboriginal. In Sydney, a survey conducted by three youth advocacy organizations reported that 42 percent of the young people who were searched by police were searched in ways specifically precluded under the act. The vast majority of people fined were the young, the homeless, Aborigines, and sex trade workers (Cohen, 2000).

The *Crimes Amendment (Detention after Arrest) Act* (1997) eroded human rights, including young people's rights, even further. Among its shortcomings was its failure to treat the detention of young people as an action of last resort, and its failure to require a shorter maximum period of detention for those under eighteen (Anderson, Campbell, & Turner, 1999). This legislation became the focus of widespread concern in progressive circles because of its selective implementation and differential impact on disadvantaged youth, most significantly, the targeting of Aboriginal youth in country towns and Indo-Chinese youth in Sydney's western suburbs. So-called reasonable suspicion on the part of the police officer was arbitrarily influenced by the age, ethnicity, social class, gender, and sexual orientation of the persons or groups under observation as well as the social location of the officer. In fact, Commissioner Ryan stated that "zero tolerance" policing—a resource-intensive approach that dealt severely with minor crime, particularly public order offenses, in the belief that this would deter more serious crime and lower the crime rate—would only be practiced in certain communities, most notably the low-income, high-immigrant areas of Cabramatta, Bankstown, Canterbury, and South Sydney (Anderson, 2000; see also Poynting, 2000). A related 1998 initiative required constant police surveillance of repeat offenders in a number of Sydney's high-crime areas; according to one media report after the program's first year of operation, "notorious criminals" would be forced to leave town before the Olympics (Miranda, 1999).

By early 2000, allegations of brutality and racism against officers involved in a zero tolerance operation in Bankstown were under investigation by the independent Police Integrity Commission. It seemed that little had changed since a 1983 observation that Australian police, in their exercise of search, arrest, and detain powers, appeared to be viewing certain groups as "a class of people who are not worth protecting or not capable of living decent lives . . . they are only fit to be exploited, ignored, or contained" (Dixon, 1999, 88).

Policing practices involving more privileged youth, on the other hand, were characterized by leniency, second chances, and diversionary programs. In one highly publicized example, when a group of eighty students from Redlands, a private school in Cremorne (a wealthy North Shore suburb), removed one-way street signs, thereby jeopardizing motorists' safety, the youth involved were praised for admitting their wrongdoing, coming forward to "help the police with their inquiries," and thus saving valuable police time and taxpayer money (Anderson, 2000). Police time and taxpayer money in Cabramatta were apparently less valuable commodities. Maher and her coinvestigators (cited in Anderson, Campbell, & Turner, 1999) reported that Indo-Chinese heroin-users in that community were searched and strip-searched up to ten times a day, with no drugs being found in their possession, and found that this kind of overpolicing failed to reduce drug trade or to minimize harm among users.

The zero tolerance model commonly associated with the New York Police Department in the early 1990s has been extensively criticized by criminologists, lawyers, and police administrators in the United States and Europe as simply another version of the traditional punitive approach. It overpoliced poor and homeless people, racial and ethnic minorities, and other marginalized people by targeting street offenses, and thereby ignoring potentially more serious issues such as domestic violence and corporate and environmental crime. Its so-called proactive approach to public order jeopardized good relations between the targeted communities and the police. Moreover, it was resource-intensive, requiring increased police strength and computerized managerial systems, and therefore expensive and short-term; there was evidence from the United States that the same drop in crime rate had been achieved by other policing strategies (Cuneen, 1999).

Of particular relevance to Olympic-related protest, the numerous critics of New York's zero tolerance policing stressed three serious outcomes: the suppression of dissent, an increase in police brutality, particularly against racial and ethnic minorities, and an increase in deaths in custody. From the time that Sydney was awarded the Games, it was clear that some Aboriginal communities and groups were planning to organize mass protests to bring world attention to the Australian government's two-hundred-year record of racism. As the 1990s progressed, a number of non-Aboriginal community groups joined this enterprise in solidarity with Aborigines, while others began to organize around social, political, economic, and environmental issues (see chapter 7). In view of the NSW Police Service's imperfect history, its zero tolerance policy in targeted Sydney suburbs, and its enhanced public order powers, the potential for police violence against protesters was high.

Law in the Olympic City

Existing public order legislation facilitated the passage of additional laws in 1999 to prepare Sydney for its role as an Olympic city, with the prerequisite constraints on public behavior. The *Homebush Bay Operations Regulation* (1999) significantly extended existing police powers, and, more disturbingly, the powers of persons "authorized" by the Olympic Coordination Authority, in all the sports grounds at the Homebush Bay Olympic site. These authorized individuals were allowed to remove anyone who contravened the provisions of the regulation, trespassed, or caused "annoyance or inconvenience" within the sports grounds. Under the new act, the officer or authorized person was not required to issue a warning, and could use "reasonable" force when removing people, a power that might well prompt resistance on the part of those being targeted. Thus, as the PIAC briefing paper pointed out, a person who objected to the direction could also be charged with resisting arrest (PIAC, 2000a).

Those charged with trespass would be banned from entering the sports ground for the next twelve months, and, if they did so, or if they were removed a second time, would incur a lifelong ban. Persons charged simply with causing "annoyance or inconvenience" could be banned for up to six months if they were to "damage/ destroy/ remove tree/ plant/ vegetation," "leave rubbish/ litter," "use indecent/ obscene/ insulting/ threatening language," "behave in offensive/ indecent manner," or "cause serious alarm/ affront." In short, when authorized officers targeted a particular person, they could call upon a wide range of behaviors, most of which were open to a wide range of interpretations, in order to eject or charge that person. Activists wearing the popular "Fuck the Olympics" T-shirts, for example, were likely to be charged under these provisions (PIAC, 2000b). Civil liberties advocates were justly concerned that these powers would be used to suppress peaceful protest, not only during the Olympics but up to March 2002 when the act would cease to be in effect.

On the question of public assemblies or processions, the *Summary Offences Act* provided for the police commissioner to authorize such gatherings. It was not an offense, however, to participate in an unauthorized assembly; authorization merely gave immunity from future prosecution on the two charges of unlawful assembly and obstruction of traffic. In the event of a refusal, the commissioner was required to consult with the rally organizers, and to obtain a court order banning the assembly. If under seven days' notice were given and if the commissioner refused consent, the organizers could apply to either the District or Supreme Court for authorization.

The *Sydney Harbor Foreshore Authority Regulation (SHFA) 1999*, in contrast, demanded that all public assemblies be authorized by the SHFA, which had the power to set dates and conditions, or arbitrarily prohibit the assembly, with no recourse open to the organizers. Thus, the new regulation gave the SHFA greater powers than those of the police commissioner. Venues constituting the harbor foreshore, not coincidentally, included the major parks in the CBD that traditionally served as gathering or dispersal points for major political protests. Equally significant was the wide sweep of the SHFA to cover not only the harbor Olympic venues but also major parks, beaches, and recreational areas in the suburbs, up to 10km away from the harbor. During designated "special event activities" associated with New Year's Eve, Australia Day, and the Olympics,

Paralympics and Cultural Olympiad, the SHFA could charge admission or prohibit entry to persons possessing alcohol or "any other specified thing" (s.8(3)). The inclusion of Australia Day celebrations was significant: Aboriginal Australians and those who supported justice for Aborigines routinely marked Australia Day, renamed "Invasion Day," with demonstrations of a very different kind. Finally, there was no sunset clause on this regulation, which would be applied to special events in these areas at least until its review in 2004.

This was not the first move toward restricting public assemblies and privatizing public space in the CBD. Constraints on activities at Darling Harbor, a redeveloped waterfront venue that included expensive restaurants, upscale shops, a marine museum and an aquarium, were implemented through the *Darling Harbor Authority Act (DHA) 1984* and its 1995 regulation. In keeping with its unequivocal profit-making designation (in the regulation) as "a public place designed to allow for activities that encourage tourism," the regulation banned unauthorized commercial activity as well as unauthorized meetings, processions, performances, or sporting events (PIAC, 2000b). The original Darling Harbor redevelopment—a 1988 Bicentennial project—was fast-tracked, and the usual social and environmental impact assessments were bypassed (Thorne & Munro-Clark, 1989). Like other developments in Olympic host cities, it provided a classic example of the "bourgeois playground" that is a prerequisite for world-class-city status (Hall, 1989). A Sydney 2000 advertising feature in the *Toronto Star* captured its attributes perfectly:

> Picturesque Darling Harbor is home to the various sports which will be staged in the Sydney Convention and Exhibition Center, but also features a delightful children's park, colorful paddle boats on a sparkling lagoon, the Maritime Museum, an aquarium, an IMAX (giant screen) theater, upscale restaurants and wine bars. (Time/CBC Viewer's Guide, 2000)

Additional "move on" powers granted to police officers and rangers by the *SHFA Regulation* closely resembled those operating in Homebush Bay: causing an annoyance or inconvenience to others, collecting money, trespassing, or sleeping overnight were typical offending behaviors. The one safeguard in the *SHFA Regulation* was the requirement that police or rangers first issue a warning that failure to comply with the request was an offense.

Special *Olympic Arrangements*

The *Olympic Arrangements Act* (2000) served to fill any gaps inadvertently left by the preceding legislation. Olympics minister Michael Knight used the occasion of the act's first reading to emphasize its key role in the Olympic transportation plan and in the prevention of "overcommer-cialization," a problem that he then equated with "ambush marketing" and "tacky street vending." The idea that the Olympics would be pro-tected from "overcommercialization" was, of course, laughable; Knight's primary concern was to protect the companies that had paid huge amounts for the privilege of exploiting the lucrative commercial and advertising opportunities offered by the Games.

On the issues of enforcement officers' powers, Knight gave Parliament the same assurances that he had offered to the media: that no Olympic volunteers would be authorized to remove or direct people. He failed to comment on the powers of minimally trained security staff or to define "authorized persons" (Knight, 2000). A few months earlier, NSW premier Bob Carr had stated that all persons engaged in Olympic security would be under the supervision of a sworn police officer (Carr, 1999). But, as Lee Rhiannon warned Parliament, the bill raised the specter of a "private army" of persons "exempt from the constraints of civil remedies, from the oversight powers that restrain the police, and from the need to carry a badge to identify themselves" (Rhiannon, 2000a). Following a meeting with Deputy Commissioner Lola Scott, Indigenous Social Justice Associa-tion leader Ray Jackson reported her statements that only the police were licensed and trained to use capsicum spray, but that the OCA-authorized persons might be issued with police batons (Jackson, 2000b).

Olympic Impact Committee members were on hand for the second reading of the *Olympic Arrangements Act* in Parliament on April 14, 2000. Several activists in the visitors' gallery succeeded in bringing about an adjournment (and subsequently getting ejected by security guards) when they stood up and read a series of statements on the threats to human rights and civil liberties posed by the legislation.

Although the two stated aims of the *Olympic Arrangements Act* were the smooth flow of traffic and the prevention of ambush marketing, it was clear that the suppression of political protest was an underlying theme. When the act was discussed in Parliament, MLAs Rhiannon, Ian Cohen, and Dr. Peter Wong were the chief critics of its no-so-hidden agenda. Wong's questions alluded to the government's hypocrisy:

> What is the motive for this regulation? Is it to show the world during the Olympics, and very likely afterwards, how successful, harmonious and organized a society we are that we do not have social problems that leave thousands of people homeless on the streets? Is it to show that we are a successful economy that can employ everyone, so that there are no beg-gars on the street? Or is it to show that we can engage our young people and artists in meaningful and fulfilling activities so that they do not have

to be a nuisance to the general public? If this is what we want to achieve, this regulation is not the way. (Wong, 2000)

Wong went on to reject the "draconian changes" to the *Motor Traffic Act* contained in the bill, which some members viewed as exceeding a reasonable attempt to protect designated Olympic traffic lanes, to control deliveries in the CBD, and to manage roads in the Homebush Bay area. The leader of the opposition, Michael Gallacher, initially shared Wong's concern about the excessive penalties—up to $2,200—for simple traffic offenses—but stated that the Olympic Roads and Transport Authority head had assured him that maximum penalties would only be imposed by the courts.

A less obvious rationale for the increased penalties surfaced in Gallacher's later statement, where he identified the need "to provide a disincentive to those who go beyond mere negligent driving and who actually manipulate the successful running of any part of the Games for a personal agenda or for some other political or set agenda" (Gallacher, 2000). In fact, deliberately causing traffic congestion is an effective "monkey wrench" strategy that has often been used to good effect by activist groups such as the probicycle group, Critical Mass.

The *Olympic Arrangements Act* made the selling or distribution of articles within 3km of an Olympic venue or facility, or an Olympic live site without OCA or local council authorization an offense, with a maximum penalty of five thousand dollars; and the possible seizure of the goods for noncompliance with police or OCA staff orders. (The live sites were seven public places in the CBD designated for entertainment and public broadcasts of Olympic events, and included the plazas at Circular Quay, the Domain, and Martin Place.) Although most provisions of the act were only in force for the duration of the Olympics and Paralympics, several Olympic live sites were already under the jurisdiction of the SHFA and the Darling Harbor Authority (DHA), whose restrictions would last at least four more years. As Rhiannon rightly pointed out during parliamentary debate, peaceful protest and free expression of political views in the Domain—a harbor-front park that was "the symbolic home of free expression and association in Australia" throughout the twentieth century—would be policed by "a private army answerable only to the bureaucrats of the OCA" (Rhiannon, 2000a).

The *Olympic Arrangements Act* legislated exactly the kinds of draconian measures that Olympic organizers had tried unsuccessfully to persuade the Australian government to enact five years earlier. In March 1995, the Senate Legal and Constitutional References Committee produced a detailed report on the copyright and trade monopoly that the International Olympic Committee (IOC) and the Australian Olympic Committee exercised in relation to the use of Olympic words and symbols for commercial purposes. The committee was instructed to investigate existing protection to Olympic words and symbols, and to determine whether further legislation needed to be enacted to prevent ambush marketing.

Although Olympic organizers argued that there were sound financial reasons for offering protection to Olympic sponsors and media-rights holders, the expensive exercise undertaken by the Senate committee revealed that some stakeholders had a political agenda that went beyond mere economics. The joint submission of the NSW government and SOCOG, for example, recommended new state legislation that would fine ambush marketers and permit Olympic organizers to apply for civil search seizure orders, and alter or seize material that infringed copyright (Senate Committee, 1995). The marketing of any clothing or banners bearing protest messages that included the word *Olympics* could probably be confiscated under such provisions. In light of the 1982 precedent, when Aboriginal political protest during the Commonwealth Games was brutally repressed by Queensland police, these proposals had particularly sinister implications (Booth & Tatz, 1994; Russell, 1996),

The Senate committee, to its credit, was not swayed by this submission, but agreed that additional precautions against ambush marketing should be taken. At the same time, it stressed the importance of the constitutional guarantee of freedom of political communication and, in this regard, suggested that press reportage and political commentary by the public should be expressly exempt from legislation, even though some limited forms of ambush marketing might result. By 2000, freedom of political communication had taken a backseat to commercial and security priorities, and the *Olympic Arrangements Act* gave police and other authorized personnel a close approximation of the powers that the Senate committee had turned back five years earlier.

Distribution of unauthorized "articles," including political or other leaflets, was prohibited by the *Olympic Arrangements Act*, with a fine of up to five thousand dollars. This section was subsequently challenged by both anti-Olympic activists and religious fundamentalists—two groups that planned to pass out their respective messages to Olympic visitors. Christian Democratic Party member Fred Nile went to great lengths to commend the government for its "reasonable and justified" approach to traffic and crowd control, which, he claimed, must include "the power to stop publicity stunts." He then proceeded to express his narrow views on protesters, alluding to the earlier actions of the Olympic Impact Coalition (OIC): "We have seen, for example, people running onto the Sydney Cricket Ground, and even people interrupting activities at Parliament. I hope the Government will take steps to prevent such people, who are simply publicity seekers, abusing the Games in some way" (Nile, 2000).

In conclusion, Nile lamented, "We cannot lock up such people for the duration of the Games, . . ." but called for ways of preventing people, particularly Aboriginal protesters such as Charlie Perkins (and probably the OIC), from "sabotaging" the Games.

Supporting the bill in general, Nile called for an amendment to exclude noncommercial items or articles "of a religious nature" from the definition of prohibited articles. He cited a number of Christian groups whose leaders were concerned that they could not distribute their publications. One such group, "Eternal Gold, an Outreach to the Sydney Olympics," had planned to hand out five hundred thousand copies of a copyrighted Christian tract in fourteen languages that had been used in Atlanta during the 1996 Games. Finally, in a token gesture toward multiculturalism, Nile called for the amendment to encompass messages from "members of the Buddhist, Hindu or Muslim faiths" in order to preserve the right to freedom of religion in its widest possible sense. Greens Rhiannon and Cohen proposed a similar amendment to exclude articles not of a commercial nature, but both attempts failed on the grounds that this would allow protesters to disrupt the Olympics. Rhiannon unsuccessfully moved several other amendments, and mounted an eloquent and courageous defense of the Greens' position in the face of continuous heckling—and an incredible level of red-baiting—from government representatives, most notably from the treasurer, Michael Egan.

The sweeping powers granted by the act in relation to the mass media provoked the greatest outrage, and, in a matter of days, their challenges to OCA and the government, backed up by international lobbying, produced results. Community workers with the NSW Council of Social Services (NCOSS) and Shelter NSW, on the other hand, had been working for months with police and the OCA to develop a homelessness protocol that would override police and security staff "move on" powers in relation to street homeless people, particularly those in the CBD's Olympic live sites. The protocol that was eventually developed comprised a code of practice for police, security, council rangers, and OCA officials and an assistance and referral service operated by street outreach workers engaged by Sydney City Council. It stated that all people, including the street homeless, had the right to be in public places during the Olympics, without fear of harassment or attempts to move them on, except in cases where they asked for help, or were a danger to themselves or others. Furthermore, the protocol required police or other officers to contact the city's outreach team before moving a homeless person (Blunden, 2000, 6–7). However, the protocol only covered Sydney's CBD, and because it was not finalized until June, it was not officially approved as a regulation of existing public order and Olympic legislation.

The SOCOG Police Handbook (2000) provided a reference guide to operating procedures for NSW Police Service personnel working at Olympic venues. In his "Welcome Message" Olympic Security Command Center head Paul McKinnon reminded officers that "The eyes of the world will be on us"; a later "code of conduct" section carried the more mundane message that trading or selling of Olympic memorabilia was prohibited while on duty. The handbook emphasized security as a key operational area, together with venue management, spectator services, transport, doping control (athletes), medical, sport, logistics, accreditation, "Olympic Family" and VIP services, and television broadcasting. They were required to assist spectator services personnel in enforcing venue house rules, which included carrying restricted items or engaging in restricted actions (distribution of unauthorized literature, busking (performing as itinerant musicians), scalping, and political or religious demonstrations). The list of prohibited items included "banners, flags of non-participating countries, signs and items with corporate branding"—for instance, T-shirts carrying a corporate (or, more likely, anticorporate) message. By September, there were reports that the Olympic "ambush-marketing police" were going to great lengths to ensure that no Olympic-related television coverage gave nonsponsors free advertising, even to the point of requiring logos on non-IBM computers in the police control room to be covered (Barkham, 2000b).

Pre-Olympic Criminalization of Disadvantage

Although Sydney City Council's response to homelessness—for example, its brokerage program (renting private accommodation when homeless shelters were full), telephone information line, and outreach service—was considered by many to be better than other councils (Plant & Roden, 1999), it was clear that the new "move on" powers granted to NSW police, security guards, and "authorized" personnel, and the absence of an effective homelessness protocol to override these powers, posed a significant threat to street homeless people in 2000.

As early as 1997, there had been reports that local business owners in the inner-city areas of Darlinghurst and Surrey Hills had asked police to move vagrants off the streets (A tale of two cities, 1998). Residents in newly gentrified neighborhoods hired private security guards, while street people in the Paddington and Darlinghurst area were moved on to make way for Gay and Lesbian Mardi Gras celebrations. Private security was also in evidence at Newington, the new residential development at Homebush Bay, where, according to a sales representative, new homeowners were protected by patroling security guards and alarm systems in every house; $300 out of their annual $1,700 strata levy (rates and maintenance fee) was directed toward this kind of security.

In 1999 and 2000, Sydney's "Street Furniture Program"—a deceptively appealing name for a blatant social control initiative similar to Atlanta's—provided park benches and transit shelter seating of a design that prevented lying down, or, in some instances, even sitting down, since the "seating" was metal tubing against which one could only lean. In another make-work program typical of the "urban face-lift" approach to hallmark events, dozens of old but still serviceable bus shelters were replaced by glass and steel structures, complete with a full wall of backlit advertising space. Westpac Bank, an Olympic sponsor, was one of the first to use the space to promote its glib Values for Life slogan campaign—a particularly cynical use of the wall in view of the fact that many of the new shelters lacked the benches that had formerly provided homeless people with a resting place and refuge from sun and rain.

Two weeks before the Olympics began, on August 30, 2000, a *Herald* story provided a detailed list of recent moves to make the CBD even less welcoming for homeless people: "There are the park benches that have sprouted armrests in the past year. Sydney City Council says the armrests improve access for the elderly; the homeless know they reduce their access to a bed for the night. . . . Three homeless hot spots in the CBD . . . have been transformed into brightly lit Olympic concert sites, forcing a re-routing of food vans that feed the needy every night." Other examples included the installation of bars and bright lighting to drive homeless people away from locales that had served as their shelters (Hill & Morris, 2000).

In another example of street sweeps, Redfern Legal Center (RLC) documented an incident on August 5, when police strip-searched a twenty-year-old man at Central Station, allegedly in public view, because he was (erroneously) suspected of having stolen property. He said the police had been searching his clothing regularly. RLC lodged a complaint on his behalf with the ombudsman's office (Blunden, 2000).

Another outcome of the privatization of urban public space in Sydney in the late 1990s was the growing inaccessibility of public or semipublic toilet facilities (in hotels, restaurants, gas stations, etc.), ostensibly to deter individuals from using them to inject drugs; special blue lighting to make veins hard to detect was installed in public toilets as an additional deterrent. Most homeless people, of course, depended on public facilities for water, toilets, and a place to wash (Boon-Kuo, 1998). And, in another kind of pre-Olympic cleanup, the NSW police began trialling an antigraffiti hotline in South Sydney in July 2000, so that callers could report graffiti activists. Postings on the Active Sydney news website in August suggested that activists could use the hotline to report "corporate graffiti" (i.e., billboards), or to complain about the police antigraffiti initiative itself.

Rumors abounded in 2000 that homeless Indigenous people were being pressured by the police to leave town before the Olympics; veteran journalist George Negus repeated these rumors in an October 13 *Herald* article (Negus, 2000), while other informal sources claimed that some

Aborigines had been "encouraged" to move to rural areas of NSW for the duration. Such rumors were generally dismissed as "urban myths" that had been circulating for years, perhaps as a racist reaction on the part of (White) local residents to any influx of Aborigines to a small country town. On the other hand, it is possible that there was a grain of truth to this so-called myth, particularly in light of the fact that Olympic organizers in Atlanta openly practiced this method of ridding the streets of homeless Black men in readiness for the Games (see Lenskyj, 2000; chapter 4).

In June 2000, the NSW Parliament passed the *Intoxicated Persons Amendment Act* that strengthened police powers to detain anyone found intoxicated in a public place and behaving in a "disorderly manner." The definition of "intoxicated" was expanded to include drugs as well as alcohol. Those apprehended by police could be released into the care of a responsible person, or, if they were violent and there was no suitable supported accommodation available, they were to be detained at the police station. Although some specific directives were given for separating youth under eighteen from other detainees, these kinds of provisions included a number of "where practicable" escape clauses.

Advocates for youth and homeless people had serious concerns about the amendment. In July, Redfern Legal Center produced a kit for welfare and community workers on all the Olympic-related legislation, and its implications for youth and homeless people. Cards were prepared for distribution to people on the street, explaining the new police powers and providing names of lawyers available to give advice after arrests, and to attend at police stations or courts. The volunteer lawyers would document infringements of basis rights and collect evidence, and Redfern Legal Center and PIAC planned to coordinate any litigation arising from such infringements after the Olympics.

As Rhiannon pointed out during the *Intoxicated Persons Amendment Bill*'s second reading, the problems of public intoxication and homelessness go together, and in a context where the centers for homeless people were being closed, there were fears that those detained under the new amendment would be left in police cells. Another critic, Opposition Leader Peter Breen, expressed the view that the bill was an attempt to extend police powers over public protest during the Olympics, a statement to which Attorney General Jeff Shaw strenuously objected. Explaining how the bill had been developed over a five-year period, he stated, "I cannot understand the degree of cynicism that would prompt members to suggest that the bill is some kind of knee-jerk reaction to the Olympics" (Shaw, 2000). One might argue, of course, that its place in a long series of similar public order bills enacted over the preceding five years provided solid grounds for cynicism. Indeed, if it really had "nothing to do with the Olympics" and was the product of long and serious deliberations and consultations, as

Shaw claimed, why was it pushed through a few months before the Games, while the more urgent Homeless Protocol encountered so many obstacles that there was not time to formalize it in law?

Call In the Troops: A New Definition of "Domestic Violence"

Finally, in an even more obvious last-minute action, the *Defence Legislation Amendment (Aid to Civilian Authorities) Act 2000* was introduced into the Commonwealth Government House of Representatives on June 28, passed without public debate, proceeded through the Senate with some amendments, and became law by September 7, four days before the World Economic Forum (WEF) in Melbourne. Not surprisingly, the NSW Labor Council condemned the bill and warned the Australian Labor Party (ALP) against supporting it, while the International Commission of Jurists, the Australian Federal Police Association, and numerous civil liberties groups raised serious concerns.

Amending an act that had been standing for ninety-seven years, purportedly in preparation for an event that had been scheduled seven years earlier, the legislation authorized three ministers, including the prime minister, to call out the military to quell "domestic violence" (civil unrest). Although section 51G specified that the chief of defense must not "stop or restrict any lawful protest or dissent," this provision had limited applicability in a city where Olympic-related legislation had classified extensive areas off limits for protesters. It gave military personnel more sweeping powers than police: for example, searching premises without a warrant and detaining without arrest. On the issue of the "use of reasonable and necessary force," section 51T prohibited military personnel from causing death or "grievous bodily harm," except in situations where they believed "on reasonable grounds" that doing so was "necessary to protect the life of, or to prevent serious injury to, another person."

Politicians and military leaders were reported to have stressed the importance of putting the act in place in time for the expected S11 antiglobalization and Olympic protests. Green Sen. Bob Brown and Democrats Sen. Vicki Bourne both attempted, unsuccessfully, to amend the act and to allow more extensive consultation and debate. Bourne pointed out that while the police have appropriate training in crowd control, the military were trained to put down riots with force (Bourne, 2000). Similarly, Brown expressed serious concern about the army's manual on dealing with civil emergencies, following media statements by a military spokesperson that the current manual was being redrafted. As Brown stated, "the ground rules for troops being used in an Olympic crisis should be debated by parliament and not left to military imagination" (Australian Greens, 2000). For his part, Minister for Defense John Moore blamed "recent media attention" for failing to note that the existing legislation was "archaic and unworkable"; he claimed that the amendments provided "appropriate controls and safeguards" and would not be used against unarmed citizens (J. Moore, 2000).

Postscript: In February 2001, it was revealed that Commonwealth Special Air Services troops had been deployed in plain clothes to help police perform crowd surveillance during the Olympics, a function that breached the military's rules on involvement in civil matters (Lague, 2001).

CONCLUSION

Against this history of Olympic-related legislation that criminalized poverty, disadvantage and difference, as well as making peaceful protest illegal in most of Sydney, it is not surprising that progressive elected representatives, human rights activists, advocates for youth and homeless people, and others devoted all their time and energy to preventing police harassment and violence in the lead-up to the Sydney Olympics. There was ample evidence to support their fears that this indeed would be the outcome in September 2000. Police powers over public behavior had been enhanced significantly, the numbers of street homeless people were increasing, and community organizations across the political spectrum were planning to use the Olympics to draw world attention to the plight of Australia's Indigenous people and to the brutal impacts of corporate globalization. In fact, as chapter 9 will demonstrate, there were relatively few instances where police, security, or other authorized officials abused the powers granted to them by this draconian legislation, an outcome largely attributable to the widespread community efforts to protect vulnerable citizens, and to government and Olympic industry efforts to avoid international embarrassment when world media attention was focused on Sydney.

3

Black and White Australia

Reconciliation and Sydney 2000

─⟪ɷɷɷ⟫─

By the end of the 1990s, Indigenous issues and race relations—specifically, the barriers to reconciliation between Black and White Australians—were commanding attention in many sectors of Australian society. As the Olympics approached, it was in government and Olympic industry interests to downplay White Australia's long and brutal history of racism toward Aboriginal peoples, and to package "Aboriginality" as a recognized and celebrated component of Australia's "multiculture."

Reconciliation, with an honorable treaty and real land rights, an end to mandatory sentencing and Indigenous deaths in custody, and compensation for the stolen generation were key Indigenous issues that demanded resolution. Flowing from these issues were the related problems of poverty, unemployment, poor health, shorter life expectancy, inadequate housing, lower school achievement, limited postsecondary options, and cultural exploitation. The problem of limited opportunity in sport was also on the list. Despite the well-known achievements of a few Aboriginal athletes who, as critical sport scholar Colin Tatz (1995b) pointed out in his analysis of Indigenous sport, seem to have crossed over color and culture lines, most were held back by the same racist systems, practices, and stereotypes that restricted other aspects of their lives. In much the same way as Black actors, musicians, and sportspeople in the United States had access to a narrow range of career opportunities, boxing, rugby league, and Australian rules football provided the entry point into sport for many young Indigenous men, while Indigenous women, facing the combined effects of racism and sexism in sport, lacked even an entry point. As recently as 1994–1995, only two of 524 Australian Institute of Sport scholarships were offered to Indigenous athletes—Cathy Freeman and Kyle Van de Kuyp (ATSIC, 1995).

A comprehensive analysis of the full range of Indigenous issues is beyond the scope of this discussion, but I will examine recent developments in key areas in order to identify the major forces driving Indigenous politics and protests during the Olympic year.

THE AUSTRALIAN GOVERNMENT AND RACE RELATIONS

Ever since the first British settlement in 1788, the legal fiction of *terra nullius*—the claim that no one owned the land before that time—has been used to justify the dispossession of Indigenous people. It was not until 1992 that the Australian High Court's *Mabo* judgment ruled that a native title to land existed in 1788 and may continue to exist under certain conditions. The *Native Title Act* (1993) provided for Indigenous people to claim ownership of their land, unless title had been extinguished under a subsequent act of government, provided they could show geographic and genealogical evidence of their ongoing observance of traditional laws and customs—itself a difficult task for people with oral traditions and for those whose land was taken over in the eighteenth or nineteenth centuries. Native title legislation met with considerable opposition from non-Indigenous Australians, particularly those who viewed it as a threat to profitable mining or other resource-based industries.

When Prime Minister John Howard's conservative government came into power in 1996, the climate was ripe for political and legal backlash to the small gains made on the native title issue. The High Court's *Wik* judgment of December 1996 determined that native title could coexist with other rights on land held under a pastoral lease. In 1998, the *Native Title Amendment Act* diluted the original 1993 provisions to such an extent that, in 1999, the UN Committee for the Elimination of Racial Discrimination (CERD) established an "early warning" watch on Australia, which then had the dubious honor of being the first Western nation to be asked to explain its race policies. Speaking to the UN Working Group on Indigenous Peoples in July 1999, Aboriginal leader Les Malezer called on other national governments to reconsider their support for Sydney 2000 unless Native Title laws were changed (Jopson, 1999). For his part, Minister for Aboriginal Affairs, Sen. John Herron, criticized the UN's monitoring of what he termed a "sensitive domestic issue" (Jopson & Martin, 1999). Later variations on this defensive theme included ministerial allegations that the UN neglected more serious human rights abuses in other member countries. In March 2000, CERD began examining reports from the period 1992 to 1998, on the issue of reconciliation, which included the issues of mandatory sentencing, Indigenous deaths in custody, and compensation for the stolen generation.

Mandatory Sentencing and Deaths in Custody

The overrepresentation of Indigenous people in detention or prison and the higher incidence of Indigenous deaths in custody are among the many markers of systemic discrimination in Australia. Australian figures for young people ten to seventeen years old in juvenile correctional institutions (1996) showed a rate of incarceration for Indigenous youth almost twenty-two times that of non-Indigenous youth, with the Queensland rate almost double that of the overall Australian rate. In the Northern Territory (NT), Indigenous adults made up 28% of the total population but 72.8% of the prison population, while in Western Australia (WA) the prison figure was 33.1%, and, in Queensland, 21.6% (ATSIC, 1999; HREOC, 1997).

The problem of high numbers of Aboriginal deaths in custody had been the subject of a Royal Commission inquiry that began in 1987, after many years of Indigenous community organizing. In 1988, as the commissioners were conducting hearings across the country and as White Australia was celebrating two hundred years of colonization, Indigenous people responded with peaceful protests tens of thousands strong. The Royal Commission released its final report with 339 recommendations in 1991; included in its findings was the fact that, in the period 1981-1991, 99 deaths had been recorded. In 1997, Mick Dodson, federal Aboriginal Social Justice Commissioner, stated that Aboriginal people would use the Olympics to draw international attention to the issue: "If our people continue to die as the year 2000 approaches, we'll make damn sure the whole world knows about it" (Dodson quoted in Mitchell, 1997).

Indigenous people did continue to die in custody—110 between the 1991 Royal Commission report and 2000—and the risk of dying in police or prison custody was twenty-two times greater than for non-Aboriginal people (HREOC, 1997). The problem was exacerbated after the introduction into the NT and WA of mandatory sentencing legislation. As the ATSIC brief on the legislation pointed out, these states' laws were particularly punitive, in that they covered a large number of common and often minor offenses, they involved mandatory imprisonment, and they generally prevented judges from using discretion in sentencing. These were the only jurisdictions to introduce mandatory imprisonment for juveniles convicted of certain offenses, while, for adults, a broad range of offenses carried mandatory prison terms. WA's "three strikes" system allowed judges to impose an additional eighteen months' detention for certain juvenile offenders who had served two previous periods of detention (ATSIC, 1999).

The federal government initially refused to use its power to override these states' mandatory sentencing laws, although it did eventually persuade NT to modify them. That this legislation contravened nineteen Royal Commission recommendations, and was potentially in conflict with sections of five international human rights conventions (Cuneen, 1999), demonstrated an obvious lack of political will to address the racist injustices embedded in law-making and law enforcement systems.

As some critics aptly observed, Anglo-Celtic Australians should have been aware of the parallels between mandatory sentencing and the harsh British penal system of the eighteenth and nineteenth centuries—a system to which contemporary NT and WA legislation bore a striking resemblance. The majority of the convicts transported for life to the new colony had been found guilty of nothing more than theft, often minor. Targeting the poor, the system punished men and women caught stealing the proverbial "loaf of bread." Stealing biscuits, pens, or soft drinks was a twentieth century equivalent, but only if the alleged perpetrator were young and Black, and lived in the NT or WA.

Zero Tolerance = Zero Equity Policing

There was an important link between mandatory sentencing legislation and zero tolerance policing, both of which posed a particularly serious threat to the human rights of Indigenous people. Analyzing these issues in 1999, criminologist Chris Cuneen reported that nearly one in three Indigenous people in police custody had been charged with public drunkenness (regardless of whether it was an offense in that jurisdiction), and, out of all the people held in custody on public order offenses (excluding public intoxication), nearly half were Aboriginal. In the NT, the 1996 figures showed that 72% of all adult court appearances for public order offenses involved Aboriginal people, who represented 81% of people sentenced to imprisonment for *any* offense in 1996 (Cuneen, 1999). ATSIC research showed that "mandatory sentencing regimes are unjust, discriminatory and undermine Aboriginal people's development of localized and effective community-based diversionary mechanisms" and create additional problems when Indigenous youth from rural areas are taken hundreds or thousands of kilometers from their families and communities (ATSIC, 1999). In one infamous case in early 2000, a fifteen-year-old Aboriginal boy committed suicide in a Darwin detention center, where he was being held on a charge of theft of items valued under fifty dollars.

On the issue of public order offenses and class/race discrimination, it is relevant to note the findings of the Australian Institute of Health and Welfare report titled *Australia's Health 2000,* which showed that, although Indigenous households were less than 2% of Australian households, they comprised almost one third of households in the category of "improvised dwellings," such as sheds, outhouses, humpies [shacks], cardboard boxes, old car bodies, or other "rough accommodation." In light of this evidence, the links between poverty, substandard housing, public order offenses, targeted policing, and discriminatory sentencing practices were quite clear.

The Stolen (Not "Separated") Generation

The 1997 report of the Human Rights and Equal Opportunity Commission's (HREOC) national inquiry documented how, in the period between 1910 and 1970, 100,000 Indigenous children had been removed, often forcibly, from their families of origin. These actions had been sanctioned by state and federal legislation, which was based on the racist belief that Indigenous children and those of mixed race ("half-caste") would be better off if they were raised in White foster families or church-run institutions. There was generally no evidence that the children were neglected by their families, and regular child welfare and protection procedures were often ignored.

In the four years following the release of the report, the Commonwealth Government provided $54m to Indigenous communities, with most funds directed toward health and aged care (ATSIC, 2000). However, on the stolen generation issue, as well as on the broader issue of reconciliation, Prime Minister Howard refused to say "sorry" because it implied "cross-generational guilt"—and he said he wasn't personally responsible for harming Indigenous people—and because a formal apology would allegedly leave the Commonwealth government open to compensation claims. His stance was universally condemned by Indigenous people across the political spectrum, and by their non-Indigenous allies, as an insurmountable barrier to progress toward reconciliation and an honorable treaty.

MESSAGES TO THE WORLD IN BLACK AND WHITE

While the complex debates of the 1990s over native title and reconciliation attracted little attention from Olympic public relations officials, the threat to the tourism industry posed by the Asian financial crisis and the One Nation political party could not be ignored. Tourism not only constituted Australia's major source of foreign exchange earnings, but was, of course, a key factor in promised Olympic benefits. As later comparisons pointed out, the 1996 Atlanta Olympics were held in a city with twenty million people within a five-hour drive, whereas, with Australia's total population only 18.7m, Sydney 2000's success depended on overseas tourists.

Launched in April 1997, the racist, anti-immigration One Nation Party entrenched existing images of Australian racism internationally. Its leader, Pauline Hanson, framed her position as patriotic and presented herself as a champion of equality for all "Australians." Like other extreme right-wing movements, One Nation coined (or borrowed) code words that became staples of their scare-mongering rhetoric: *multiculturalists* and the *multicultural industry, Aboriginalism* and *Aboriginal industry, Asianization* and *internationalization* were all concepts designed to convey the message that White Australians' tax dollars were subsidizing, and in fact encouraging, non-White Australians to remain unassimilated (R. Hall, 1998). (Racist characterizations of government-funded programs as the "Aboriginal industry" should not be confused with the internal critiques of Aboriginal bureaucrats, as discussed in the next section.)

With Hanson's views on Asian immigrants widely reported in Asian countries, Australian Bureau of Statistics figures for May 1998 showed sharp falls in tourism from Korea (78%), Thailand (59%), Malaysia (36%) and Indonesia (23%) (Lenthen, 1998). Confirming Asians' fears was the fact that Howard's coalition party placed One Nation above Labor in their recommended preferential voting system for the 1998 Queensland elections, a move that was widely criticized by tourism industry leaders and others.

As the Olympic year approached, it was obviously in the government's best interests to counter the image of White Australian racism symbolized by Hanson. The messages presented on the Commonwealth government's official media website, which was managed by the Department of Foreign Affairs and Trade (DFAT), reflected attempts to put the best face on its relationship with Aboriginal people. Since the website was designed to serve as the electronic starting point for most international media, trade, and tourist inquiries, its impact was significant. Called "Australia-Media Focus," this interactive "virtual media center"—mediafocus.org—was launched in November 1999 for the purpose of providing international media representatives with "accurate information on contemporary developments in Australia" and "official responses to emerging issues" in the period leading up to the Olympics (DFAT, 1999a).

In the DFAT fact sheet on Aboriginal people and the Olympics, the Sydney Organizing Committee for the Olympic Games (SOCOG) manager for Aboriginal and Torres Strait Islander Affairs and former football player, Gary Ella, presented Sydney 2000 as "an opportunity to show the world the rich culture of Australia's Indigenous people ... [by encouraging] employment, promotional, business and cultural design and ceremonial opportunities" (DFAT Fact sheet 11, 1999b). The fact sheet proceeded to profile several successful Aboriginal Olympians and Paralympians, and to note the success of the first Olympic Arts Festival in promoting the "continuing involvement" of Indigenous artists and performers in Australian culture. Another fact sheet, titled "Indigenous Australians excel in many fields," also took this outdated and patronizing "great achievements" approach. One only need consider public reaction if a DFAT fact sheet were titled "Australian women excel in many fields" to understand the assumptions underlying this perspective.

Two other fact sheets—on native title and reconciliation—were similarly self-serving. The first noted the $50m government support for the Aboriginal Land Fund, and the fact that the 2 percent of the population who are Indigenous owned or controlled about 15 percent of the country. The document also stated that it did not accept the UN's criticism of its land rights actions (DFAT Fact sheet 5, 1999b). On reconciliation, the government's position was presented in a favorable light, and the fact sheet offered the usual rationale—the (alleged) implication of government responsibility—for not supporting a formal apology to children of the stolen generation, which it erroneously referred to as Indigenous children who were simply "separated" from their families under state and territory welfare laws (DFAT Fact sheet 8, 1999b).

This offensive term *separated generation*—one that might have been coined by a One Nation speechwriter—implied that Aboriginal parents and children merely lost track of each other, and were happily reunited at some future date. The public testimonies of those who, as children, were permanently removed from their families, provided ample evidence that this was more than just a temporary "separation." And, given a life expectancy about twenty years shorter than non-Aboriginal Australians, many of these parents died long before their adult children managed to find them. Equally traumatic was the alienation of Indigenous children from their traditional communities; they had no sense of belonging to the dominant culture, from which they were largely excluded, and few links with their culture of origin.

A few months after the DFAT promotional material was posted, Australia's international reputation on Indigenous issues again came under attack with the release of Australian filmmaker John Pilger's documentary, *Welcome to Australia*. Like the DFAT fact sheets, it profiled Aboriginal sportspeople and reviewed land rights legislation, but, unlike the government materials, it examined Indigenous athletes' experiences of discrimination and alienation from the early 1900s to the present, and identified the serious threat to land claims posed by the 1998 Native Title amendments. As Pilger accurately predicted, "Against this turmoil, Australia prepares for the Sydney Olympics; this is to be Australia's glittering showcase when all the picture postcard images and delights of 'Oz' will be on show" and when Aboriginal art and artists will be co-opted "to ensure the 'multicultural' face of the Games" (Pilger, 1999).

Further evidence of the plight of Australia's Indigenous people was provided in the national report titled *Australia's Health 2000*. Released three months before the Olympics, it identified significant differences between the health of Indigenous and non-Indigenous populations on a wide range of health measures. Life expectancy was in fact close to that of non-Indigenous Australians born almost a hundred years earlier, a finding that prompted the *Herald* headline "Indigenous health a century behind" (Metherell, 2000a). In terms of age distribution of deaths, 53 percent of deaths of males and 41 percent of deaths of females occurred before age fifty. Unemployment, lower personal and household incomes, larger households, and more improvised dwellings than other Australians were all identified as socioeconomic health risk factors (Australian Institute of Health and Welfare, 2000).

In the lead-up to the Olympics in 2000, a series of inexplicably inflammatory statements by government ministers served to fuel the already volatile situation on Indigenous issues. In April 2000, Aboriginal Affairs Minister, Senator John Herron, prepared a submission to a Senate committee inquiring into the stolen generation, in which he denied that there was actually a "generation" of "stolen children" and claimed that the proportion of children "separated" was "no more than 10 per cent." At the same time, to add insult to injury, the minister for family and community services was reported to have accused Aboriginal people planning Olympic protests of being "unAustralian" (Grattan & Jopson, 2000).

There was widespread outrage at these statements, and the late Indigenous leader Charlie Perkins, in his customary impulsive style, was reported to have predicted violence in the streets—"burning cars"—and to have urged tourists to stay home. He later withdrew these statements, but not before the Sydney tabloid *Herald Sun* had published a completely unrelated photo of a burning car next to an image of Perkins. Commenting on the situation, the Real Games anti-Olympic website <realgames.org> claimed that, ignoring their long history of peaceful protest, "the Australian government, in league with the media, appear to be deliberately portraying Indigenous people as violent and out to disrupt the Olympic Games" (So this is Australia? 2000).

ABORIGINAL POLITICS AND ORGANIZING

It is both difficult and inappropriate for non-Aboriginal commentators to present themselves as authorities on the internal politics of Indigenous people. As Ray Jackson, leader of the Indigenous Social Justice Association (ISJA), stated in reference to the Aboriginal Tent Embassy, political differences among Aboriginal groups are not the business of (non-Aboriginal) government officials. There is ample historical and contemporary evidence of the ways in which racist individuals and institutions have exploited apparent rifts—particularly the alleged lack of solidarity—within minority communities. In these scenarios, the dominant group often co-opted minority leaders into "advisory" roles—a pattern evident in Sydney when several prominent Aboriginal people, including sportspeople, were invited to work for the Olympic industry in paid or voluntary capacities.

Equally important in the Australian context was the recruitment of Aboriginal leaders into government bureaucracies, and critics were quick to identify the tokenism at work when Olympic organizers recruited men and women from government-subsidized Indigenous organizations, such as ATSIC, which, they claimed, were not genuinely representative of their people or respectful of traditional Aboriginal laws and protocols. Moreover, Aboriginal participation in, and potential co-optation by, the Olympic industry frequently produced political disagreements between those who were on the inside and those who were not. In these kinds of situations, Aboriginal solidarity suffered serious damage, while the Olympic Coordination Authority (OCA) and SOCOG maintained their reputation as organizations that had at least attempted to be inclusive.

Aboriginal activist and academic Roberta Sykes identified some of these internal problems in 1989. Having reviewed Aboriginal gains in the areas of medicine, education, public and private employment, politics, and the arts, she went on to explain,

> This is not to say that all is well in the Black community and everyone is doing their bit. Nepotism, factionalism, racism, jealousy and disunity constantly threaten to disrupt our fragile progress. Constant vigilance is required to develop systems of reciprocally beneficial emotional, financial and political support, and the community needs to discipline the talking heads and show ponies who abound, to our detriment, in the community. (Sykes, 1989, 228)

Although it will become clear that the range of Indigenous responses to the Sydney Olympics reflected very diverse political standpoints and strategies, mainstream political labels such as liberal and radical are not always appropriate. Indigenous activists such as Sykes and Gary Foley (1998, 1999) identified the divisions between traditional and urban Aboriginal peoples, and between political activists and government bureaucrats, rather than using categories derived from mainstream (White) political organizing. In fact, as Foley (1998) pointed out, Aboriginal activists themselves coined the term *Aboriginal industry* twenty years earlier to describe ATSIC: a "vast gravy train" which, as late as 1994, had only 38 percent Indigenous employees.

As environmentalist Drew Hutton explained in relation to the boundaries between Australian social movements, Indigenous resistance has its own internal culture, values, protest styles, and agendas (Hutton, 1987, 7). "We don't organize things the way a whitefella might," one Aboriginal protester explained (Jopson, 2000a). The *Herald* attempted to categorize what it saw as the three main Indigenous positions on the Olympics, drawing on the views of nine leaders. A group labeled "the radicals" called for boycotts and/or demonstrations, while "the politicians," including Metropolitan Aboriginal Lands Council chair Jenny Munro, wanted to use the Games to educate international visitors about Aboriginal issues, particularly poverty. The third group—"Olympic insiders"—comprised former ATSIC chair Lowitja O'Donoghue and ATSIC commissioner for Sydney, Charlie Perkins, both members of SOCOG's National Indigenous Advisory Committee (discussed in chapter 7); Perkins shared the politicians' goals, while O'Donoghue wanted to focus on the Games and Aboriginal successes (The factions, 1999). The full political picture was, however, even more complex than the *Herald* proposed.

Sydney Metropolitan Aboriginal Lands Council (MALC)

The activities of the Sydney land council demonstrate some of the complexities of Indigenous political organizing. In a context where Europeans' total disregard for Aboriginal laws and protocols had devastating impacts on their traditional relationship with, and ownership of the land, MALC called for recognition of the traditional elected custodians of land used for Olympic venues, thereby questioning the (White) SOCOG system of appointing people from elsewhere in Australia to various Olympic committees simply because they were high-profile Indigenous leaders, bureaucrats, or athletes. And while MALC organized the Aboriginal art and cultural pavilion inside the Homebush Olympic site, it also planned to hold highly visible protests in Sydney to draw visitors' attention to the Australian government's treatment of Aboriginal people. MALC Chair Munro's public statements left no doubt that she was a strong critic of the Howard government and Olympic minister Michael Knight.

In May 2000, at a meeting of 188 NSW land councils, MALC was given the mandate to coordinate Aboriginal protests during the Games. But, like many Indigenous groups, MALC emphasized that they did not want their protests to detract from Aboriginal athletes' Olympic achievements, or to convey anti-Olympic messages. In fact, Munro reported that their relationship with OCA over three years had produced some good results, including Indigenous employment opportunities in construction and landscaping on the Homebush Olympic site.

The cultural pavilion itself had a conflicted history. When OCA called for tenders, a subsidiary of MALC submitted a proposal that was subsequently accepted, but, in a strange intervention, OCA initially vetoed the inclusion of any boomerangs or spears in the cultural displays. As Munro pointed out, this seriously compromised Aboriginal cultural integrity, already a concern because most of the program had been put together by a non-Indigenous person (Munro, 2000). In fact, OCA had censorship power over the entire contents of the pavilion, and its contract with MALC stated, "OCA reserves the right to review the text of all material on display in the pavilion other than text describing works of art" (Jopson, 2000d).

A few months later, another controversy erupted over plans to use the pavilion as the dispersal point for various Indigenous protest marches. Needless to say, OCA officials realized too late that they may have inadvertently provided some of the most radical Indigenous groups in the state with official access to the Homebush Bay Olympic site. Not to worry: they quickly fell back on IOC bylaw 61 prohibiting political protest in or near Olympic venues. But, as Munro pointed out, it was a "fantasy" for OCA to threaten to close the pavilion if any "political" activity were conducted on the site, since "Every breath I take is political in one way or another. . . ." Ironically, according to Jopson's *Herald* account, Knight had given MALC control of the pavilion partly in an attempt to minimize potential protest (Jopson, 2000d).

In May 2000, MALC began efforts to organize a tent embassy at Wilson Park, Silverwater, adjacent to the Homebush Bay Olympic venues. Although Auburn Council supported the project in principle, it had no jurisdiction over the park during the Games, because it was under OCA control. For its part, OCA claimed that soil remediation at the Wilson Park site would not be finished until January 2001, although MALC had originally been given a September completion date. Wyatt Park, further from the main Olympic site, was proposed as an alternative. Munro reported that Auburn Council at first misunderstood MALC's position. The purpose of the proposed tent embassy was not to promote anti-Olympic protest but to focus on government mistreatment of Aboriginal people over the last 212 years.

Aboriginal Involvement In the Olympics

Indigenous people were represented in the bid process team and enshrined in the bid. Sydney's seven-minute part in the closing ceremonies at the 1996 Atlanta Games also featured "Aboriginality", with Indigenous people playing didgeridoos [traditional musical instruments]. The official Sydney logo has incorporated a boomerang into its design and the Sydney Olympic torch is inspired by the shape of a boomerang. . . . The Australian leg of the torch relay will begin at a sacred Indigenous site, Uluru, and the first torchbearer will be Indigenous Olympic gold medallist, Nova Peris-Kneebone. (Hanna, 1999, 15)

These examples, along with the bid committee appointment of Aboriginal leader Perkins (who, as other sources point out, received a warmer reception in England than in Australia as a soccer player) were presented as positive evidence of Olympic organizers' association with Indigenous people in Michelle Hanna's *Reconciliation in Olympism* (1999). Many critics (e.g., Godwell, 1999a, 1999b) would challenge Hanna's liberalism, and would argue that such examples demonstrated how the bid and organizing committees continued the well-established White Australian tradition of exploiting Aboriginal people and culture for their own ends.

Hanna did acknowledge, however, that with Beijing as Sydney's main rival for the 2000 Olympics, it was important at the outset for Olympic organizers to present Australia as "a nation that seemed to embrace its traditionally oppressed minority culture" and that their inclusion may have been "a calculated political move" (Hanna, 1999, 16, 25). As Sydney bid committee head Rod McGeoch stated in 1994, "We were particularly keen to have the support of the Aboriginal community. . . . We knew we would also have to be prepared to answer questions about race relations in Australia. . . ." (McGeoch & Korporaal, 1994, 144–45). In the early 1990s, McGeogh could not have predicted how the land rights issue would unfold, or how the Howard government's position on reconciliation would attract international censure by the end of the decade.

"Aboriginality" and Olympic Symbolism

In the late 1980s, when the Melbourne committee bidding for the 1996 Olympics had discovered that the International Olympic Committee (IOC) "loved the Aboriginal angle," it located an Aboriginal didgeridoo player to perform at every official function. And when Samaranch requested a dot-style painting that incorporated the Olympic rings, the bid committee found an artist to produce one (Godwell, 1999a). Sydney's lobbying of the IOC during the bid invariably included some "Aboriginality"—usually in the form of music and dancing. The prerequisite Aboriginal dance troupe accompanied the Sydney bid committee to Monte Carlo when the IOC met to select the 2000 host city, and former tennis star Evonne Goolagong Cawley was a member of the bid presentation team.

The cover of the bid committee's glossy *Share the Spirit* magazine in June 1993 carried a paternalistic image of a beaming IOC president Samaranch resting his hand on the bare shoulder of a young male dancer, one of a group of Aboriginal schoolchildren who "entertained" the president during the IOC visit to Sydney. And, in one of the last photo ops of this genre, in September 2000, Samaranch was filmed trying to play the didgeridoo that had been used by Aboriginal performers during Sydney 2000's welcoming ceremony (DiManno, 2000a).

Plans for the Olympics cultural program did not overlook Aboriginal people as artists and performers. "With the dawn of the new millennium, peoples of the earth will look to the Olympic Movement for renewed inspiration" gushed the writer of promotional material in 1993. Australia's "multicultural character" was to be the theme of the cultural program, which would seek, among other goals, to promote "knowledge and appreciation of the unique culture of the Australian Aboriginal Peoples" (Sydney Olympics, 1992). At the symbolic level, a little bit of "Aboriginality" was identified by McGeoch as the missing component of the proposed designs for the Sydney bid logo (McGeoch & Korporaal, 1994, 68), and images such as a boomerang or dots, to signify a Central Desert Aboriginal painting style, soon became essential features of the Australian Olympic industry. As Aboriginal activist Darren Godwell explained in his analysis of "Olympic branding of Aborigines," the exploitative use of a narrow range of images entrenched the "primitive" stereotype of Indigenous people in limited roles as artists, dancers, and performers; moreover, their cultural work was consistently underestimated and undervalued (Godwell, 1999a, 1999b).

Support or Boycotts: Debates Among Indigenous Communities

Throughout the 1990s, there were divergent views among Indigenous people on the question of Olympic boycotts. Shortly after the IOC announcement that the Sydney bid had been successful, some Aboriginal leaders threatened a boycott to force the Australian government to revise its land rights legislation. Predictably, politicians and the mainstream media presented proposed boycotts as a threat to "Australia's dream"—in other words, un-Australian. There was support for demonstrations and boycotts at a 1993 meeting of seven hundred Indigenous leaders in Canberra where native title issues were discussed. Perkins subsequently called for an alternative Aboriginal Olympics in 2000 when SOCOG failed to include any Aboriginal people on its board. Seven years later, the board remained unchanged in terms of Indigenous representation.

On his 1996 visit to Sydney, IOC president Samaranch warned Aboriginal people against "hijacking" the Games. Perkins claimed that SOCOG had orchestrated these remarks, and had failed to consult with Aboriginal people. Michael Knight had issued a similar warning a week before (and would do so on several more occasions), so Perkins was probably correct. And, as political analyst Stuart Russell argued, the IOC unnecessarily transformed "a threat of peaceful protest into a criminal act of terrorism" (Russell, 1996, 14).

In August 1999, mainstream media reported that many Indigenous leaders had decided to abandon the boycott plans, and instead to use the opportunity provided by the Olympics to draw world attention to the Australian government's treatment of their people—an approach that the *Herald* labeled

The Shame Games. An Aboriginal Embassy would provide information and education, as well as offering international media, VIPs, and others the opportunity to see living conditions in urban and rural Indigenous communities; Thailand's IOC member Nat Indrapana was reported to have shown interest in such tours (Jopson, 1999). In reality, Indigenous groups were investigating the full range of possibilities of politicizing the Olympics from both the inside and the outside.

Cathy Freeman: The Perfect Symbol?

In a 1999 essay titled "Cathy and the Olympics," Aboriginal activist Gary Foley explained his response when asked about the potential significance of Cathy Freeman winning a gold medal:

> whether she won or not was ultimately completely irrelevant to the on-going history of oppression and racial persecution of Indigenous people. Nor would it have the slightest effect on the 200 year old historic struggle for justice in this country. It would not change one hard-core racist attitude and will not create one opportunity for the army of Indigenous unemployed youth. Nor would it free a single one of the thousands of Kooris in Australian jails. (Foley, 1999)

Foley went on to explain that the Olympics provided an unprecedented opportunity for Indigenous people to tell the world about their plight. (I would argue, too, that while millions of non-Indigenous Australians celebrated Freeman's gold medal, their reaction would have been markedly different if Freeman's traditional people had lodged a native title claim.)

While some other Indigenous leaders shared Foley's position regarding Freeman, the mainstream view was, predictably, very different. With several high-profile Indigenous athletes working with SOCOG and OCA, and others, including Freeman, making public statements about their focus on winning races, rather than on the politics of race, White politicians could readily exploit the "Freeman factor." Following the backlash to Herron's stolen generation denials, John Howard was reported to have claimed that most Aboriginal people agreed with Freeman about keeping "politics" out of the Olympics (Gratton, Metherell, & Seccombe, 2000). A few months earlier, Michael Knight had been quoted as saying, with incredible arrogance, "The best thing for Aboriginality would be for Cathy Freeman to win a gold medal" (Knight quoted in "Ratbags," 2000).

This is not to suggest that Freeman was apolitical. In 1994, in an action that commanded international attention, she ran a victory lap carrying both the Australian and Aboriginal flags after winning gold medals in the 200m and 400m events at the Commonwealth Games in Victoria, Canada.

Subsequent criticism by team officials was countered by the widespread community support that she received in Australia, and the 1999 approval of the Aboriginal flag in the list of official flags to be flown at the Sydney Olympics (although only at six selected sites) was believed to have been helped by her action.

In November 1997, the Nyungah Circle of Elders from WA called for a boycott and specifically requested Freeman's support. "We ask you not to run. Stand and mourn with us," they wrote in an open letter, prompted by restrictions on Aboriginal land rights that were soon to be debated in Parliament. The *Associated Press* story quoted Black American sprinter Carl Lewis's advice to Freeman to ignore the request, while Freeman's manager criticized what he saw as the inappropriate use of her name to "drag her into the land rights debate" (Lewis tells Freeman, 1997). Knight, predictably, warned that any groups' attempts to hold the Olympics "hostage" would create a backlash against them (Boycott threats, 1997).

Like some other Indigenous athletes, Freeman at first tended to keep a low profile on Indigenous political issues before the Sydney Olympics. But by July 2000, government denials of the existence of the stolen generation prompted her to break the silence. At that time, she publicly denounced the Howard government's stance during an interview with a British journalist, to whom she gave an account of her own grandmother's experiences as a member of the stolen generation (Gratton, Jopson, & Metherell, 2000).

Permission to Protest: Denied

Aboriginal activists, like other protest organizers, generally expected and received a chilly response from police and Olympic security officials. In March 2000, when ISJA head Ray Jackson and four other Indigenous leaders met with Roland Tisdale, superintendent and precinct commander for Sydney Olympic Park, their plans to march and camp in Bicentennial Park were met with "apoplectic indignation." They were told that only 200 of the anticipated 10,000 Aboriginal protesters could camp outside the Olympic site. More sinister, in Jackson's account of the discussion, was Tisdale's threat that Aboriginal people entering the Olympic site would be stopped by force, "Whatever the cost. Whatever the pain" (R. Jackson, 2000a, 9).

Tisdale refused a second request to meet with ISJA representatives, who then asked for, and were granted meetings with Knight and his staff, and later with representatives from Sydney police commands and shire councils. At one point, David Darcy of the Sydney Command said that he would intervene on ISJA's behalf so that 1,000 Indigenous representatives could camp in Bicentennial Park.

ISJA then met with the mayor of Strathfield, the police, and SOCOG personnel to discuss camping in Bressington and Mason parks (outside the Homebush site). They were told, first of all, that the wildlife protection area near the parks would be disturbed by camping. Then, as Jackson described the discussion,

> [The Mayor] informed us that at the bottom of Bressington Park was a manmade hill. The hill contained quantities of toxic material which was unknown to Council or anyone else. The argument put was their concern for our young female supporters of childbearing age, who could possibly be made sterile by a toxic zap from this toxic hill. At least this concern, and honesty, of the known toxicity of the Homebush Site and its environs was most refreshing. Environmentalists, including Greenpeace and others had complained long and loudly of the major toxic problem that is the Homebush site, only to be put down by the government, SOCOG, and others as being alarmists at best, mischievous at worst. (R. Jackson, 2000c, 1)

On the day of the opening ceremony Green Games Watch 2000 warned protesters against camping in Bressington or Mason parks, because potentially dangerous levels of dioxin and other contaminants made them dangerous places for camping, particularly for children, pregnant women, and people with chemical sensitivities (Symington, 2000).

In further meetings with Deputy Police Commissioner Lola Scott to discuss plans for Indigenous protests at Bicentennial Park, the "no marching" law was reiterated, and Jackson and other leaders were threatened with "swift and forceful removal" by police if protesters entered the park (Jocelyn, 2000).

Speaking at the inaugural meeting of the Anti-Olympic Alliance (AOA), Jackson predicted that thousands of Aboriginal protesters would be converging on Sydney from NSW and other states in order to take part in a march to Homebush Bay and a peaceful camp on Aboriginal land in Bicentennial Park. He referred to the 1988 precedent when huge numbers had protested the Bicentennial "celebration" (of one hundred years of White occupation of Indigenous land). Like other speakers, he emphasized his people's proud tradition of nonviolent protest and their intention to be leading the march, and possibly facing the police batons. Just two weeks after the AOA meeting, on May 28, an unprecedented number of Australians—up to 250,000—marched across Sydney Harbor Bridge in support of reconciliation and to protest the prime minister's continued refusal to apologize.

The Aboriginal Tent Embassy

The original Aboriginal Tent Embassy in Canberra was established on Crown land near the Old Parliament House on January 26, 1972 to assert

Northumbria University
Library & Learning Services
City Campus
Items borrowed

Title: Olympic Games : a social science
perspective
: 200638726X
Due: 20/08/2010 23:59

Title: best Olympics ever? : social impacts of
Sydney 2000
: 2005917028
Due: 20/08/2010 23:59

Title: Olympic games : a social science
perspective
: 2003817638
Due: 10/09/2010 23:59

Title: Olympic event organization
: 2006976117
Due: 10/09/2010 23:59

Total items: 4
/08/2010 21:08

Please keep your receipt in case of queries.
Checked out our electronic books yet?
books are just a click away!
http://librarycat.northumbria.ac.uk/
alisPrism/

Aboriginal sovereignty. Long celebrated by White Australia as "Australia Day," this day in January is commonly termed *Invasion Day* by Indigenous Australians. In 1927 on the same site, two older Aboriginal men had protested against the construction of Parliament House on land to which they laid claim as traditional owners, and there was archaeological evidence that Aboriginal people had lived on that land for centuries. Indigenous people were exempt from the usual prohibitions against camping on Crown land, and the camp survived for six months—and attracted world media attention and a groundswell of public support. A new law was passed empowering police to remove the campers by force, and subsequent events were recorded by journalists and television crews as concrete evidence of police brutality toward Aboriginal people (Sykes, 1989, 93–97).

The Tent Embassy was reestablished in 1992 on its twentieth anniversary, following a two-day occupation of Old Parliament House to draw international attention to Aboriginal sovereignty, and the site has been maintained ever since. The Fire for Justice was lit in April 1993 to symbolize the Aboriginal struggle and to commemorate freedom fighters and activists who had died since the struggles began. In 1995, the embassy was recognized by the Australian Heritage Commission as a site of special cultural significance.

Isabell Coe, a veteran and elder from the Canberra tent embassy, set up the Sydney branch in Victoria Park near Sydney University on July 14, 2000. Its initial stated purpose was to inform Olympic visitors and the media about the suppression of Indigenous rights by past and present governments, and specifically "to highlight how the Aboriginal people are regarded as 'aliens' in our own land" (Aboriginal Tent Embassy, 2000a).

Eviction Notices, Legal Battles

Eleven days after the Sydney tent embassy was set up, South Sydney Council charged the group with unlawful occupation of the park, and demanded that they agree to a number of council conditions related to health, safety, and noise if they wanted to remain. These included limiting the group to one tent and caretaker's accommodation in a designated 100 square meter area, having a maximum of four overnight occupants, containing the fire within a metal drum, banning drugs and alcohol, and taking out a $10m public risk insurance policy.

The council's action was somewhat unexpected in light of its initial cordial reception, as well as its reputation as at least "on the progressive side of conservative councils" because of its endorsement of the annual Gay and Lesbian Mardi Gras (pride parade), and its support of safe houses for prostitutes and drug-users (Connor, 2000a). However, the racist efforts of some of Sydney's radio "shock jocks," who called the embassy "a disgrace" and encouraged listeners to complain, no doubt helped fuel the council's and Sydney residents' racist reactions.

Discussing other council concerns, Mayor John Fowler cited noise complaints from nearby residents, loss of amenity for daily park users, and "the broader motives of other participants" (Jopson, 2000c). It should be noted that concern about inconveniencing "daily park users" had been conspicuously absent a few months earlier when politicians voted to convert six other downtown parks and public domains into Olympic "live sites," thereby subjecting the users of these spaces to the full force of legislated police and security constraints on public behavior during the Olympics (as discussed in chapter 2). Moreover, like every inner-city park, Victoria Park was frequented by homeless people, whose rights were not usually given such a high priority.

On the issue of "other participants," it became clear that a "divide and rule" tactic was at work. A letter to the council, dated August 21, from ISJA leader Ray Jackson provided a detailed account of his discussion with Grahame Dearsley, the council's director of health and community services, who told him that the council's problem with the camp was not the Aboriginal people, but rather the non-Aboriginal participants such as "hippies, greenies, uni students and other 'odd types.' " When Jackson explained that these people were supporters and helped to protect the Aboriginal people, he was told that protection was a task for police, not for those "loonies." A council spokesperson was also reported to have referred to Isabell Coe as a "lunatic" (Connor, 2000a; Jackson, 2000b).

For their part, embassy organizers pointed out that the council's requirements interfered with their ancient right to assemble and to hold a corroboree (ceremonial gathering), as well as with the camp's safety requirements and functions as a community. Because it was a ceremonial center, drugs and alcohol were already banned, and, as they explained, it was inappropriate to contain the sacred fire for peace and justice in a metal drum. The fire had been lit from ashes brought from Canberra according to rites which, as Indigenous organizers pointed out, were more "real" and ancient than the Olympic torch relay (which had its origins in Hitler's 1936 Olympics) (Jopson, 2000c).

Supporters of the tent embassy quickly mobilized, the numbers of overnight (Indigenous) occupants were boosted through the "Sleepout for Sovereignty" initiative, several fund-raising and educational events were held on the site, and calls for donations of money and goods (tents, seating, etc.) were sent out through the Internet. In early August, the council applied for an injunction with the Land and Environment Court in order to be able to evict the Tent Embassy at any time. The Indigenous Students' Network and other supporters launched a telephone and e-mail campaign targeting South Sydney Council, and set up a mobile phone alert registry so that notification of a police raid of the embassy could be circulated immediately through an automatic message service. Protesters were asked to bring cameras and sound recording equipment to document any illegal police action.

During the first court proceedings, the judge issued suspended orders, to take effect on August 23, requiring Coe to cease occupying Victoria Park and restraining her from doing so without the council's permission. The "nearby residents" who complained of noise, the decision revealed, lived in a hotel and a university student residence—not exactly noise-free premises themselves. And, capitalizing on an (alleged) breach of traditional Aboriginal law when it suited the purposes of the White legal system, the judge noted that the tent embassy activities were not "supported" by either the NSW or the Metropolitan Aboriginal Land Councils (*South Sydney City Council v. Coe*, 2000).

The council eventually agreed to let the tent embassy remain in Victoria Park on condition that the fire was monitored at all times, vehicles were removed, noise was restricted at night, and toilets were installed (although Sydney University, adjacent to the park, had been providing access to their toilet facilities). By September, the camp comprised about one hundred fifty people.

It was generally believed that fear of negative international media coverage during the Olympics was the key factor that forced South Sydney Council to back down. Indeed, just as the international viewing audience was led to believe that Indigenous content in the opening and closing ceremonies signified progress toward reconciliation, many (non-Indigenous) international visitors saw the existence of the embassy as evidence that human rights, including the right to peaceful protest, were not under threat during the Olympics (e.g., Kidd, 2000).

Divide-and-Rule Tactics Prevail

It was widely rumored, and substantiated by some Indigenous sources, that Olympic organizers and NSW police had "bought off" any Aboriginal leader who might become a problem. A highly visible presence at the tent embassy, police made daily visits to monitor participants and engaged in "friendly chats and advice" to leaders to evict "troublemakers," particularly anyone associated with the Melbourne S11 protests against the World Economic Forum, or with the Anti-Olympic Alliance; several Indigenous participants had to leave as a result of this pressure. It was believed that the police had one or two undercover officers at the camp, and that they had also infiltrated other groups considered anti-Olympic or anticapitalist; like most community groups with a "very loose anarchic structure," the Anti-Olympic Alliance held open meetings and gave little thought to the need for security—in this case, to monitor undercover plants (D. Clark, 2000; Jackson, 2001).

Original plans for the tent embassy area to serve as the assembly point for the mass protest march were changed at the last minute by embassy leaders, in what was probably another example of White authorities' successful divide-and-conquer strategies on two fronts: between Indigenous and non-Indigenous protesters, and between more radical and less radical Aboriginal people (Jackson, 2001). It is important to establish that all Indigenous groups (and their non-Indigenous supporters), in keeping with their tradition of resistance, planned nonviolent protests; however, as Ray Jackson (2001, 1) explained, while the so-called Peace Games were "emblematic of peace, love and brother/sisterhood," in no way did they symbolize the more radical goal of "peace and social justice with the Indigenous peoples of this land."

Negotiations between AOA and the tent embassy proved complicated. Initially, AOA representatives, including Indigenous Students' Network member Kim Bullimore, had asked Isobell Coe for permission to hold the September 15 rally at the embassy, which would serve as the starting point for a mass protest march. Four thousand posters were to be printed with details of the time and place, along with the four AOA demands: real land rights and treaty now; stop mandatory sentencing; apologize to the stolen generation; and fund public transport, health, and education, not the Olympics. Agreement had been reached on these matters at a joint meeting in July. Subsequently, one particular line on the poster—which referred to anti-Olympic protest—was removed at the embassy's request.

As Bullimore explained, this and later events demonstrated to the AOA that there had been a change in the original political basis on which discussions had been held. In an unexpected move on September 11, Coe circulated an urgent media release declaring that the embassy had not consented to any anti-Olympic protest. It went on to state that organizers had sought legal advice concerning (alleged) "unauthorized use of the Aboriginal Tent Embassy name along with names of supporters and traditional elders for the Anti-Olympic rally" (Aboriginal Tent Embassy, 2000b). AOA, of course, agreed to withdraw from any organizational role in the opening day rally, and to communicate clearly to the media and other activists that the rally was solely an Indigenous initiative (Bullimore, 2000). By this time, embassy organizers were emphasizing the peace and healing functions of the camp over political protest, and were publicly disassociating themselves from any Indigenous or non-Indigenous groups with a stated anti-Olympic position.

Walking the Land—For Peace and Healing

On June 10, 2000, the Aboriginal Walk for Peace set off from the shores of Lake Eyre in South Australia, led by Arabunna elder Kevin Buzzacott who carried the Sacred Fire for Peace. The walk initiated by the Keepers of Lake Eyre—"a journey for peace, freedom and healing the land and its peoples"—traveled over 3000km. through small country towns and cities, inviting all people to join at any point. After seventy-two days, the walkers, about fifty in number, were welcomed by the elders of the Canberra Aboriginal Tent Embassy. While in Canberra, they participated in traditional ceremonies with a group of about 20 Native Americans, Americans, Japanese, and Australians known as the Sacred Runners, who were running a 14,000km route around Australia, to be completed just before the Olympics. Two MPs—a Labor and a Green representative—greeted the group, which increased in number to about one hundred by the time they left Canberra (Szentkuti, 2000).

On September 2, eighty-five days after they set out, the Walk for Peace arrived at "The Foot"—the Sydney suburb of Kurnell—and celebrated by planting the Aboriginal flag at the Captain Cook Monument (which symbolized the official European "discovery" of Australia by Capt. James Cook in 1770). For the next six weeks, the group visited Sydney area Aboriginal communities and land councils, as well as organizing a walk from Newtown Square to the Sydney Tent Embassy, where a celebration of peace and healing was held. The group invited John Howard to sit with them at the peace fire on September 13, but received no official response.

CONCLUSION

By the end of September 2000, the "symbolic reconciliation" presented to the world through the Olympic ceremonies and cultural programs was the only evidence of change on the race relations issue. The popular (White) notion that the mere hosting of the Olympics Games would help ameliorate social problems facing Indigenous people was, of course, flawed. Indigenous activists and their allies, however, had more realistic goals: to capitalize on the opportunity that Sydney 2000 provided to draw international attention to the Howard government's shameful record on reconciliation and related issues. But the limited capacity of progressive individuals and groups to work together in coalition on Olympic-related issues—a challenge for both the fragmented non-Indigenous groups that constituted the Australian left, and for the politically diverse Indigenous community—was further undermined by police, government, and Olympic industry officials. The outcomes were evident in September, as chapter 9 will demonstrate.

4

"You Can't Share the Spirit If You Can't Pay the Rent"

Housing and Homelessness in the Olympic City

━━◦◦◦◦━━

The widespread negative social impacts of hallmark events and megaprojects on host cities have been extensively documented and analyzed (Hall, 1989, 1994, 1998; Olds, 1998; Rutheiser, 1996). A study commissioned in 1994 by Shelter NSW, a peak housing body, examined the impact of six international events on local communities—the America's Cup in Fremantle, the Brisbane Expo (trade fair), Sydney's Bicentennial, the Barcelona Olympics, the Atlanta Olympics, and Melbourne's bid for the 1996 Olympics—as well as the potential impact of the 2000 Olympics on Sydney. The report provided irrefutable evidence that, in the absence of appropriate policy measures, hallmark events had a negative impact on housing, particularly on low-income private renters. Monitoring the housing market, strengthening existing planning controls and residential tenancy legislation, controlling private rentals, and increasing the supply of low-cost accommodation were identified as key policy recommendations (Cox, Darcy, & Bounds, 1994). And on the related issues of human rights, hallmark events in Australia and internationally were often accompanied by enhanced police powers, harassment of street homeless people, and suppression of public protest (Cox, 1998; Russell, 1994)—as discussed in chapter 2. Other Australian studies, largely supporting international findings, showed patterns of urban gentrification, displacement of low-income tenants and boarding house lodgers, and the privatization of urban public space (Cox, 1998, Hall, 1998; Lye, 2000; Phibbs, 1999, 2000; Ritchie & Hall, 2000).

GENTRIFICATION: WHO WINS? WHO LOSES?

The common urban pattern of gentrification, in evidence in Sydney in the 1980s and 1990s, resulted in cheap rental accommodation being upgraded

and low-income tenants evicted to make way for middle-class professionals who chose to rent or buy newly renovated premises close to the CBD,
where employment opportunities in information technology, in particular,
were expanding (Blunden, 2000; Hansson & Ans, 2000).

A cynical view put forward by the Sydney Housing Action Collective
captured the combined impacts of capitalism and globalization in Sydney
as the Olympics approached:

> Look at the scale of urban gentrification in Sydney at the moment—
> doesn't look like abating in the near future does it? Relax. It is only
> natural—the strong over the weak. It is just space, not place. One day—
> when you can afford to purchase property of your own—you will under-
> stand. And you too will give the gift of rental accommodation to someone
> who has enough money to afford it but not enough to return the gift.
> And they will give you the security you need for further speculation in
> real estate. Everyone's a winner. Sydney 2000 Yes! (SHAC, 2000a).

In 1973, Australia became a signatory to the UN Convention on Economic, Social, and Cultural Rights, which required member states to guarantee, through laws and policies, that all citizens had the right to adequate
shelter. In no Australian state, however, was there legislation guaranteeing
tenants security of tenure (Sullivan, 2000). In NSW, under the 1987 *Residential Tenancies Act,* landlords could increase rents and evict tenants
without cause, with sixty days' notice. The Residential Tribunal allowed
tenants to appeal excessive rent increases, a difficult procedure since the
onus of proof lay with the tenant to prove that the rent was excessive in
comparison to the market. In the pre-Olympic period, with rents going
through the roof (to use a Rentwatcher's term) all over Sydney, appeals
were unlikely to be successful. Boarders and lodgers lacked even these
minimal legislative rights since they were specifically exempt from the act.

In June 1999, the Green Party, in consultation with tenants' services
and community legal centers, introduced an amendment to the *Residential
Tenancies Act* to protect tenants, calling for a limit of one rent increase per
year until December 2001, and putting the onus on landlords to show just
cause for evictions. But, as Greens councillor from Leichhardt, Jamie Parker
explained, both the opposition and the government acted as if the Greens
were "nefarious smashers of the private property system," and in October
the amendment was soundly defeated (Parker, 2000).

In its rationale for opposing the amendment, the government claimed
that "NSW tenancy laws already provide protection for tenants against
unscrupulous landlords . . . there is no evidence of Olympic-related rent
increases" (Greens bill defeated, 1999, 5). It went on to announce an
education campaign on the rights and responsibilities of tenants and landlords, with the Department of Fair Trading publication "The Renting

Guide" marking the first stage, and a focus on "dampening any speculative activity of landlords" for the second.

Housing advocates were in agreement in condemning the government's failure to acknowledge any negative Olympic-related impact, and its overall inaction on any of the pressing social impact problems. There was a clear lack of political will on the part of both the state Labor government and the opposition to enact any kind of preventive or protective legislation that would tip the balance toward tenants' rights rather than landlords' profits. Community leaders drew public attention to the social divide between two increasingly disparate groups: those with adequate housing and those without. In a country that traditionally promoted home ownership, an unprecedented 31% of people in NSW were tenants in 1999. While the Commonwealth Government's 1992 Affordable Housing Strategy set an "affordable housing benchmark" at 30% of a household income—a high level by most standards—Department of Fair Trading figures released in 1998 showed that 94% of very low-income renters spent more than 30% of their income on rent, a problem termed *housing stress* (Blunden, 2000). A June 1998 report from the Smith Family, a charitable agency, found that figure to be 40% (*Rentwatchers Report*, 1998). Sydney rents were 40% higher than those in Melbourne, a city of comparable size but with the advantage of not having hosted the Olympics since 1956.

The gap between Sydney residents who were adequately housed, and those who were not, was graphically illustrated every Saturday in the real estate pages of the *Sydney Morning Herald*. A section called *Title Deed* at the front of the real estate pages was devoted to a report of top-end auction sale results, accompanied by gratuitous personal details about the buyers and sellers involved. The format typically listed the former owners, their occupations and/or claims to fame, the selling price when the property last changed hands, the latest selling price, and details about the new owners and their lifestyles. Sydney's rich and famous dominated these pages; properties valued under $1m rarely warranted inclusion. This crass display of conspicuous consumption—a 1990s version of newspapers' and women's magazines' "society pages"—stood in stark contrast to the accounts of rent increases, evictions, hardship, and homelessness that regularly appeared in the front section of the paper in 1999 and 2000. Between 1992 and 2000, the waiting list for public housing in NSW had increased by 38%; in 1999, with 100,000 applications, 2,000 fewer people were housed than in 1992 (Nash, 2000).

Indigenous People and Housing

Systemic racism and other systems of discrimination and oppression had clear impacts on housing and homelessness. For example, 1996 Census figures showed that Indigenous people were the most inadequately housed of any group in Australia. Representing less than 2% of Australian households, they comprised almost a third of households living in "improvised dwellings"; 69% of households were renting, compared to 27% of non-Indigenous households; about half of overcrowded dwellings (ten or more people) were Indigenous households; and Indigenous people were twenty times more likely to be homeless than non-Indigenous people (HREOC, 2000; Australian Institute of Health and Welfare, 2000).

In Sydney, the area in Redfern known as the Block had been home to urban Aborigines and a center of Black organizing in Australia for decades (Laanela, 1999). Activists were determined to draw international visitors' attention to the Block's long-standing and complex problems, and overseas journalists did, in fact, cover many of these issues. The Block also attracted the attention of human rights advocates in the period leading up to the Olympics. Police drug raids in the Block escalated in August, and in a typical dawn raid on August 27, just over two weeks before the Games began, 120 police stormed the area and laid over 55 charges. Some Indigenous activists believed that these raids, characterized by the usual intimidation tactics directed at Aboriginal communities, served primarily for security practice purposes (R. Jackson, 2001, 5). Witnesses alleged that police pointed firearms at residents, including young children who were asleep in their beds, and Redfern Legal Center lodged a complaint with the ombudsman and the police, seeking compensation for stress and trauma experienced by the children (Dwyer, 2000).

A Lucrative Olympic Corridor

When Sydney won the 2000 Olympics in 1993, one of the purported strengths of the original Olympic design was the concentration of sporting competition in one area. The western suburb of Homebush Bay, formerly an industrial area, was the site of most new Olympic construction, and the bid promised that all venues would be within thirty minutes' travel of the Olympic village at Homebush Bay (Sydney Olympics 2000 Bid, 1992). This would only be achieved after major (and costly) improvements to the public transport system. The influx of public and private money, together with state-of-the-art sporting amenities and new infrastructure in the traditionally underserviced western suburbs, were touted as major Olympic legacies. By 2000, however, it was clear that not all legacies were positive.

Early patterns of rent increases and rising house prices in the five-year period leading up to 2000 indicated that the suburbs most affected were within the "Olympic corridor," a 12km spine going west from the CBD to Homebush Bay and Parramatta. Sydney house prices rose by 7% above inflation in 1998, compared to the usual 2% historically (Real Estate

Institute, 1999). In the Olympic corridor, according
provided by the developers Mirvac Lend Lease, t
from 13.7 to 23.6% in 1997–1998 (Newing'
Rentwatchers analysis of Department of Fair Trading
March 1997 and 1998 reported rent increases ranging from 1つ い
these suburbs (*Rentwatchers Report*, 1998). Many of these communities
had been home to low-income tenants, with high proportions of unskilled
and unemployed workers, immigrants, Indigenous people, and single parents—groups that were particularly vulnerable to Olympic-related impacts
on their housing arrangements.

In the local government area (LGA) of Auburn, where Homebush was
located, a 1998 council study investigated the long-term financial implications of the $2b Olympic construction project for local ratepayers. Among
the factors contributing to the rate revenue problem was the loss of $3.7m
in property tax revenues from the former state abattoir site when the
government changed its rating status to accommodate Olympic construction. Planned residential developments in and near the Olympic site were
expected to increase the population by 40% to about 70,000, but the
housing would not be fully occupied and rate-paying until 2007, and it
was predicted that any long-term increase in rate revenue would not come
about until 2010 (Davidson, 1999). Auburn LGA was one of the most
disadvantaged areas of Sydney, with the 1996 Census figures showing a
median personal income of $234 per week, 30% lower than for the median
for Sydney residents, an unemployment rate of 14.3%, nearly double the
overall rate for NSW, as well as significantly lower levels of educational
attainment. With close to half of the Auburn population born outside
Australia and having English as a second language, the combined effects
of social class and ethnic discrimination were in clear evidence (James,
1998).

From the perspective of real estate agents and investors, inner-west and
western suburbs represented a gold mine. The term *Olympic corridor* was
coined by one of Australia's major real estate companies, L.J. Hooker,
whose 1993 research report identified thirteen sites in the planning or
construction stage, and another eighteen sites, including waterfront land,
which could be redeveloped. The broader Sydney real estate context was
also conducive to development in these suburbs: a long housing boom,
low interest rates, and significant urban consolidation since 1994 (G. Moore,
2000a; Cox, 1999). As the Mirvac Lend Lease promotional material
"Newington News" (1999) enthused, in typical real estate jargon that
rendered human suffering invisible, "the changing nature of the [Olympic
corridor] area from semi-industrial dormitory suburbs to a near-city waterfront residential location" had produced an "upsurge" in house and
apartment sales, new housing starts, and, most significantly, higher prices.

e predicted key components of the "Olympic factor" in boosting real
te development were new amenities, improved transport services, con-
ntration of expenditure and employment, and the "re-imaging" of the
western suburbs property market as a desirable target for buyers and
investors (Cox, 1999, 50–51; Dunn, 1999). Developers' subsequent marketing of Homebush Bay—"The Natural Heart of Sydney"—and the logo
that appeared on Olympic Coordination Authority (OCA) publications in
2000—"Homebush Bay: The New Heart of Sydney"—captured this "re-
imaging" campaign. With the adjacent suburb of Parramatta commonly
recognized as the geographic center of Sydney's metropolitan region, and
the Millennium Parklands at Homebush Bay promising to be Sydney's
largest park, the "natural heart" claim had some legitimacy. On the other
hand, if the "center" of Sydney were to be measured by other criteria,
such as its location on public transport grids, employment opportunities,
access to cultural and recreational activities, or proximity to beaches and
the harbor—Homebush would not be at the top of the list.

By 1999, rises in rent and house prices were no longer confined to the
original Olympic corridor. Rentwatchers coordinator Beth Jewell reported
that the NSW government now agreed that the new Olympic corridor
stretched from Bondi to Penrith, a distance of over 55 km. In terms of
housing impact, its new north-south boundaries, as Jewell pointed, were
from Newcastle, about 160 km north of Sydney, to Wollongong, about
100 km south, and southwest to the Southern Highlands, which, not
coincidentally, was the area where horses brought from overseas for Olympic
equestrian events would be housed before the Games.

In February 2000, Tenants' Union data documented sharp increases
since 1998 in calls to twenty tenant advice services, with callers requesting
information and help regarding rent increases and no-cause evictions. In
the inner ring of suburbs (5–10 km from the CBD), in particular, the last
half of 1999 saw dramatic increases in the number of inquiries related to
terminations by landlords. This change was not simply a function of increased calls; there was clear evidence from Tenants' Union statistics of an
increasing proportion of termination-related calls. During the same month,
it was reported that an average of 125 termination-related applications
were being dealt with by the Residential Tribunal each day (Rentwatchers,
2000). During 1999, calls to the inner-city tenant services doubled while
calls to the eastern suburbs services tripled; in late 1999, it was reported
that about 250 people were evicted from the South Sydney local council
area alone (Sullivan, 2000).

As Tenants' Union president Nick Warren explained, landlords usually
found it easier to evict than to raise the rent of current tenants, who might
well challenge unfair increases (Warren, 2000). Tenant services documented
a pattern of no-cause evictions and subsequent rent increases, with land-

lords failing to carry out needed repairs, or even to complete superficial improvements, before putting the premises on the rental market again. Other common landlord strategies were to evict and renovate, or to evict, demolish, and redevelop.

Rent increases, of course, produced an increase in the number of homeless people. With a shortage of shelter beds in Sydney in 1997, community organizations provided emergency shelter of up to two weeks in private accommodation beds purchased by Sydney City Council and the NSW Department of Housing—a system termed *brokerage*. The Council's Homeless Persons' Information Center (HPIC) coordinated the service, which had about 29,000 calls per year. HPIC reported that the number of homeless people in Sydney almost tripled between 1992 and 1999, and its 1997 surveys revealed the new profile of shelter users: 60–70 percent had never used shelter accommodation before, increased numbers had psychiatric disabilities, and over half were from outside the city, including the Olympic corridor suburbs of Parramatta near the Homebush Bay Olympic site, and Blacktown, where the Olympic baseball and softball facilities were located (Cox, 1999; *Rentwatchers Report*, 1998).

Eastern Suburbs: The Corridor Expands

The late addition of Bondi as site of the beach volleyball competition, and the routing of the marathon, triathlon, and cycling events through Kensington, Centennial Park, and Bronte, had the effect of bringing Sydney's eastern suburbs into the Olympic picture by the late 1990s. These developments, along with the long-standing appeal of the eastern beach suburbs for tourists, backpackers, and others seeking ready access to sand and surf, had a significant impact on real estate and the residential tenancy market.

By the late 1990s, Bondi—traditionally a suburb with a mix of "battlers" (working-class people), people from the arts and cultural community, and summer visitors—was perceived by many locals as being overrun by "backpackers" and other "transients." Some of these negative perceptions unfairly targeted young tourists from Great Britain, who allegedly flooded the casual labor market in hotels and restaurants and crowded out Australian youth. For their part, hotel and restaurant managers were likely to be displaying class bias in their preference for middle-class British employees over working-class Australians. Moreover, Australia's immigration policy provided overseas visitors aged eighteen to twenty-five with temporary work permits, thereby encouraging exactly the kind of working holiday that permanent residents viewed as contributing to the "transience" problem in beach suburbs such as Bondi and Coogee.

At the same time, however, the number of inadequately maintained backpacker hotels was identified as a serious problem in these suburbs, particularly in the municipality of Randwick, which had one of the highest number of illegal backpacker operations in Sydney. Providing relatively cheap dormitory-style accommodations, these residences were justly viewed as undesirable neighbors because of high noise levels day and night, as well as poor maintenance practices. While the stereotype of the young backpacker who "doesn't care" about the neighborhood often held true, there was ample evidence in Bondi and Coogee that greedy and irresponsible operators and owners also earned the reputation as "bad neighbors" when they failed to control noise or to maintain clean premises.

A pattern of absentee landlords emerged in these suburbs, and elsewhere in Sydney, as the Olympics approached. Property owners found alternative temporary or permanent accommodation, and then extracted high rents from groups of backpackers or other temporary tenants. In one Coogee example, an unfurnished two-bedroom apartment, shared by an unspecified and constantly changing number of young tourists, produced a weekly rent of six hundred dollars for the landlord, and a weekly output of dozens of beer bottles dumped in the driveway beside the building.

Boardinghouse Residents: Disenfranchised Citizens

Although a clear pattern of conversions of boardinghouses to backpacker hotels was evident in Sydney in the 1990s, conservative arguments routinely held that this was not an Olympic-related effect, but merely a product of "changing demographic patterns." In Toronto, for example, loss of boardinghouse stock since the 1980s was largely attributable to the gentrification of inner-city neighborhoods, rather than to that city's relentless attempts to mount Olympic bids since 1989. However, there is also evidence that hallmark events precipitated this trend, and clearly the Olympics and the gentrification trend were complementary factors behind the dramatic changes in Sydney's housing market during the late 1990s (Lye, 2000). When Sydney hosted the 1988 Bicentennial events, over 5,000 inner-city rooms were lost, either converted to backpacker accommodations or budget hotels; in Brisbane, preparations for the 1988 Expo resulted in a loss of 13 boardinghouses, conversion of a further 22 to tourist accommodations, and house price increases of 56 percent in some neighborhoods (Cox, 1999; Jewell, 2000a).

Before the Bicentennial, the NSW government introduced the *State Environmental Planning Policy No. 10—Retention of Low-cost Rental Accommodation* (SEPP 10) in an attempt to restrict the redevelopment of boardinghouses and other low-cost rental housing into residential apartments or hotels (strata-titled residences). Amendments introduced before the Olympics, as a result of pressure from Rentwatchers, the Tenants' Union, Shelter NSW, and New South Wales Council of Social Services

(NCOSS), required Department of Housing and local governments to reject a development application if it resulted in a loss of low-cost rental housing, and where existing demand could not be met by comparable accommodation in the locality. However, landlords could escape the restrictions of this act if they were simply converting to tourist or backpacker lodgings, as long as they complied with zoning and other local council policies. Equally important, SEPP 10 was a policy document only, and did not give boarders legal enforceable rights (Lye, 2000).

There was extensive statistical as well as anecdotal evidence of dramatic increases in conversions, renovations, demolitions, and new developments in the lead-up to the Sydney Olympics, and housing advocates consistently argued that these changes were prompted by property owners' hopes of an Olympic bonanza. For tenants, these changes represented rent hikes, increases in no-cause evictions, $1,000–$3,000 in moving and relocation expenses, and general uncertainty and anxiety about accommodation for themselves and their families. In this downward spiral for tenants, the new rental premises were inevitably of poorer quality, and after several such moves, many low-income people ended up in emergency shelters (G. Moore, 2000b).

In 1998, the Inner Sydney Boarding House Report predicted that, with the current rate of loss, most Sydney boardinghouses would be converted within a decade. The vast majority of boardinghouse residents were elderly, or had physical or mental disabilities, and/or were living on social security. In the inner-city area of South Sydney, 76 percent of boardinghouses had been converted over a ten-year period. Most former residents had been paying between $70 and $100 per week, well below the median rent even for the cheapest one-bedroom apartment (Boarding houses, 1998).

A speaker at the March 29, 2000 Rentwatchers' meeting at the Newtown Neighbourhood Center documented how, in the inner-west suburb of Camperdown, twenty-five boarders had been evicted from a facility that had operated for twenty-five years for recovering alcoholics, despite the fact that every resident on the street had signed a petition asking the minister for health to prevent these evictions. The boarders were now housed in different accommodations all over the city, while the landlord began the minimal upgrading necessary for the backpacker conversion. In an equally disturbing example, one of the Rentwatchers' case studies documented how twenty elderly and disabled people living in a Darlinghurst boardinghouse were given three weeks' notice to leave in December 1999. At least two of these men ended up sleeping in parks the week before Christmas, while the landlord leased the property to someone planning to operate it as a backpacker hotel (Rentwatchers, 2000, 10).

In another Rentwatchers example, in September 1999, the operator of about twenty inner-city boardinghouses for low-income people evicted twenty residents as part of a program of converting the residences to backpacker accommodation (Crunch time, 1999). Interestingly, a *Herald* journalist interviewed Rentwatchers staff, who substantiated these facts, but the story was never printed. According to a *Herald* source, the journalist failed to deliver a newsworthy story backed up by evidence. It seems likely, however, that the possibility of libel charges initiated by the boardinghouse operator had a chilling effect.

On a similar note, a June 2000 *Herald* story reported that In-West, a company that had operated thirty-five inner-west boardinghouses—comprising 80 percent of such housing—had closed twelve of its premises, after twenty years in the boardinghouse business, because it was no longer "viable" (Morris, 2000c). With the Olympics imminent, this move threatened to make up to three hundred people homeless. It was not clear from the article whether In-West was entering the more "viable" backpacker business in time for the Olympics.

THROUGH THE ROOF: SYDNEY RENTS

A Rentwatchers analysis of Department of Fair Trading figures for January–March 1997 and 1998 provided clear evidence of rent increases—ranging from 15 to 40 percent—in all Olympic corridor suburbs (*Rentwatchers Report,* 1998). By 2000, with the imminent implementation of the Goods and Services Tax (GST) exacerbating Olympic-related increases, Sydney rents became the topic of news items and human interest stories on a regular basis, a common theme being no cause termination notices issued to tenants of long standing. A June *Herald* story even carried the alarming news (for some) "Now rent rises hit the more affluent" (Morris, 2000d). This impact was substantiated anecdotally: for example, international students and academics, and business and professional people who had been transferred to Sydney often complained privately about the high rents, particularly when contrasted with cities in Scandinavia, Canada, and the United States, where monthly rents were not much higher than Sydney's weekly rate.

In March 2000, Rentwatchers published eighteen case studies involving rent increases and unfair evictions, many involving groups of tenants, in the information kit *We Can't Share the Spirit If We Can't Afford the Rent* (Rentwatchers, 2000). First-person accounts of hardship resulting from landlords' attempted Olympic profiteering could be heard at every Olympic-related community meeting. Rentwatchers also documented some disturbing precedents during recent hallmark events. Exploiting the opportunity provided by 1999 New Year's Eve festivities on Sydney Harbor, including fireworks displays that were televised around the world, several owners of harborfront rental properties took over common areas such as rooftops in order to host private, commercial New Year's Eve parties. With a number of Olympic events taking place on the harbor, it was feared that these practices would be repeated, with tenants having to pay for the privilege of accessing common space for which they had already paid rent.

Finally, in blatant examples of landlords' rent gouging, tenants in some Sydney suburbs reported being told that rents would increase for the duration of the Olympics. Rentwatchers obtained a lease dated February 9, 2000, for $550 per week rent for premises in the inner-west suburb of Balmain, with the following handwritten "additional terms and conditions": "Tenant agrees that rent shall be $1,000 per week during the 3 week Olympic Games period" (Jewell, 2000a).

Affordable rental accommodation in the eastern suburbs, inner-city, and inner-west became virtually nonexistent by 2000. A pattern of eviction and renovation, or eviction, demolition, and redevelopment, was particularly in evidence. In a typical eastern suburbs example, two older semidetached houses were sold and demolished to make way for a block of six home units, with the original rents doubling or tripling by the time the new units went on the market. And, in a Bondi example that attracted national media attention, a landlord evicted all the tenants from an eight-unit block of apartments after he had been issued with a fire defect notice by Waverley Council, arguing that the improvements could not be done unless the property was evacuated (Wade, 1999).

Another potential source of Olympic-related income for homeowners was the Olympic Homestay Homehost program, managed by Ray White Real Estate, which provides vacant furnished rental or bed and breakfast accommodation for visitors. These arrangements, at first glance, appeared to fit the needs of the considerable number of Sydney residents who had decided to leave Sydney during the Olympics and wanted to reap the tourism benefits by renting their houses. By February 2000, however, it appeared that the supply of housing was greater than the demand. Ray White reported a ceiling of about $20,000 a week, with "superior" houses starting at about $8,500, while Hooker gave $3,000 (one-bedroom) to $20,000 (three-bedroom) as the range for apartment rentals during the Olympics, but warned homeowners that long-term bookings were more secure than three- or four-week Olympic rentals with long vacant periods before and after the Games. Some newspaper accounts of "executive rentals," however, continued to boost homeowners' dreams of Olympic windfalls. In February 2000, the *Herald* reported a four-week city apartment rental to an American firm for $200,000, as well as an overseas client prepared to pay $500,000 for a harborfront property, and in May, the *Daily Telegraph* carried the story of a Balmain penthouse to be rented to a Japanese investment company for $720,000 (Grennan, 2000; Martin, 2000).

At the other end of the Olympic rental scale, youth workers in Sydney predicted that some young Australians would hitchhike long distances in order to see the Olympics. As a result, they emphasized the need for advanced planning to ensure that these young people had safe, secure accommodation. Figures for March 2000 showed that the youth crisis accommodation in Sydney was already stretched, and it was not designed for Olympic overflow. Moreover, it was feared that young people of identifiable ethnic minority backgrounds—Aboriginal, Arabic, and Vietnamese, for example—would be targeted by police, rangers, and security guards if they attempted to sleep in parks or on beaches (Tonkin, 2000).

OLYMPIC HOUSING: MYTHS AND REALITIES

Contrary to prevailing Olympic myths about housing legacies, all new permanent housing at Homebush Bay was to be sold or rented at market value. Most apartments in the luxury $90m riverfront development known as Mariners Cove were sold by March 2000, with some three-bedroom units still available at that time priced from $495,000 to $785,000. Like other premises near Olympic venues, Mariners Cove apartments were available, for a price, to Olympic visitors: $10,000 per week (for a three-week block booking only), which, as one real estate company advertisement boasted, was under $250 per night per person, and even less if nine rather than six people shared the space. The proximity of these apartments to the water raised some safety concerns, since it was well established that the water and sediment in Homebush Bay (the actual *bay*, not the suburb) were highly contaminated, and that remediation would take several years to complete.

The first phase of Mirvac Lend Lease's somewhat more modest Newington development, comprising 100 houses and 130 apartments, was completed and on sale by 1999, with houses ranging from $380,000 to $540,000, and apartments, $295,000 to $525,000. The 500 houses and 300 apartments that formed the Athletes' Village represented Phase Two, with prices starting at $300,000. Other village accommodation consisted of demountable components that would subsequently be sold and removed from the site. Phase Three, to be built by 2006, would bring the total number of Newington residents to about 5,000.

During the first half of 2000, Phase Two buyers were encouraged to "beat the GST" by investing before July, and were promised new kitchens, carpet, and interior painting post-Games. A leaseback arrangement allowed buyers to generate rental income—a guaranteed 6 percent return on the purchase price—until 2001, when they could take possession. Despite the reputed real estate boom, Phase Two sales were aggressively marketed in 2000, and *Newington News* for Autumn 2000 noted that thirteen different home lenders were on site every weekend to facilitate sales. At this stage, according to the promotional material, "we are proud to be able to boast" a supermarket, a retail center with a dozen specialty shops, a business park, a community center, and the Millennium Parklands. A forty-place childcare center was due to begin operation in 2001, while the public elementary school would open in 2002—even though by April 2000, 210 households had already moved in (Taylor, 2000).

Overall, while fulfilling the promise of becoming the world's largest solar-heated suburb, the housing development at Homebush Bay had some major shortcomings, especially for families with young children. For example, in the Australian context, where the quarter-acre lot was seen as standard, the very small backyards, zero lot lines, and the higher density housing—covering 90 hectares of the 262-hectare site—were viewed negatively by some buyers. Rising to this challenge, promotional material invariably pointed to the adjacent 450 hectares of public parkland as evidence that residents could enjoy "secure, quality, parkland living"—not a particularly persuasive argument for those who simply wanted adequate backyard play areas for their children.

Despite Newington's stated goal of reducing dependence on car use and resulting carbon dioxide emissions, there were challenges for residents who relied on public transport. The Olympic Park railway station was a fifteen-minute walk from Newington; the ferry terminal was a five-minute bus trip, and the light rail system was to be developed at some future date. Moreover, the fact that the larger houses had two-car garages, and the others had a garage and designated parking space, would seem to cast doubt on this original goal.

CREATIVE HOUSING SOLUTIONS: THE BROADWAY SQUATS

The Sydney Housing Action Collective (SHAC) was organized in order to facilitate the use of unoccupied housing in the inner-city area by squatters. As a SHAC representative explained at the May 2000 Olympic Impact Coalition meeting, squatting was a physical manifestation of the housing crisis. For the two years before the Olympics, squatting had become increasingly criminalized, and houses with activist squatters were reported to be the first to be closed down, purportedly because of the alleged "terrorist threat" posed by these particular squatters. The SHAC website, shac.net, provided addresses and photos of potential squats, as well as the squatters' handbook, a comprehensive legal and practical guide to squatting, including advice on communication with the media and the use of e-mail and the internet for research and support. Citing some of the advantages of squatting, the SHAC handbook explained,

> Despite the "threat of eviction" squatting actually gives you a high degree
> of control over where and how you choose to live . . . to organize a place
> according to your individual and collective desires—a privilege usually
> reserved for owners of private property to enjoy. And when you create
> that kind of autonomy you tend to actively participate in maintaining it
> rather than simply waiting for the government / rental market to try and
> provide it for you. . . . (SHAC, 2000a)

On the issue of eviction, the handbook suggested that citing the *In-closed Lands Protection Act* (1901), section 4 (which authorized the "occupier" of premises to request persons to leave if they were conducting themselves in an "offensive manner") might be effective in forcing "an unauthorized wannabe evictor to back off for a while" (SHAC, 2000a). It acknowledged, of course, that the act could equally be used to evict squatters (and in an interesting parallel, it had in fact been invoked to secure the area of Bondi Beach for stadium construction—see chapter 8).

In March 2000, about fifty people who would have otherwise been homeless as a result of Olympic-related rent increases began occupying three empty buildings owned by South Sydney Council. As the SHAC handbook explained, "People used to squat [in] government-owned buildings . . . because it was thought that there was more room to negotiate with 'public' authorities with a 'conscience' than with 'private' property speculators and companies who were more obviously concerned with 'making money' " (SHAC, 2000a). And, in the lead-up to the Olympics, public authorities were no doubt more concerned than private landowners about maintaining a humane public face.

These council-owned buildings were located on Broadway, a major artery running from Central Railway, past the University of Technology Sydney (UTS), to the University of Sydney, and only a short distance away from the Sydney Organizing Committee for the Olympic Games (SOCOG) headquarters. The council, in a joint venture with the multinational construction company Australand Walker, planned to demolish the block in 2001. Original plans to include affordable units in the new development were changed, however, to a proposed office complex and luxury apartments—a change supported by a council that had earlier "proclaimed an ardent dedication to relieving homelessness among its constituency" (Connor, 2000a).

The squatters cleaned the rooms; repaired the floor and roof; fixed the shower and toilets; secured doors and windows; and installed a sink, refrigerator, smoke detectors, carpet, lights, power points, and fire extinguishers. Much of the equipment was recycled, including food thrown into dumpsters at local supermarkets (Predator, 2000).

The State Fights Back: Eviction Notices

Three weeks before the Olympics, the Broadway squatters were notified that they had to leave by August 28, and that failure to do so would result in a police and/or tactical response unit raid. SHAC quickly organized defensive actions, including a protest, a street party, and solidarity sleepovers. They asked supporters to send letters to the mayor and councillors asking that residents be allowed to stay until after the Olympics. As the squatters explained, "It is clear that in the circumstances where council has vacant livable unoccupied premises, that policy and protocols to allow residency for those members of the community squeezed out by a lack of affordable housing are not only necessary, but legally manageable" (SHAC, 2000b)

Some squatters and their supporters attended the September 7 council meeting, but were not permitted to speak. Councillors eventually decided, behind closed doors, to evict the squatters immediately; failure to leave would incur $1.1m in fines. It was reported that councillors' fear of personal liability if squatters were injured on the premises prompted this decision. The timing was obviously another factor: the council decided to play hardball after their first eviction attempt failed and the Olympics were approaching. They were aware, of course, that international journalists were scouring the city for precisely this kind of "behind-the-scenes" Olympic-related story. On September 15, the council sought an injunction from the Land and Environment Court to evict the squatters because the premises did not comply with fire safety regulations. Represented by a solicitor from the Public Interest Law Clearing House's law firm, the squatters achieved a small victory when the judge found that one building did not pose a fire hazard. Because it would be a hardship for them to vacate it immediately, the squatters were given ten days in which to find alternative accommodation.

In the interim, four Labor councillors and the Greens councillor agreed to put forward a motion to the October 11 meeting calling for the council to drop court proceedings, and to implement a joint plan developed by SHAC and the University of Sydney's Fell Housing Research Center to give caretaker status to the squatters—an innovative and workable approach that would help to address South Sydney's housing crisis. As SHAC spokesperson Gavin Sullivan explained, the majority on the council (five out of nine) felt that the "council should be negotiating not litigating" (Sullivan, 2000). This policy proposal promised to break new ground by formalizing a mutually beneficial relationship whereby the council made vacant properties available for short-term accommodation, while residents with skills in basic repairs and fire safety kept the places clean and secure until their demolition.

But the threat of eviction continued. On September 25, a message was circulated to supporters via e-mail that council employees would arrive at 8:00 A.M. the next day to board up the squats. Unexpectedly, just after midnight, about eight police officers arrived on the premises, tried to kick down the doors, and "aggressively pushed, searched and harassed sleepy squatters," according to the account posted to the Sydney Independent Media Center (IMC) by one of the squatters (Skive, 2000). (Most squatters posting news items on the IMC website followed the SHAC handbook advice to use pseudonyms to avoid being identified by police intelligence or other officials.) Police behavior was reported to have been intimidating and racist; they accused some residents of "not being able to speak English" and not looking "Australian"—presumably implying that they were (illegal) immigrants. Ironically, while searching the premises, police found a printout of a message, posted by Inspector Dave Darcy and Superintendent Ron Mason to the IMC on September 25, which guaranteed no police raids on the squats. It stated in part, "we have no intention of launching a tactical strike and casting them onto the streets. In terms of police action this matter will be progressively worked through with an emphasis on consultation and negotiation" (Darcy & Mason, 2000). The police then left the premises.

When the municipal workers arrived at 8:00 A.M., the squatters, along with a building trades union representative, explained their situation, the potential occupational health and safety risks to the workers, and the ongoing negotiations about caretaker status. The workers eventually agreed that the situation was too confusing for them to proceed. By that time—the fifth week of squatters' resistance—four building trades unions were supporting the residents in a twenty-four-hour picket line, which council workers who were union members refused to cross. The aim at this stage was to keep a strong public presence to protect the premises and residents until the October 11 council vote. Although the mayor opposed the caretaker status motion to the end, the majority voted in favor. But, as one squatter pointed out, "it never ends." A few days later, the *Daily Telegraph* began a "trash the squatters campaign," beginning with a distorted story titled "Squatters living free and easy on Broadway" (2000) in which they were portrayed as middle-class people with jobs, cars, mobile phones (and "brand-name shampoo") who were living rent-free, thanks to the council's "generosity." In typical *Telegraph* style, the Vote Line question of the day was phrased negatively: "Is it wrong for councils to give squatters caretaker status in empty buildings?" Activists quickly circulated the article so that supporters could help balance the inevitable "yes" response that the *Telegraph* was inviting.

STUDENT HOUSING = PRIME OLYMPIC RENTALS

A short distance from the Broadway squats, students at the University of Sydney and UTS were also experiencing serious housing problems as the Olympics approached. A significant proportion of these universities' academic buildings, sporting facilities, and student accommodations had been contracted out to SOCOG for Olympic purposes.

At the end of March 2000, the University of Sydney sent out letters calling on students to offer temporary housing (e.g., sofa beds or inflatable mattresses) to their peers who normally lived in on-campus residences, for the duration of the Olympics (Heath, 2000a). Concerned about the threat to student housing, the Student Representative Council (SRC) posed a number of questions to the university senate. By May 4, having received no response, it forwarded the same inquiries to the vice-chancellor regarding, in particular, the arrangements that the university planned to make for vulnerable groups including overseas students, those from remote rural areas, those who were homeless or had no parental home, and those working on placements or ongoing projects and needing access to university facilities during September/October (Humphrys, 2000; Verco, 2000).

Summarizing these events in August, SRC president Natasha Verco reported that many students in university-owned, on-campus accommodation signed contracts agreeing to give up their rooms during the Olympics, because they believed they would be denied access to housing if they resisted. As a result, they felt "disempowered, alone, and very pissed off at the university administration." They were required to vacate their rooms for four weeks within twenty-four hours after the semester ended, and to pay for storage space and reconnection fees for electricity and telephone service when they returned (Scully, 2000). For those who left, one week's rent rebate was provided and they were guaranteed further accommodation in 2001. Students who chose to stay were warned that they may be housed in alternative accommodation for the four-week period. Of the private colleges, all except one (with a capacity of only forty rooms) were renting space to SOCOG, but these colleges had made efforts to ensure that students were not left homeless (Humphrys, 2000).

UTS, a university with two of its campuses located in Sydney's central business district, did not evict any students during the Games, largely because of the hard work of its Housing Department and Students Olympic Housing Project to ensure no loss of accommodation and no Olympic-related rent increases in university-controlled housing. Whereas, in 1997, the university's housing committee only received about 400 inquiries per semester, by 2000, with Olympic-related impacts seriously affecting the rental market, the number had risen to 10,000. Between February and

April 2000, less than 1% of students who made these inquiries found housing. In terms of non-university-owned student housing, 12 to 15 landlords were withdrawing their offers from the UTS housing registry each week, while only about 1% of landlords surveyed said they would rent to students during the Olympic period. SOCOG even attempted, unsuccessfully, to rent UTS-owned student housing during the Olympic period by offering to pay UTS 75% higher than market value (Heath, 2000b). On the other side of the city, it was reported that colleges at Macquarie University were asking about ten times the student rate for rooms booked by SOCOG for visiting sports officials (Bita, 2000).

Additional problems faced the thousands of new international students who arrived in Sydney in July and August, just before the Olympic tourists. Most were unfamiliar with Sydney's rental market and therefore were vulnerable to exploitation by dishonest landlords. In one example that came to the UTS housing committee's attention, an international student signed a six-month lease and paid the full $250 per week in advance for one room in a ten-room house in Newtown, only to find when he arrived that most students paid $100–$150 for this kind of accommodation. UTS Students' Association president Ryan Heath was a highly visible and active advocate for student housing issues in the lead-up to the Olympics, correctly believing that it was essential to keep up public pressure and scrutiny of landlords in order to avert a student housing crisis.

CONCLUSION

A compilation of the personal experiences of tenants from a range of socioeconomic backgrounds and geographic areas, backed up by results of extensive surveys conducted by the Tenants' Union, Rentwatchers, and other groups, produced indisputable evidence of a widespread social problem of housing and homelessness that increased in the years before the Olympics. Whether the Olympics constituted the major cause or one of many causes, the onus was on all levels of government to address the obvious crisis in housing by protecting tenants' rights and preserving affordable rental accommodation. The state government, for its part, refused to strengthen tenants' rights through legislation, and the provisions of SEPP 10 were generally too weak to protect the existing stock of affordable rental housing. In short, the Olympic impact exacerbated the gap between those who had adequate housing, and those who did not.

5

Olympic Values, Impacts, and Issues

The Real Legacy

Discussing the humane values that Toronto—at that time an Olympic bid city—used to hold as a vision of its future, *Toronto Star* environment writer Cameron Smith wrote in January 2001, "That was before the phrase 'world-class city' became a substitute for imagination, before the Olympic bid and other megaprojects came to be the solitary definition of progress" (Smith, 2001, B5). Developments in Sydney following its 1993 selection as an Olympic host city provide clear evidence of the ways in which Olympic industry goals threatened values rooted in democracy and social justice. Olympic-related impacts on housing and homelessness, together with the escalating criminalization of disadvantage and difference, constituted the most significant social problems confronting Sydney activists and community leaders in the late 1990s, as the preceding three chapters have demonstrated. This chapter will examine other social issues related to the staging of the Olympic Games: the real legacy questions, the struggle for fair wages, volunteer recruitment and training, the ticket sales fiasco, "Olympic Opportunity" tickets, and corporate-sponsored "Olympic education" programs aimed at children and youth.

OLYMPIC LEGACIES: WHO WINS? WHO LOSES?

Olympic industry rhetoric holds that cities reap extensive benefits from hosting the Summer Olympics, and the promised legacy of state-of-the-art sporting facilities usually heads this list. In the case of Sydney 2000, the (partial) remediation of Homebush Bay, the provision of sporting facilities and venues for the previously underserviced western suburbs, and the larger and more accessible premises for the annual Royal Agricultural Show were generally viewed as the most significant legacies. But, as NSW Council of Social Services (NCOSS) director Gary Moore stated, the whole community should benefit from the Olympics, and any costs should be evenly shared and not borne by specific groups, because, if there were a deficit, as Moore warned, "NSW taxpayers will wear it" (G. Moore, 2000a).

Social service leaders pointed out that, with Olympic-related spending taking the lion's share in the five years before the Games, core spending in health, education, welfare, and transport had suffered; therefore, they demanded a government commitment to correct this imbalance by directing spending to those areas in the next five years. Similarly, they called for a government capital works initiative to promote employment in areas of Sydney and regional NSW that missed out on Olympic benefits.

The hidden costs of staging the Olympics, incurred when government agencies were expected to absorb additional expenses into their own budgets, were identified in the 1999 Performance Audit Review. This report stressed the inconsistencies and inaccuracies of an Olympic budget that only included *direct* costs but allowed *indirect* revenues to be counted. It pointed out that, even with incomplete estimates from government agencies at that time, direct costs totaled $44.8m, a figure that failed to appear in the Games budget. It was well-known by then, of course, that the budget did not include capital works and infrastructure costs. Finally, the review identified the potentially negative impact of new sporting facilities on existing ones in relation to future use and foregone revenue. In the area of discretionary costs, it included extra demands on police, ambulance, fire brigades, and local government, the latter including garbage collection, traffic diversion, and possible compensation to shopkeepers for disruption and loss of business during the Games (Performance Audit Review, 1999).

Community leaders were concerned about the lack of government attention given to transport, health, and social services to the inner-city, eastern suburbs, and Olympic corridor during the Games, when there would be road closings, traffic restrictions, and a huge influx of tourists. There were over twenty-five thousand older residents and people with disabilities who relied on the daily delivery of services into their homes: Meals on Wheels, community nursing, mental health services, and others. Increased pressure on public hospitals in these same suburbs during the Games was another issue that community leaders believed was not fully addressed by the relevant government departments.

As late as April 2000, the Olympic Roads and Transport Authority had not yet developed an adequate transport plan to address these potential problems. Another serious transport problem involved the deployment of thirty-five hundred private buses from elsewhere in Australia during the Olympics. As a result, people in regional areas of the eastern states who relied on private buses, as well as people with disabilities who needed accessible buses, would have reduced or nonexistent transport services.

Olympic organizers unsuccessfully sought an exemption from the Disability Discrimination Act in order to commission wheelchair-accessible buses from Victoria and Queensland.

Finally, there was concern that the introduction of the Goods and Services Tax (GST) on July 1, 2000 would exacerbate Olympic-related social impacts. It was feared that the private business sector would blame Olympic-related price increases on the GST, since businesses were not required to change their cash registers to specify the amount of tax. Equally important, the added GST produced rent increases that exacerbated the already widespread problem of housing stress in Sydney.

According to a number of sources within social service and community activist circles, NSW premier Bob Carr and his so-called do-nothing government did not want to acknowledge that the Olympics were having *any* negative impacts. As a result, ministers in state departments of health, housing, and fair trading were not at liberty to reveal their Olympic preparations. At the same time, social service leaders faced two major challenges in their dealings with the government: first, to prove increased need in these areas, and second, to show that the Olympics were exacerbating existing social problems.

OLYMPIC EMPLOYMENT: STRUGGLES FOR FAIR PAY

Depending on one's political agenda, Olympic employment could be said to encompass the construction of every Olympic facility and venue, including those that were in progress or completed before 1993 when Sydney was awarded the Games. While it was in the bid committee's interests to maximize the number of existing facilities in order to impress the International Olympic Committee (IOC) with the city's state of readiness, the organizing committee would probably lay claim to many of the same structures as evidence of Olympics-generated work in the building trades. Hosting the Olympics also necessitated a number of infrastructure projects, including improvements to highways and the airport. Funded by the NSW government, these projects provided construction work in the Sydney region from 1993 on. Employment in the construction industry, however, was clearly stratified by gender, ethnicity, and social class, and Olympic-related boosts in this area did not necessarily benefit all job-seekers.

Principles of Co-operation between the Sydney Organizing Committee for the Olympic Games (SOCOG), the Sydney Paralympic Organizing Committee (SPOC), and the Labor Council of NSW were signed on November 21, 1997, for the purpose of "promoting harmonious industrial relations" at Olympic sites and facilities, developing a multiskilled workforce, and establishing high standards of service and "world class sport venues" (OCA, 1997). Consistent with these goals, two major awards (industrial agreements) were subsequently negotiated.

The first, the *Olympic Coordination Authority Staff (State) Consolidated Award 1997* covered members of the Australian Workers' Union (NSW), employed by the Olympic Coordination Authority (OCA) or a subcontractor and working in the areas of leisure/recreation and venue management. Rates of pay (1998) for weekly employees ranged from $12.15 to $18.20 per hour, and the award was in operation until the end of November 1999.

The *Sydney Olympic and Paralympic Games 2000 (State) Award* was passed on January 29, 2000. Wages and conditions for private sector workers (cleaning, catering, housekeeping, venue/events services, and security) were set out in the award, which overrode thirty existing industrial agreements. The award was in effect only for the duration of the Olympics and Paralympics, did not apply to the volunteer workforce, and did not set precedents for the future operations of facilities used during the Olympics.

All employees were required to pass probity checks before being permitted to work in SOCOG/SPOC-controlled areas. If existing venue staff did not satisfy the probity check, attempts would be made to give them alternative employment. Provision was made for training and consultation with the union over disputes. The maximum shift was 12 hours per day, or 152 hours over not more than 28 days, and at least 8 days off in a 28-day cycle, with overtime provisions for shifts exceeding these guidelines, and extra pay for late night and weekend work.

In addition to the rates of pay set out in the award, employees were to receive an attendance bonus of $1.50 for each paid hour worked, but only on completion of all allocated shifts—a provision described by SOCOG deputy chief executive Jim Sloman as an incentive "to stay in the job and a disincentive to poaching by other areas or by other employees" (SOCOG, 1999b). Chamber of Commerce sources warned employers about workers at the Atlanta Olympics who switched jobs several times until they got the best rates, and it was feared that this might happen again in Sydney (Vincent, 2000).

Hospitality Union Struggles

The Liquor, Hospitality and Miscellaneous Workers Union (known as LHMU) led a six-month campaign to win their Olympic award. In July 1999, the union began by sponsoring a register for members to apply for 50,000 part-time and casual Olympic jobs; the other 50,000 jobs were expected to be filled by volunteers. By 2000, the campaign's success was evident in the bonuses, higher hourly rates, and extra leave secured through concerted lobbying and protest efforts. LHMU members received an average of $20 per hour for Olympic work, as well as free transport and refreshments, in an award that its leaders hailed as the "best rates of pay for working at an event ever negotiated in Australia" (LHMU, 1999). More hospitality workers were needed, however, and in April 2000, it was reported that about 30,000 bar and restaurant trainees were to be brought to Sydney from tourism and hospitality colleges in other cities, with Olympic work counting as credit toward their certificates (Morris, 2000a).

By mid-2000, the LHMU faced the challenge of securing Olympic bonuses for members employed in all Sydney hotels, following agreement by the Starwood Hotel group to pay an additional $7.25 per hour ($550.00) for the two-week Olympic period to their 1,500 employees. At that time, the management of a number of hotel groups, including Accor, with its signature Olympic hotels at Homebush and Darling Harbor, had refused to enter into discussions about bonuses. Accor's offer of $2.00 an hour, subsequently upped to $3.00, was called "insulting" by LHMU negotiators, who planned to start an industrial campaign to put more pressure on management (LHMU, 2000a). By late August, the Australian Hotel Association, which had initially opposed any Olympic bonus, was advising its members to offer no more than $2.00 per hour extra, but LHMU viewed the Starwood bonus as the benchmark and rejected any lower amount.

Another Olympic-related issue emerged on August 28, when it came to light that the Regent Hotel, where Samaranch and other "Olympic family" members would be staying in luxury suites at up to $4,350.00 per night, was importing 30 workers from another Four Seasons hotel in Djakarta, where they received significantly lower wages. LMHU immediately contacted the Indonesian Hotel Workers Union to investigate. The need for additional staff—between 10 and 15 percent—was not unexpected, but big hotel groups were planning to bring them from their branches outside Sydney, not from outside the country (Cass, 2000; Morris, 2000a).

The same day, about 120 Regent Hotel workers held a protest concerning management's refusal to discuss the bonus claim, and as the LHMU newsletter reported, the new issue of cheap Indonesian labor "just added extra international value to the pre-Olympics coverage of the international media contingent" (LHMU, 2000b). Protesters also complained about the new security system that required fingerprint identification of all staff, presumably because of the high-level security surrounding "Olympic family" venues.

More Olympic Bonuses—But No Big Mac

In August, 1,300 City Rail security officers from Chubb Security won an attendance bonus of $4.50 per hour for the duration of the Olympics. Also in August, LHMU was successful in its demands to get Coca-Cola to pay a bonus to its Olympic workforce at Homebush Bay: forklift drivers, production workers, maintenance technicians, and distributors. From August 1 to November 1, interstate workers received an additional $100.00 a day, and local workers, $30.00 a day (LHMU, 2000b). Interestingly, while Coca-Cola was attempting to improve its image in Australia with Olympic bonuses and environmentally friendly refrigerants (see chapter 7), the company's head office in Atlanta was settling a racial discrimination lawsuit brought by Black employees, and paying out a record $US192.5m (Schafer, 2000).

The 1,200 employees working at seven Olympic Park McDonalds outlets were less successful in getting fair Olympic pay rates, because McDonalds, as a major sponsor, was reportedly exempt from the Olympic award. As a result, the generally younger workforce, already employed in other Sydney outlets, would earn their regular rates: that is, between $3.00 and $5.00 an hour less than their counterparts who were covered by the Olympic award. A fifteen-year-old, for example, would earn $10.30 per hour at other jobs on the Olympic site, but only $5.55 per hour at McDonalds. Justifying these arrangements, a McDonalds spokesperson claimed that employees would return to their regular jobs after having had "an outstanding Olympic experience" (Kerr, 2000).

This view that Olympic "goose bumps" would somehow compensate for the poor wages, longer travel times, and significantly tougher working conditions at Olympic venues was both patronizing and insulting—but it was not surprising. After all, the average young female worker behind the McDonalds counter was more malleable than the Coca-Cola forklift operator or the Chubb security guard. Indeed, from early 1999 on, the media were reporting threats of Olympic-related strikes by a number of male-dominated unions, including railway workers, police, and construction trades.

Another instance of top-down attempts to sell Olympic-related employment as a "once-in-a-lifetime" experience was found in the newsletter circulated to public housing tenants in November 1999. Reproduced in the *Rentwatchers Report*, it offered a *gem of a job opportunity*—Rentwatchers' cynical term—to work in a short-term hospitality job during the Olympics. The letter explained that the Department of Housing's Tenant Employment Project was helping companies recruit workers in food and beverage and housekeeping jobs. No doubt assuming that public tenants needed a timely reminder about good work habits, it went on to warn prospective employees,

> If you are successful in getting a position, you need to be committed to honoring your promise to work during the Games. If you live outside Sydney you will need to ensure you have accommodation in Sydney (ideally with family or friends as private accommodation will be hard to find). (Department of Housing, 1999, 7)

But, as Rentwatchers pointed out, the letter failed to mention that tenants' Olympic earnings would probably result in rent increases.

The *Bus 2000 Olympic Games and Paralympic Games (State) Award*, which was passed in April 1999, provided bus drivers with a bonus rate of $1.50 per hour and an extra $200.00 per week for the six-week Olympic and Paralympic period, but suspended overtime and other extras. One rationale for the bonus was to provide an incentive for drivers to complete all their rostered shifts. Many of the 10,000 drivers came from regional or country areas of NSW, and retired drivers were recruited to help fill the roster; they were provided with free accommodation, meals and laundry services.

In other public service areas, the NSW Labor Council and the Public Service Association demanded $3.00 per hour Olympic bonuses for public servants, regardless of whether or not their jobs were affected; the NSW government offered $1.50 per hour to a selected group of employees deployed in Olympic work. By April, police, fire and emergency services, transport workers, and medical staff were all seeking Olympic bonuses. In May, rail workers demanded $300.00 per week attendance bonus and an extra week's leave, and after subsequent negotiations were granted an Olympic bonus of up to $4.50 per hour, well below the original claim, but up to three times the amount offered to other public servants.

Hidden Olympic Costs: The Public Service Contribution

In the struggle to fill the thousands of required Olympic workforce positions, the NSW government asked all department heads to assess how many staff could be redeployed for Olympic work. As *Herald* Olympic editor Matthew Moore explained, with yet another round of cuts to the SOCOG budget, the public service was "the only place to find a large, professional group of people that is available at no extra cost." It was estimated that about 14,500 government staff would not be required by their agencies during the Games; by April, 1,200 employees had offered to do Olympic-related work at their normal pay rates. A less apparent advantage of the reassignment of public servants, as Moore pointed out, was the fact that taxpayers were footing the bill while Olympic organizers benefited from the public servants' "free" services (M. Moore, 2000b).

This figure—as high as $1.7m if public servants averaged the same $20 per hour rate as LHMU members—was unlikely to appear in any official Olympic budget. Similarly, overall costs to state government departments and services, officially listed as $430m, were believed to be significantly understated because many departments, such as Health, Fair Trading, and Housing, were asked to "absorb their Olympic-related costs into their existing budgets" (G. Moore, 2000a).

With government agencies trying to persuade staff to take leave during the Games to help minimize the number of people traveling to the CBD, particularly on public transport, the planned reassignment of public servants helped to address traffic as well as staffing problems. Some employers investigated ways that staff could "telecommute" from home, but most jobs outside the white-collar sector did not lend themselves to this arrangement. A number of private companies urged employees to take their annual leave, and schools, colleges, and universities extended their holidays to include the entire Olympic period, for the dual purposes of alleviating demands on public transit and freeing up students and staff to volunteer. Those who were uninterested in volunteering or attending the Olympics—inconceivable as that might seem to Olympic boosters—faced the prospect of taking an unwanted holiday at the end of winter in a city where the usual leisure activities were closed down or inaccessible by public transport. A more serious problem for low-income families was the fact that, despite the additional week of school holidays, parents did not receive additional child care funding for that period (G. Moore, 2000b, 2000c).

When IOC transport commissioner Anita DeFrantz visited Sydney in April 2000, she told residents that they would have to change their travel habits during the Olympics, and stop using public transport during times of high visitor demand. Community groups, environmentalists, and employer groups were justifiably outraged at this high-handed statement. A *Green Left Weekly* article summed up the incident: "The latest IOC representative to grace Sydney with a whistlestop tour has probably managed to do more to harm the Olympics cause than several years of organizers' blunders" (Ranald, 2000, 7).

Filling Olympic Jobs—Equitably?

The Olympic Labor Network, comprising eight major personnel and recruitment companies, was launched on March 12, 2000 under the management of Adecco, "the world's largest staffing company" and an Olympic sponsor. A special supplement to the March 12 *Sun-Herald*, the newspaper with exclusive rights to publish the network jobs, bore the catchy title *Work the Dream*. Olympic rhetoric continued inside its pages: "Join the Hype! Be a Part of These Exciting Hospitality Positions"; "Team Leaders—Help Run the Greatest Show on Earth!" and "Fast Track Your Hospitality Career at the Games . . . A Once-in-a-Lifetime Opportunity." (*Work the Dream,* 2000). A vacuous celebrity sidebar (p.3) quoted Australian sprinter Matt Shirvington: "Workers help run the event and the running of the event is vital to the whole Olympics."

By mid-2000, volunteer recruitment was 7,000 below target, and with unemployment rates in Sydney only 4.6 percent, Olympic labor shortages were a pressing issue. An Olympic work-for-the-dole (workfare) scheme had been introduced earlier in the year to staff areas such as cleaning, transport, and waste management; in one example, the Redfern Aboriginal Construction Company worked on landscaping projects at the Homebush site.

In June, 57,000 registered job-seekers living in Sydney, the central coast, and the Illawarra (south coast) were warned that they had to direct at least 50 percent of their efforts to finding Olympic-related jobs, or face a cut in their payments. Welfare groups were critical of these coercive tactics, which required some job-seekers to travel up to two hours each way to short-term Olympic jobs, when they needed permanent employment closer to home. It was reported that people at one dole seminar were told that, with the shortage of cleaners, those who didn't get jobs beforehand would be expected to do cleaning work during the Games. More offensive were the parallels drawn between Sydney's Olympic work-for-the-dole scheme and Atlanta's solution to the cleaner shortage during the 1996 Olympics, when low-security prisoners from the local jail had been used as free labor (Crackdown, 2000; Sentas, 2000b).

In August, as a further incentive to job-seekers from regional and rural areas to take up Olympic work, the federal government temporarily suspended the rule that penalized those who returned home to areas of high unemployment after working in a high-employment area. But, as NCOSS director Gary Moore explained, employer attitudes played a major part in determining who benefited from the much-touted Olympic employment boom. Many Olympic contractors wanted people who were already employed, skilled, and having the "right attitude" to work, while a lot of the long-term unemployed and those from areas of high unemployment were not getting Olympic jobs. Social service providers also reported communication problems between the Jobs Network program and SOCOG's labor recruitment agencies (Herbert, 2000b; G. Moore, 2000b, 2000c). In short, the promised Olympic employment bonanza did not live up to expectations.

VOLUNTEERS: A "ONCE-IN-A-LIFETIME" OPPORTUNITY

Olympic organizers, politicians, visitors, and the mass media were all unanimous in their praise for the volunteers who ensured the smooth running of the 2000 Olympics and Paralympics, and there is no doubt that their contributions were invaluable and their motivations genuine (Booth, 2000b). However, the widespread use of volunteer labor in the hosting of the Olympics has been justly criticized in the past for its negative impact on unionized labor and its displacement of volunteers from work of greater social value (Bread Not Circuses, 1990). And, as Kevin Dunn and Pauline McGuirk (1999, 29–30) point out, although volunteers' direct participation helped to promote public support and "a widespread sense of possession" of the Sydney Games, it was clearly at the "easier end" of the citizen participation ladder. In other words, the huge volunteer workforce enhanced Sydney 2000's image as a community-supported event, but failed to make any difference to the Olympic industry's pattern of bulldozing local communities.

Another important consideration was the fact that, just as volunteer and community work—valued at over \$18b in 1992, according to Australian Bureau of Statistics figures—was excluded from Australia's gross domestic product, it was also an invisible component of the Sydney 2000 budget. With an estimated $50,000 \times 140$ volunteer hours in September and October—the period where a (paid) unionized hospitality worker averaged \$20 per hour—Olympic volunteers' invisible contributions may have been as high as \$15m.

Various sociocultural factors, including increased female participation in the labor force and the abolition of compulsory retirement, changed the composition and availability of the Australian volunteer pool in the last decades of the century. In 2000, Sydney had the lowest rate of volunteerism in Australia at 10%, compared to the national average of about 17% (Nixon, 2000). Welfare, community, educational, and youth development organizations attracted 55% of Australia's volunteers in 1995 (Encel & Nelson, 1996). With over 50,000 people volunteering for the Olympic industry in September and October 2000, it is reasonable to assume that at least some of these men and women had to reduce their other volunteer commitments. Their motivation was not, of course, a mystery; this "once-in-a-lifetime" opportunity, to use Sydney 2000's most overused cliché—obviously trumped Meals on Wheels.

As just noted, Olympic organizers originally planned to use volunteers for half of the 100,000 labor force required to stage the Olympic Games. The final count of about 55,000 included 6,000 performers, mostly students, in the opening and closing ceremonies, members of voluntary organizations such as the Rural Fire Service, St. John's Ambulance, State Emergency Service, Rotary and Lions service clubs, as well as about 40,000 other volunteers.

Glossy volunteer recruitment publications called for a wide range of jobs to be filled: from doctors and nurses to ushers and media messengers. Volunteers had to make a commitment to attend at least three training sessions, and to work about 12 shifts of 12 hours each, with a rest day every 5–6 days. As one volunteer information sheet cheerfully warned, "Of course, it is important that you are fit for this demanding role!" It is illuminating to compare these requirements with the NSW Volunteers Center guidelines (based on the International Association on Volunteer Effort) calling for a 16-hour per week maximum on voluntary work, in order to avoid possible problems of organizations exploiting volunteers (Darby,

1996). Most jobs only required work for the two-week duration of the Olympics or Paralympics, but some called for availability for three weeks.

Just as the marketing of other SOCOG "properties" was distributed, official promotion of the volunteer program was the exclusive domain of Fairfax, publishers of the *Sun-Herald, Sydney Morning Herald, Melbourne Age*, and other major papers, which had to be purchased in order to obtain the "registration of interest" application form. Early volunteer recruitment information, along with the numerous Fairfax newspaper articles that served as recruitment tools in 1998–1999, stressed that, while the uniform would be provided by SOCOG, there would be no free tickets and no travel reimbursement for volunteers. By mid-2000, with the response well below target levels, new perks were introduced: free travel regionally as well as on Olympic routes; tickets to a dress rehearsal for the opening or closing ceremony; and tickets to selected athletics competition, including morning sessions that still had 250,000 unsold tickets a month before the Games (M. Moore, 2000e).

In April 2000, volunteers were in the news in a *Herald* story about a private boys' school in Parramatta, one of the many schools and universities capitalizing on the Olympics. It was revealed that the King's School planned to charge $19.50 for breakfasts for the Rural Fire Service volunteers who would be housed there during the Olympics. The $58.00 per night cost for (boarding school) beds was to be covered by SOCOG, but not, apparently, the conference rate that King's was charging for breakfast (M. Moore, 2000c). Interestingly, a 1998 press release from NCOSS pointed out the double standard at work when SOCOG had refused to meet essential costs of the St. John's Ambulance Service while "proposing more favorable treatment for Rural Fire Service volunteers" (NCOSS, 1998c). This was one of many occasions when NCOSS called on SOCOG to establish transparent rules and policies.

Despite the government's incentive of five days' special leave for public servants who contributed five days of their own leave to Olympic volunteer work, in yet another hidden taxpayer subsidy to the Olympic budget, only five thousand had signed up as Olympic volunteers by April 2000 (Morris, 2000b).

Undercover Training as Olympic Volunteers

The Technical and Further Education division (TAFE) of the NSW Department of Education and Training was awarded the Olympic volunteer training contract in March 1998. Like all things Olympic, the training program was cloaked in secrecy, and my various phone calls and e-mails to the TAFE manager and other staff over a nine-month period in 2000 produced no results. In an initial call in 1998, I was told that their proposal would not provide the detailed information about teaching approaches, aims, and objectives that I was looking for. I was able to obtain a copy of an unsuccessful proposal that confirmed that the emphasis was on persuading SOCOG of the organization's track record and capacity to do the job, rather than on developing detailed curriculum and program goals. However, even after the training was completed, my requests to TAFE were ignored, including a final e-mail in which I explained that, if details of the training were classified information, that fact itself would be useful for me to document in my book. When a post-Games news item revealed that the training program was going to be marketed internationally (Nixon, 2000), my suspicions of a "commercial-in-confidence" agreement were largely confirmed.

Despite the secrecy, various official and unofficial sources provided some details of the volunteer training. Attendance at a minimum of three two-hour basic training sessions was required by all volunteers. The first was a core training and orientation session held in Sydney and some interstate capitals, followed by a venue training session to familiarize volunteers with the specific competition and noncompetition sites where they would be working. Finally, job-specific training, through seminars and interactive sessions on site, was designed to give volunteers skills for their particular role.

The two-hour initial orientation session was, for some, a "propaganda" exercise and "a waste of time." Participants were subjected to a video and motivational talk, during which they were "repeatedly asked to clap, cheer, make a lot of noise, stand up, sit down and pat each other on the back" (Sharma & O'Brien, 2000, 14). Not everyone was critical: an elderly man at one orientation session seized the chance to take photos of the Olympic official who was addressing the group. Returning to his seat, he told those near him that the opportunity to photograph this famous "Olympian" had "made it all worthwhile."

According to some reports, the venue-specific training was equally weighed down with propaganda. During the press operations volunteer training session, "aspiring journalists" were told that "real" journalists did not want to be their friend; "Just get them their coffee and give them space," Tracy Holmes of Channel 7, the official Olympic television station, was reported to have told participants (Sharma & O'Brien, 2000, 14). This was not an isolated incident; some test event volunteers also reported organizers' arrogant and patronizing attitudes. Ironically, TAFE's "cultural awareness" pamphlet, distributed to volunteers to give them practical tips on verbal and nonverbal communication, preached the message of "respect for others and treating them as you would like to be treated."

More SOCOG Secrecy: Keeping Volunteers in Line

The thirteen-item agreement and consent section of the volunteer application form dated September 1998 protected SOCOG's commercial interests first and foremost, while volunteers' rights were barely visible. Unauthorized "public speaking activities or promotions" regarding SOCOG, SPOC, or the Games, or "other activities which may adversely affect" Olympic interests were prohibited, and volunteers had to agree to keep confidential all information regarding the Games that they knew was confidential. While some of these provisions legitimately helped to maintain the traditional mystery surrounding the opening and closing ceremonies, the ban on speaking to the media was more difficult to justify. It was suggested that if one disgruntled volunteer complained to the media about SOCOG, this would cause considerable damage to the recruitment and training process, even if that person's experience were atypical. However, it seems equally likely that the prohibitions were yet another example of Olympic industry attempts to stifle public criticism and prevent ambush marketing.

SOCOG also protected its commercial interests in the area of intellectual property, with the consent form requiring volunteers to notify SOCOG "of any ideas or materials which you may create relating to your provision of voluntary services and . . . transfer to [SOCOG] all rights and interests in these creations. . . ." In other words, SOCOG was not only harnessing what some critics called volunteers' "slave labor" but was also planning to put its own trademark on their creativity and intellect. For example, if a volunteer planned to write a memoir for commercial publication, SOCOG could conceivably claim the copyright and royalties.

The issue of security background checks on Olympic volunteers raised considerable concern when it was first made public in 1995. The consent form required prospective volunteers to agree that the NSW Police Service could check their records for details of adult or juvenile convictions and prison sentences, dating back over ten years in some instances. The federal attorney general's department, part of the Olympic Security Working Committee, conducted the screening, which the NSW Privacy Commission considered excessive. Moreover, with Indigenous people overrepresented in the prison population, it was likely that the screening would discriminate against that minority group. For their part, SOCOG justified the security checks as a means of ensuring that nothing in a volunteer's background would "hurt the Games" (Vass, 1995).

In May 2000, I had telephone conversations with two SOCOG representatives regarding what I viewed as SOCOG's potentially discriminatory volunteer recruitment procedures that required a passport-size photograph to accompany applications for placard bearer roles during the ceremonies. The first person, a volunteer, seemed mystified by my inquiry, but assured me that organizers didn't want to "disclude" anyone but just wanted "to see what people will look like"—thereby inadvertently confirming my suspicions.

The second person, a SOCOG employee, made repeated attempts to reassure me that everything was aboveboard, and concluded by saying that I would simply have to trust SOCOG, which, after all, was the focus of widespread scrutiny. The employee then tried to end the discussion with the *non sequitor* that "Australians understood" what SOCOG was doing to guarantee a multicultural show. Clearly, this employee read my blended Australian/Canadian accent as North American, and, frustrated by my apparent lack of understanding, resorted to the converse of the "un-Australian" label—that is, the charge that I was an outsider who couldn't possibly be expected to understand SOCOG's rationale or to trust their good intentions.

Of course, it was possible that the volunteer interview process did in fact screen for appearance covertly. The explicit requirement that applicants have "smart presentation and grooming" appeared in print, apparently without contravening any equal opportunity legislation, on the list of "qualities" that were needed for paid employment in the Games workforce; these were primarily jobs in cleaning, service, and security areas, as advertised in the March 12 *Sun-Herald* "Work the Dream" supplement. And, more discreetly, volunteer recruitment articles and ads—for example, the call for transport volunteers in the *Herald Good Weekend* on March 11, 2000—included the message, "You'll be a part of the public face of Sydney Olympic and Paralympic Games."

This is not to suggest that organizers planned to exclude any specific ethnic group; on the contrary, the *Sun-Herald's* Olympic job supplements for March 11 and May 14, 2000 included images of Asian and other minority workers—all "smartly groomed," of course—while the opening and closing ceremonies relied heavily on Indigenous performers. And the National Broadcasting Company (USA) (NBC) was reported to be looking for Indigenous people for short-term paid employment, mainly as "runners" and production assistants, in order to have a diverse workforce (Local knowledge, 2000). In short, it appears that organizers and sponsors generally wanted the Olympics to have a "multicultural face" and that, to some extent, they succeeded. The degree to which the symbolism represented genuine commitment to diversity, and, more importantly, to reconciliation with Indigenous people, rather than political and corporate self-interest, will be discussed in chapter 9.

SELLING OLYMPIC TICKETS: A FAIR GO?

The question of "ordinary" Australians' access to Olympic tickets was raised regularly in the years preceding the Sydney Games. As *Herald* journalist Jacqueline Magnay predicted in 1997, "nothing will fuel the ire of the local populace more than the suspicion that it might prove impossible to get a ticket, especially since taxpayers have footed the bill." In the wake of a greatly undersubscribed share market float of about 30,000 Stadium Australia $10,000-seat packages, many Australians believed that stadium seats would either be priced beyond their reach, or already be allocated to sponsors and shareholders. Their fears were not unfounded: estimates in mid-1997 showed that about 60 to 80 percent of the 110,000 stadium seats were allocated to overseas visitors, Stadium Australia developers, SOCOG, AOC, and "Olympic Family" members (Magnay, 1997).

In May 1999, it was revealed that 25,000 seats to popular Olympic events would go on sale to those who had purchased gold memberships as part of the (failed) Stadium Australia scheme. These were not bargains; it was reported that SOCOG was charging premiums that more than doubled the face value of the most expensive package of tickets. In the same manner, SOCOG offered "season tickets" guaranteeing seats at every session of a particular event at a premium of between 30 and 100 percent (Evans, 1999c; M. Moore, 1999d).

Another false start in the ticket marketing plan was the November 1997 launch of the world's first Olympic Club, the "official club of the Sydney 2000 Olympic Games." Publicly promoted by Australian Olympic Committee (AOC) director and former Olympic runner Herb Elliott, and marketed though letter box drops, media advertising campaigns, shopping mall displays, and, in a last-ditch effort, door-to-door salespeople, it offered a "Welcome Kit," "exclusive collectables," an "Olympian for a day" gimmick, and "many chances to win free tickets" in draws. With individuals paying $150 and a family membership costing $300, the club was seriously undersubscribed. By early 2000, there was widespread dissatisfaction with the quality of tickets allocated for sale to club members, who, unlike Olympic volunteers, were free to make their complaints known to the media—and did so (e.g., M. Evans, 2000a).

"We Might Have Overdone Ourselves": SOCOG's Ticket Fiasco

By October 1999, *Herald* journalist Matthew Moore was trying to reconcile the number of Olympic events reportedly "sold out" through the public ballot with the ticket sales numbers provided by SOCOG (as discussed in chapter 1). It came to light that Sydney's Tattersall's Club and other organizations that attracted wealthy members were being offered premium ticket packages, with a markup averaging 2.6 times face value, from a hidden supply of about 800,000 tickets. Representing the best seating at the best events, these tickets were kept out of the public sales process through a marketing ploy that critics later referred to as "executive scalping" (Moore & AAP, 1999).

The most galling aspect of this revelation was the fact that Olympic organizers had been assuring "average" Australians for years that they would have a fair chance to purchase tickets for any Olympic event. SOCOG's 1999 promotional flyer, "All you need to know about our

Olympic Games," promised, "This way all Australians will have a fair chance to get tickets."

Although SOCOG and OCA had conveniently arranged to be exempted from NSW *Trade Practices Act* in order to protect Olympic business interests, they were subject to fair trading provisions at the federal level. The ticketing process was subsequently investigated by the Australian Competition and Consumer Commission, and an independent review was conducted for the NSW Legislative Assembly by the Sydney law firm Clayton Utz and Deloitte Touche Tohmatsu. The review found management and oversight failures, lack of transparency, "carelessness," and an absence of internal controls and safeguards, particularly in relation to the ticket inventory, thereby damaging the public's faith in SOCOG. Furthermore, it found that advertising of the premium package program—by word of mouth—failed to take "proper account of the public interest in having access to tickets" (Clayton Utz, 1999).

The independent review noted that SOCOG had released an additional 524,000 tickets, and that the board, through Michael Knight, had issued an apology, although, during the first disclosures in October, it was reported that four key board members—Knight, Kevan Gosper, Graham Richardson, and John Coates—had all refused to apologize (Magnay & Evans, 1999). Numerous *Herald* articles and editorials criticized SOCOG, an organization that it described as having "a culture of secrecy and a lack of accountability," and a "sense of superiority" and arrogance: "This fed a perception that SOCOG is a club where the wealthy and well-connected hobnob with the political elite (more particularly the elite of the Labor Right), and everybody else should be merely grateful for their efforts" (Challenge for SOCOG, 1999).

These characteristics made SOCOG well suited to membership in the "Olympic family" as a subsequent news item demonstrated. In a statement that reflected the IOC scale of moral values, Samaranch was reported to have said that this "small scandal" merely demonstrated that "Australians are very much interested to buy tickets to attend this very important event" (Alcorn, 1999). Eventually SOCOG admitted that efforts at testing the market had been based on an inflated number of tickets in the premium pool (Moore & Magnay, 1999). It recognized the need to stop deceiving the public regarding ticket inventory and availability, and an internal ombudsperson from the Department of Fair Trading was appointed to oversee future ticket sales. At this stage, SOCOG was reported to have admitted, "We might have overdone ourselves."

The system of cascading tickets that SOCOG had introduced contributed further to an inequitable situation. Unsuccessful orders for A class tickets were put into a B ballot, and, if unsuccessful again, into a C ballot, but no orders "cascaded" into the D category. SOCOG's advice to telephone inquiries, also publicized in newspapers in June 1999, was to maximize one's chances of winning a ticket by requesting a combination of A and D class tickets. The fact that this advice discriminated against poor people apparently escaped SOCOG's attention until NCOSS director Gary Moore wrote a letter of complaint to SOCOG CEO Sandy Hollway. Both Moore and Uniting Church Board for Social Responsibility director Harry Herbert pointed out that the system advantaged the rich by increasing their options, while limiting the supply of tickets that poor people could afford, and SOCOG eventually admitted that this was a mistake.

The *Herald* was not particularly helpful on this issue. Although a June 3 article (M. Moore, 1999e) reported on Moore's and Herbert's concerns, a piece titled "How to reduce tickets trauma" (1999) that appeared the next day repeated the advice about requesting A and D tickets, even while it noted that this strategy had been criticized for undermining the purpose of affordable D class tickets.

A Neilson opinion poll conducted at this time revealed a widespread perception that tickets were too expensive, with only 9 percent of Australians with household incomes of under thirty-thousand dollars planning to buy tickets (M. Moore, 1999f). By the end of June, with ticket sales below expectation, SOCOG began distributing ticket order booklets to news agencies and to every household in NSW and the Australian Capital Territory, as well as to selected high-income neighborhoods on the south Queensland coast and elsewhere. But right up to September, the ticket sales program remained complicated and mysterious, characterized by surprise announcements of newly generated blocks of tickets, some as a result of ticket inventory reviews, others by adding more seating to venues. It soon became clear that the fine-tuning of ticket availability and pricing was largely based on SOCOG's efforts to balance its budget in the lead-up to the Games.

SOCOG and Equity: Not a Concept

Social service leaders tried for many years to persuade SOCOG to offer discounted tickets to disadvantaged groups. With Olympic venues and associated infrastructure funded with public money, equality of access to Olympic tickets for low-income people was an important social equity issue. But, as members of SOCOG's Social Impact Advisory Committee (SIAC), including Herbert and Moore, reported, SOCOG had no understanding of fairness or social equity. As Herbert explained, SOCOG considered a process to be fair if "everyone has the same chance" and if no one (except perhaps the wealthy) received "special treatment."

SIAC unsuccessfully raised the ticket issue with SOCOG in the mid-1990s, when Mal Hemmerling was CEO. The next CEO, Sandy Hollway, responded more positively, and SIAC, through OCA, commissioned a report on best practices in past Olympics regarding ticket allocation. But Herbert reported that SOCOG's preoccupation with fairness in the ticket *allocation* process surpassed any interest in the fairness of getting into the ballot in the first place. SIAC urged more of the D class tickets to popular events such as athletics, swimming, and opening and closing ceremonies to be sold at discounted prices, and to be available only to people entitled to concessions. And, in a June 24, 1998 press release, NCOSS proposed a number of ways that the cheaper tickets could be distributed to low-income people: through disadvantaged schools, public and community housing organizations, senior citizen and child care centers, the Aboriginal and Torres Strait Islander Commission (ATSIC), Land Councils, and other Aboriginal community organizations. Anticipating the worst, Moore stated, "It would be grossly unfair if the cheapest Olympic tickets to premium events are snapped up by high income people and companies" (NCOSS, 1998a).

SOCOG's ticketing policy, announced on August 26, immediately prompted a critical response from NCOSS. Even the cheapest tickets for popular events, for example, $95 for the swimming finals, were still beyond the reach of low-income people, NCOSS pointed out. In an equitable system, these cheap seats would have been kept out of the open ballot and reserved for low-income people (NCOSS, 1998b).

In a number of media appearances on the ticket issue, Herbert suggested that SOCOG could raise the price of A tickets as much as the market would bear, in order to subsidize D tickets—a proposal that SOCOG rejected even though the premium ticket scandal had proven that a markup of more than 200 percent was acceptable to wealthy ticket-buyers. SOCOG's eventual "Olympic Opportunity" ticket plan for community and welfare groups did not offer discounted tickets, but simply packages of low-price tickets ($10–$19) to less popular events that would probably not have been sold otherwise. One cynical but probably accurate view, offered a few years earlier, was that SOCOG wanted to swell the television audience at events in which Australian spectators had little interest (e.g., handball, fencing, and badminton), while appearing magnanimous by giving poor people cheap tickets (Magnay, 1997).

In a farcical sequence of events, the 1.5m Olympic Opportunity tickets promised in August 1998 dropped to 1.1m the next year, partly as a result of a decision to "raid" the pool of cheap tickets to add to the public ballot in yet another controversial feature of the ticket fiasco. By February 2000, the number of Olympic Opportunity tickets had been reduced to 735,000, and the next month it was revealed that SOCOG planned to make the initial sales offer to schools, and to postpone sales to welfare groups till later in the year.

Reflecting what some critics now viewed as a predictable absence of planning, SOCOG assumed, without consultation, that it could readily enlist the help of school staff to sell Olympic Opportunity tickets to students, parents, and teachers. The Public Service Association (PSA) and its School Administrative and Support Staff (SASS) members first learned about the ticket plan through a newspaper article, which had produced an immediate barrage of phone calls to school offices. With office staff already facing an increased workload with the introduction of the GST, PSA delegates for SASS staff quickly resolved "That a ban be placed on Olympic ticketing in the light of the Department [of Education]'s refusal to allocate extra resources to assist in the organization of issuing of tickets" (PSA, 2000).

Unlike their counterparts in universities, PSA leaders examined the extra "complex and time-consuming" demands on staff time, and documented at least ten separate stages in the process of booking and allocating tickets to more than 160 sessions, and handling the money and receipts for group excursions, school groups, or parents and families—additional work that would constitute both the exploitation of SASS labor and a hidden, publicly funded subsidy to the Olympic industry.

By June 2000, having only sold about 109,000 tickets, SOCOG abandoned the Olympic Opportunity plan and put these so-called dog tickets on the general market, where again they proved difficult to sell. NCOSS repeated its proposal that SOCOG should discount the $65 seats for welfare groups, rather than leaving them empty—again without success—and social service leaders were in agreement that SOCOG's attitude was mean-spirited, to say the least. The only small victory on this front was a donation by Olympic sponsor John Hancock Financial Services of over 2,000 tickets (worth about $120,000) to schoolchildren in low-income areas in the Sydney region (M. Evans, 2000e; Evans, Peatling, & Jacobsen, 2000).

Meanwhile, SOCOG's ticketing sales program had been investigated again by the Australian Competition and Consumer Commission, because of the proposal that Visa credit cards would be the only acceptable means of payment—a privilege that Visa, as an Olympic sponsor, argued that it had purchased. Eventually a somewhat more "consumer-friendly" plan was put in place—one that protected Visa's monopoly while accepting checks or cash as well. In May 2000, the new ticketing supremo, deputy CEO Michael Eyers, echoed SOCOG's earlier promise and reflected SOCOG's failure to understand the difference between equality and equity: "Everyone who calls the telephone line will have an equal chance to get tickets" (Horan, 2000).

OLYMPIC BRAND EDUCATION: START YOUNG

Corporate targeting of children and adolescents was not a new phenomenon; indeed, since the 1980s, establishing brand loyalty at an increasingly young age was a mark of success for the multinationals pushing their unique brand of clothing, toys, computer games, sporting goods, soft drinks, and snack food on youthful consumers (Klein, 2000). It therefore came as no surprise that Olympic sponsors seized the youth marketing opportunities offered by Sydney 2000. Their cynical exploitation of "Olympic spirit" rhetoric and pseudo-educational initiatives were key components of the campaign to reach children and youth. On a broader scale, it could be argued that any Olympic education program serves to promote not only sport-related values (excellence, achievement, etc.) but also the values of the Olympic industry and its corporate partners, thereby socializing children to become "global consumers" (Schimmel & Chandler, 1998). The following "educational" examples, initiated by Olympic sponsors Coca-Cola, IBM, Visa, Westpac Bank, and Westfield Shoppingtowns, will illustrate this trend.

Coca-Cola and IBM sponsored Sydney 2000's Olympic Schools Strategy. Olympic education kits, aimed at promoting "Olympic ideals"—a few years before they became tarnished by the bribery scandals—were sent to every school in Australia in 1995, and 1998 Winter Olympic kits and SOGOG newsletters were subsequently distributed to every schoolchild. Kimberley Schimmel and Timothy Chandler (1998, 12) pointed out a serious contradiction in the program: despite the fact that the IOC prohibits corporate advertising within stadiums, these kits were "literally framed by corporate logos." And, as Tara Magdalinski and John Nauright reported, connections between the Olympics, the 1998 Olympic kit, and corporate sponsors were clear from the outset: AOC president John Coates's introduction began by acknowledging Berlei Sports (women's sportswear), Fairfax publishers, IBM, and Seven Network. Thus, they concluded, "Olympic education . . . seeks to capture adherents in their youth and create brand loyalty that will enhance the interests of the Olympic movement's leaders and their multi-national sponsors" (Magdalinski & Nauright, 1998, 6).

Their predictions about Olympic branding among children were substantiated in August 2000, when a *Herald* story, bearing the strange headline "Basic Skills Test *Forces* 200,000 Students to Play Games" (emphasis added), reported that the annual NSW literacy and numeracy tests for grades 3 and 5 students had a Sydney 2000 Olympic theme. What was particularly illuminating—and problematic—was the reported discussion between the journalist and three children, aged 10–11, after the test. Suggesting alternative children's Olympic events, one girl said that there should be a contest "to see how much McDonalds you could eat in an hour" (Baird, 2000). Other children joined in to boast about their own consumption of Big Macs and quarter-pounders. The connections they made between McDonalds and the Olympics, her generic use of "McDonalds" to connote hamburgers, and the *Herald*'s free advertisement for McDonalds products all served this transnational corporation's interests very effectively.

Visa's "Olympics of the Imagination" program, which challenged school-children "to create an original piece of art representing what the Olympic motto . . . (faster, higher, stronger) means to them," was announced in the *Herald*'s Olympic Insight section on February 26, 2000. Promising winners from thirty-five countries the chance to attend the Olympics, the ad went on to note that entry forms and posters were to be distributed to all Australian primary schools—where, no doubt, teachers would be expected to assist with the next stage of the competition, thereby serving as Visa and Olympic industry volunteers.

Meanwhile, SOCOG's "Share the Spirit Art Program—Welcome World" produced 54,000 entries from schoolchildren across Australia. The best artwork would be hung in the Olympic village—obviously, an honor for those selected. But the "real" prize winners would see their designs featured on Sydney 2000 merchandise (mugs, ties, pins, and T-shirts)—in other words, their labor would be commercially exploited and their artwork copyrighted for Olympic industry profit. This was not in itself an unusual outcome for a commercially sponsored children's art competition, but, in this case, the commercial purpose was hidden behind Olympic spirit rhetoric.

Beginning in 1997, Westfield organized a traveling exhibition, comprising twenty-eight displays of Olympic memorabilia, titled the "Olympic Journey." Its arrival in Westfield Shoppingtowns in regional and metropolitan centers across the country was marked by parades, entertainment, Olympic and Paralympic athletes, sporting events, and "guest appearances" by the Olympic mascots—in other words, children's toys. (Promotion of Olympic mascot toys, thinly disguised as an educational activity for younger children, was also a function of the "activity sheets" found on the Sydney 2000 children's website.) In April 1999—no doubt as an Easter holiday children's attraction—the "Kids 2000 Olympic Games Arena" opened at Westfield Parramatta shopping mall. Children were invited to try various sporting activities and to "pit themselves against Olympic athletes," according to the April 3 ad in the *Herald*'s Olympic Insight.

The Sydney 2000 National Education Program, sponsored by Westpac and supported by Fairfax and IBM, included five editions of a free student newspaper for all grades 3 to 12 students across Australia; an interactive school resource kit with materials designed to "capture the spirit of the Games" and to "live on in schools" beyond 2000; and the children's Internet site. Westpac's Olympic advertising "imagineered" the banking company as a good corporate citizen as well as a generous Olympic sponsor and supporter of Australia's best athletes (thereby glossing over the fact that it was a major financier of the controversial Jabiluka uranium mine). Westpac distributed over 3,000 free tickets to its customers and their partners through its 500 Day Countdown Competition (lottery). And, for the children, Westpac sponsored the 2000 Pacific School Games, held in May 2000 in the Homebush Olympic venues, and funded the high-profile "Values for Life" Olympic youth program, advertised in classic liberal hyperbole as "a way for us to help today's 3.1 million schoolchildren achieve their full potential in any chosen field."

Olympic Ideals: Which Ones?

Not too surprisingly, Olympic-focused education in the schools uncritically promoted so-called Olympic ideals. Magdalinski and Nauright identified numerous distortions and inaccuracies in the Olympic kits' written materials, and concluded, "the uncritical writing of Olympic history that foregrounds myth and virtually ignores struggle and contestation serves to create the captive audience loyal to the ideal brand of ideal sport idealized in the Olympic Movement" (Magdalinski & Nauright, 1998, 7).

The Wespac-sponsored "Real Ideals" competition exemplified "corporate idealism." Teams of schoolchildren, "with help from their teachers" (of course), were invited to complete projects that demonstrated "Olympic ideals." The best teams won visits from Olympic athletes and souvenirs, while five grand prize-winning teams and two teachers received trips to Sydney for the Games. A two-page color advertisement in the *Herald*'s Good Weekend (March 4, 2000) presented photos of the winning teams' projects, two of which were murals. According to the fine print in the contest's terms and conditions, these would become the property of Westpac, including copyright and any other rights. Interestingly, one of the winning murals depicted the five Olympic rings, thereby infringing the IOC copyright even before Westpac had the chance to brand it with its own logo.

Westpac used children in its "Values for Life" Olympic billboard series, displayed in Sydney bus shelters and elsewhere in 2000. One of these showed a small, unathletic-looking boy holding a soccer ball, with the caption, "I might never be an Olympic athlete but at least I can think like one." This was arguably a dangerous message to promote among children—or even among adults, for that matter. In 1999 and 2000, some of the least admired, and least admirable, members of Australia's "Olympic Family" were former Olympic athletes—Kevan Gosper, Phil Coles, and John Coates—as were many of the IOC members from other countries who resigned or were expelled in 1999 following the bribery scandals (see Lenskyj, 2000). From another perspective, to "think like" one of the many Olympic athletes who took performance-enhancing drugs was hardly a worthwhile goal.

Obviously, the notion that Olympians were all worthy of emulating was seriously flawed. A 1999 *Herald* story, for example, revealed that a former Olympic swimmer was "scalping" a package of swimming tickets on an

Internet auction site at four or five times their face value. As a result of the *Herald*'s disclosure, the AOC, which had spent $16.1m on cost-price tickets for these former Australian "Olympians," had to write to all recipients reminding them that they could not sell or use the tickets for commercial purposes (M. Evans, 1999f). And, as the Games approached, there was no shortage of trash-talking "Olympians" whose macho posturing was presented in the media on a daily basis: again, not an example for young people to follow. Nevertheless, the Olympic industry's marketing tradition of glorifying the "pure Olympic athlete," especially in messages to children, was alive and well (Lenskyj, 2000).

ACCESS TO OLYMPIC LEGACIES: FOR A PRICE

Among the key issues that social service and community leaders raised during Sydney Olympic construction were concerns about the future management, funding, use, and accessibility of Olympic facilities. The notion that Olympic facilities constituted a legacy of affordable recreation venues and services for local communities found little support in the operations of various centers at Homebush Bay in 1999 and 2000, and OCA's early attempts to capitalize on visitor and tourist interest provided a warning of things to come. Its glossy 1999 brochure titled "Homebush Bay Olympic Site Seeing" promoted guided tours (at unspecified prices) to the completed sport facilities and Bicentennial Park at Homebush Bay. "A rich variety of experiences for the people of Australia and our international visitors" was promised, and Asians constituted about 50 per cent of the faces in the photographs. In mid-2000, Stadium Australia was offering seven or more one-hour tours daily, at a cost of $20 per adult and $10 per child; for the SuperDome, the rates were $14 and $9. The three- and four-star Olympic Park hotels, the Novotel and Ibis, were open for business in 2000, as was the Heritage Café near the train station, where prices were almost double those of a comparable café in the Sydney CBD.

With post-Olympic management of Olympic venues still not finalized in mid-2000, there was a valid concern that facilities fitted out for elite sport would not be appropriate for general public use, and that admission prices would not be affordable. It was predicted that the velodrome would be underused, and that the SuperDome would be a white elephant within two years because of the overprovision of facilities in the 20,000–40,000 seat range (M. Moore, 2000e). In the case of Stadium Australia, which opened in 1999, soccer fans had been outraged at the high-priced tickets—ranging from $39 to $250 and averaging $72—for the Australian Socceroos versus FIFA World Stars game. Organizers argued that, with sports stars earning as much as rock stars, such an event constituted "entertainment" rather than "sport"; attempting to cash in on the stadium's future Olympic role, they also reminded fans that they were "sitting on a piece of history" (Dennis, 1999). By the end of 2000, it was clear that the white-elephant predictions were well-founded, and by May 2001, the NSW government had allocated $50m to promote commercial development at the site so that it would eventually become self-supporting (M. Moore, 2001).

Privatization of publicly subsidized Olympic facilities after the Games was a serious concern. The Olympic velodrome was to be managed by Bankstown Sport Club for the next fifteen years under a contract with OCA, with the NSW government paying the full maintenance costs, estimated at $1.5m per year. Following a similar pattern, the Ryde Olympic water polo venue, to which Ryde Council had contributed about $24m, was part of a new, privately managed leisure center that included three pools, a licensed restaurant and bar. Replacing the former council-owned and operated six-pool community center, only half of the new facility would be accessible to the general public, while the other half would be operated as a private leisure club.

In early 2000, when a church group planning to take children to the Olympic Aquatic Center at Homebush Bay found that costs for the trip would total $12.00–$13.00 per child, they canceled their plans. At that time, guided tours of the center cost $12.00 per adult and $8.00 per child, pool admission was $5.00/$4.00, and there was a $2.50 fee for (non-swimming) spectators. In the low-income municipality of Auburn, it was reported that the council-run swimming pool was getting increased use because of the high admission costs to the Aquatic Center (Herbert, 2000b). It was fortunate that Auburn experienced some small benefits, since it shouldered additional and largely hidden Olympic-related costs on the other side of the ledger, such as the extra demands on garbage collection, street cleaning and police services, and compensation to shopkeepers.

NCOSS, Shelter NSW, and others sought a NSW Parliamentary Committee to hold an inquiry into the costs and benefits of the Games and the true nature of the Olympic legacy. It was proposed that a public inquiry take place six to nine months after the Olympics and Paralympics in order to produce a report and recommendations to Parliament. Furthermore, these groups stressed the need for full disclosure by Michael Knight regarding post-Olympic ownership, management, and financing arrangements for all Olympic venues and related sites (G. Moore, 2000d).

CONCLUSION

Except for the construction industry, a high proportion of Olympic-related employment was temporary, low-skilled service work, volunteers accounted for about half of the Olympic labor force, and there was evidence that the much-touted boost to employment was not always new job creation, but largely job-churning. Although there was a marked increase in training opportunities for people in the hospitality and security industries, these did not necessarily translate to permanent post-Olympic employment. And, given prevailing employer attitudes, a currently employed skilled worker or tradesperson had a distinct advantage over an unemployed job-seeker or a person from a low-employment area in regional or rural NSW—in other words, a stereotypical "dole bludger" in the eyes of a prejudiced Olympic employer.

In other social impact areas, the ticket sales program—particularly the complicated application process, the premium ticket scandal, and the failure of the Olympic Opportunity initiative—all reinforced the image of SOCOG as dishonest, arrogant, and unconcerned with the desire of the "average" Australian to "share the spirit." Meanwhile, schoolchildren's brand loyalty was being established by Olympic sponsors under the guise of "Olympic education." Overall, there were strong indications that "Olympic legacy" benefits would accrue to the already privileged sectors of the population, while the disadvantaged would disproportionately bear the burden.

6

Productive Partnerships

Corporatized Universities Meet the Olympic Industry

═══⟨ℰℰℰ⟩═══

Trends in universities in Australia, Canada, the United States, Europe, and elsewhere in the last two decades of the twentieth century included partnerships with global corporations and, by extension, with the Olympic industry. The impact of global economic restructuring on universities was marked by changing relationships between the university and the state, and increased corporatization of the university at regional and national levels. From a global systems approach, it was possible to identify similarities in patterns of university reforms across a wide range of sociopolitical contexts: cutbacks in state subsidies; increased reliance on private funding; the growth of market-driven programs, usually in business and technology; and the development of partnerships with private corporations, who, by providing capital or grants, purchased the right to influence the direction of research and to hold exclusive licenses on patentable discoveries. In some instances, tenure was abolished, and, with it, academic freedom (Pannu, Schugurensky, & Plumb, 1994).

Olympic vs. Liberal University Ideals

A 1992 University of Toronto statement of purpose provides useful criteria by which to assess the new corporatized model: "the rights of freedom of speech, academic freedom, and freedom of research . . . are meaningless unless they entail the right to raise deeply disturbing questions and provocative challenges to the cherished beliefs of society at large and of the university itself. . . ." (quoted in Love, 2000, 2); and, one might add, the equally cherished beliefs in many university departments of kinesiology and physical education regarding the privileged place of the Olympic "movement" discourse in programs and curricula.

In addition to documenting the obvious changes in universities' relationships with the welfare state and institutional capitalism, Raj Pannu, Daniel Schugurensky, and Donovan Plumb (1994) made important connections between economic restructuring and the increasing commodification of culture. No longer were scholarly debate and academic research automatically valued as the by-product of a liberal university; part of their worth now lay in their global market value. These insights shed some light on universities' complicity in the Olympic industry, not only at the level of finance and research, but also in the equally important realms of values and ideas.

One of the earliest academic debates on the Sydney Olympics took place in the pages of the Australian Society for Sport History (ASSH) journal *Sporting Traditions,* where Colin Tatz and Douglas Booth (1994) developed an incisive critique of the bribery and corruption underlying Sydney's bid process. In one of the rebuttals, Canadian academic and former Toronto Olympic bid committee member, Bruce Kidd, asserted that the modern Olympics had "affirmed the importance of intercultural communication, fair play, inclusion and whole person development far more consistently than another other major sport organization" (Kidd, 1994, 26). In Canada, Kidd continued, they had provided a "humanistic alternative to the misogynist, instrumental, xenophobic nationalism often preached and practised by the leaders of professional ice hockey." It could be argued, however, that setting the ethical bar at the level of North American professional sport was not a particularly high standard for the Olympics to attain.

The rationale for a precedent-setting University of Technology Sydney (UTS) sixteen-month graduate course in sport management for fifty students from Greece—the first such course to be cosponsored by the International Olympic Committee (IOC) and an Olympic organizing committee —stood in marked contrast to earlier defenses of the Olympics based primarily on humanistic values. In addition to the obvious benefits to the scholarship recipients—free tuition and preparation for a "promising professional career" in the Athens 2004 Olympic organizing committee—the program, according to one of its organizers, served IOC interests by advancing "the Olympic education and training agenda" and ensuring that "a great deal of the know-how from the Sydney Games [would] be transferred to Athens in addition to SOCOG's written Transfer of Olympic Knowledge program" (Gargalianos, 1999).

For their part, UTS gained "a considerable income from tuition" and SOCOG saved money through the extensive volunteer work required of the Greek students as part of the degree program; a *Herald* article reported that the arrangement saved SOCOG $4.2m in salaries (M. Evans, 1999a). Although the UTS account made a passing reference to "lifelong memories and friendships," thereby evoking humanistic "Olympic spirit" ideals, the primary emphasis was market-driven, as befitted the restructured university of the twenty-first century.

Given a university's mandate to encourage free and open academic exchanges and debates, including challenging "cherished beliefs" about the "Olympic movement," one might well ask why a "Transfer of Olympic Knowledge" program was housed in a (largely) publicly funded institution of higher learning rather than, for example, in a private institute for corporate education, known in the United States as a "corporate university." After all, past and present Olympic sponsors such as Coca-Cola, McDonalds, IBM, Master Card, Reebok, and Xerox all have their own corporate universities in the United States (Global Learning Resources, 1998). Of course, university-based management training itself was not a new concept, but one with an explicit (Olympic) corporate brand was noteworthy.

A second example will illustrate how the demise of the liberal university has served Olympic industry interests. In April 2000, in a ceremony covered by the official Olympic television station Channel 7, Australian IOC member Phil Coles made a donation of a large number of historical and contemporary "bid books"—the expensive bound bid documents submitted to the IOC by each bid city—to the library collection of the University of NSW (UNSW) Center for Olympic Studies. In his speech thanking Coles, Prof. Chris Fell, UNSW deputy vice-chancellor, alluded to the great value that the books would have for future students, who could learn from them what successful and unsuccessful Olympic bids looked like. Fell's statement implied that it was unproblematic, and indeed quite appropriate, for UNSW to view the training of future Olympic bid committee members as part of its mandate. Interestingly, in the same month only one year earlier, Coles had been *persona non grata* in the Australian and international media because of his role in preparing "character assessments" of IOC members and their spouses in order to provide appropriate gifts and services that might influence their votes (see Lenskyj, 2000).

Australian Universities: Thoroughly Corporatized

Economic restructuring and the corporatization of the Australian university had its beginnings in the 1970s, with the amalgamation of universities and colleges of advanced education, and a two-thirds reduction in the number of postsecondary institutions (from 99 to 32) between 1975 and 1991. Although the former colleges of education had taken a more vocationally oriented approach than universities, some had degree-granting status and included a balance of vocational and liberal arts subjects; therefore, even the new hybrid universities of the 1980s and 1990s shared some common ground with the liberal model of tertiary education.

Neoliberalism produced a situation where higher education was "displaced from its relative autonomy within public policy practice—it is now a pawn in macroeconomic policy" (Patience, 1999/2000, 65). Similarly, "entrepreneurialism"—evident, for example, in the aggressive recruitment of (full fee-paying) international students—became a typical Australian university response to globalization (Pratt & Poole, 1999/2000). A 1988 policy had the effect of making universities compete with one another for resources, while the line between private and public, in both finance and governance, became blurred.

A reward system based on achievement and efficiency promoted *the commercialization of university research,* as some scholars termed it (Pannu, Schugurensky, and Plumb, 1994). Faculty members were subjected to increasingly quantitative evaluation based on research grant income, numbers of scholarly publications, and student assessments. The emphasis was on efficiency rather than equality of opportunity or other liberal and nonquantifiable goals. And, in Australia's conservative political climate, many radical scholars were unlikely to perform well, or indeed to survive the tenure and promotion process, when judged by these criteria—unless of course they compromised by "playing the game" until they achieved some job security. For their part, the more conservative and/or compliant university "experts" were readily co-opted by the government and corporate sector to add their weight to the prevailing economic ideology.

These trends fitted well with Herman and Chomsky's (1988) propaganda model of the mass media, specifically in relation to their analysis of ways in which academic "experts" were used to add legitimacy to media messages that served the interests of corporate elites. Similarly, Australian environmentalist Drew Hutton (1987) identified the pattern whereby "intellectual dissenters" were displaced by "safe" academics in positions of power in Australian universities. The Olympic industry was one of many global corporations to benefit from these university practices, as the following discussion will show.

Public Intellectuals at Risk

It is ironic that one example of the corporatization trend and its resulting "partnerships" with industry, as piloted in Canada at the University of Waterloo, has been termed the *service university model.* In a different usage of the word, tenure and promotion criteria in Canada and elsewhere often included *service* to the university, the profession, the field, and the community. In practice, this meant that a faculty member's voluntary work, for example, as a member of a board of education subcommittee, or as a leader of a community organization, was recognized as a valid component of an academic career. In the Australian context, although there is no shortage of academics with a critical analysis of the political issues of the day, it appears that their activities as "public intellectuals" are more seriously constrained by systemic forces that dictate what their academic, professional, and even political priorities should be.

With 37 universities, about 50 campuses, and a population of only 18.7 million, Australia is well supplied with academics and students, but, as one Labor Party commentator argued, "universities take a dismayingly low profile in public debate," and the key critical voices tend to come from outside the academy (Jones, 1999). Barry Jones went on to identify the barriers facing academics in a context where private industry increasingly sponsors university research, and where fear of litigation limits critical public debate. He went on to claim that the academic "super-specialist writes in a coded private language that can be interpreted by his/her peers, not by a broader community." In a nation which, a decade ago, renamed itself the "clever country"—but nevertheless a country that takes pride in its egalitarian roots and cuts down its "tall poppies"—there is some obvious ambivalence over the role of the university "expert."

Academic Freedom in the Entrepreneurial University

An anthology titled *Why Universities Matter* (Coady, 1999), as well as the 1999/2000 issue of the *Australian Universities Review*, are among the many publications that have documented the attack on academic freedom posed by recent trends in Australian universities. Of particular interest are the examples of two academics who were disciplined by university administrators for going public with their critical views, regarding, in the first case, the administration itself, and, in the second case, the Commonwealth government.

The first example is particularly pertinent in light of the furor at the University of NSW in May 1999 when a Sydney newspaper revealed that Vice-Chancellor John Niland had spent $245,000 on a corporate box at the Olympic Stadium, largely as a public relations gesture. In a similar incident at the Victoria University of Technology (VUT), a professor, Allen Patience, had his e-mail access temporarily suspended when he used it to communicate his critique of the university's rental of a corporate box at the new Docklands Stadium, at an initial cost of $100,000 for the year. Like UNSW, VUT had experienced budget cuts to teaching and research programs, staff morale was low, and the decision was based largely on fund-raising and "friend-raising" rationales. Patience subsequently received a letter from the vice-chancellor warning of possible legal action against him. Furthermore, he was asked (and refused) to sign a guarantee that he would abide by the university's e-mail regulations. As he later wrote, one positive outcome was the strong collegial and community support he received for this attack on academic freedom and the university's failure to engage in public debate of such issues (Patience, 1999/2000).

The second case involved a UNSW lecturer, Cathy Sherry, who wrote a letter to the *Sydney Morning Herald* editor, in which she was critical of the federal government's record on native title settlements. A federal member of Parliament contacted the vice-chancellor in an attempt to curtail this kind of public initiative (Fraser, 1999). In another UNSW example, I learned that a proposed university publication of conference papers, which included a strongly worded critique of Australian prime minister John Howard by an Aboriginal leader, would have to be vetted by the university's lawyer before it could be published.

There are clear similarities between these academic freedom issues and university administrations' disciplinary measures directed at other kinds of "whistle-blowers." Graham Pratt and David Poole (1999/2000) documented a number of examples of academics who raised ethical concerns about the recruitment of underqualified—but full fee-paying—international students; lecturers who questioned these students' admission, or issued failing grades to them, were suspended, disciplined, or "forced" to lower their standards. Further complicating this situation was the possibility that these "whistle-blowers" would, justly or unjustly, be labeled racist if they questioned the ability of minority students, particularly in a context where such a label would serve the university administration's interests by silencing its critics. Interestingly, in January 2001, when the *Herald* published a series of reports on allegations of "soft grading" of international students and the chilly climate for whistleblowers, the Australian Vice-Chancellors Committee responded with outraged indignation, claiming that there was no real evidence to support the charges—this despite the fact that Poole and Pratt's article, which included several documented accounts, had been published a few months earlier.

On a related topic, the recruitment of international students, who comprised the country's fifth highest source of foreign exchange earnings, was threatened by the racist and anti-immigration One Nation political party in the late 1990s. At UNSW, Australia's largest university (and SOCOG's major university "partner"), over a third of the student body came from overseas, and 40 percent of Australian students had English as their second language. UNSW Vice-Chancellor John Niland represented Australian university vice chancellors in their efforts to reassure Asian academics and potential Asian students that One Nation did not speak for all of Australia; in his June 1998 speech to the University of Singapore, he devoted about 15 percent of the presentation to the "unhappy Hanson phenomenon" (Niland, 1998).

Although it would be naive to assume that financial concerns were not paramount in the universities' attempt to allay Asian students' fears, one might hope that some of the rhetoric about Australia's pride in its multicultural and multiracial makeup would be reflected in the climate of the university community, particularly in relation to Indigenous students. However, less than a year after Niland's goodwill mission to Asia, University of Wollongong administration saw fit to invite *Daily Telegraph* columnist Piers Akerman—who shared considerable ideological ground with One Nation—to deliver the keynote address at the May graduation ceremony. As was the usual practice, this speech was vetted by the vice chancellor before being delivered to an audience that included, not coincidentally, the first graduating class of Aboriginal students in the fine arts program. When Akerman proceeded to make racist comments about the "Aboriginal industry," several of these students walked out "disgusted by his fascist diatribe" (Dennis, 1999).

Academic Freedom and the Olympics

The suppression of academic freedom in relation to Olympic issues began shortly after Sydney was awarded the 2000 Games. In 1993, University of Wollongong engineering professor Sharon Beder completed an article exposing Olympic organizers' cover-up of toxic contamination at the Homebush Bay Olympic site, and critiquing the proposed remediation process. After it was accepted for publication in the journal *New Science*, two senior NSW government officials who held Olympic managerial positions visited her and the head of her department, and as a result she was initially prevented from publishing the article, which did not appear until 1994 in the *Current Affairs Bulletin* (Beder, 1994, 1999). Australian academics also reported that attempts to engage in critiques of the Olympics during conferences were silenced (Holmes, 1997), and, although I uncovered other anecdotal evidence of the chilly climate for university-based critics, most of these academics were unwilling to make their experiences public.

Many of my own professional and academic colleagues who took issue with my Olympic critique resorted to name-calling rather than engaging substantively with my arguments. On one memorable occasion, my colleague Anthony Hughes kindly presented a paper—"The myth of the pure Olympic athlete and pure Olympic sport"—on my behalf at the UNSW Center for Olympic Studies 1999 Conference, *The Olympics in the New Milennium* (see Lenskyj, 2000, 99-105). My critique of Olympic myth-making provoked many angry responses, starting with Kevin Berry, who in 1998 was named the center's first "Olympian member." When the chair told the audience that the session should not turn into a character assassination (in my absence), the discussion waned dramatically, although Professor Emeritus John Lucas, the official Olympic historian, proceeded to denounce my paper, along with my earlier research, as "rubbish." With this kind of response representing "academic" debate, Olympic critics should not be surprised by emotional reactions from the community at large.

This was not the only controversy at the 1999 conference. Two IOC members, Anita DeFrantz and Jacques Rogge, gave presentations which, to many listeners, lacked depth and merely rehashed the IOC "party line." (Of course, it could be argued that nonacademic IOC members can hardly be expected to deliver scholarly speeches.) More importantly, DeFrantz and Rogge joked about the gifts that they had received from the UNSW conference organizers, and asked delegates to "forgive" them for accepting this gesture, a response that, as academic Tara Magdalinski aptly pointed out in the *Australian Society for Sports History Bulletin,* "makes not only a mockery of the reform process, but denigrates those who are genuinely concerned about these allegations of corruption" (Magdalinski, 1999, 27). Her critique of Rogge's and DeFranz's behavior was not well received by the conference organizers, who unsuccessfully sought an apology from Magdalinski. The matter was finally resolved—favorably from an Olympic industry perspective—when the ASSH executive itself voted to issue an apology. As Olympic scholar and critic Doug Booth interpreted this decision, the ASSH executive decided that "nothing, least of all freedom of academic speech, should jeopardize possible future funding from the Olympic industry" (Booth, 2000, 124).

There was no dearth of Olympic boosterism emanating from Australian universities, as evident in the numerous national and international conferences on Olympic themes. A liberal, pro-Olympic approach characterized the majority of papers presented at the 1999 UNSW conference just mentioned, and at the September 2000 joint conference of UNSW and the University of Western Ontario (UWO) Centers for Olympic Studies (with partial funding from the IOC)—a trend that had been firmly established in UWO's biennial conference since 1992. One small difference, however, was the predictable inclusion (in liberal Australian contexts) of an Aboriginal dance troupe performance to open the Sydney conference.

An interesting attempt at "balance" was evident in choice of keynote speakers: IOC vice president Richard Pound versus University of Queensland sport sociologist Jim McKay. Both discussed Olympic crises, with Pound's address titled "Managing through crisis" and Jim McKay's presentation "Shame and scandal in the family." The latter included an incisive critique of contemporary Olympic mythology and an analysis of media coverage and public response to Australian IOC member Kevan Gosper's decision to allow his daughter to run the first leg of the torch relay in Greece (McKay, Hutchins, & Mikosza, 2000).

In September 1999, the University of Sydney hosted a conference with the promising title "The Politics of the Olympics" that boasted 10 "high-powered speakers" representing government (2), Olympic organizing bodies (3), and academia (5) (Nougher, 1999). Of the latter, one was the official Olympic historian, one was a member of the Toronto 2008 Bid Committee, one taught the sport management course for Greek students cosponsored by the IOC and SOCOG, and two worked in centers for Olympic studies that received funding from either IOC or national Olympic committee sources. In other words, no academic, and certainly no government, Olympic Coordination Authority (OCA) or SOCOG representative who spoke at this university-sponsored conference, was free of Olympic industry ties.

Universities and Olympic Promotion

Universities' attempts to capitalize on the Sydney Olympics took a variety of forms, ranging from small sport-related programs to major research projects and, in some instances, contracts handing over entire campuses to Olympic organizations. Indeed, as a result of discussion at the March 1998 NSW Vice-Chancellors' Conference, each university agreed to designate an Olympic contact person to liaise with SOGOG. For their part, SOCOG gave overall responsibility for university liaison to its group general manager as well as naming a second staff person as principal SOCOG contact. No NSW university escaped Olympic-related impacts—some positive, many negative.

All educational institutions in NSW extended their spring vacation by at least two weeks, with a break from September 11 to October 6 in order to accommodate the Olympics, and, specifically, to allow students eighteen and over to work as Olympic volunteers. Thus, tertiary students had to take a long break at a time of limited access to university libraries and changed employment opportunities, often with negative consequences for their studies and their jobs. Moreover, as just discussed, many had to leave their university residences for up to four weeks.

Disruptions experienced at the Sydney campuses of the Australian Catholic University exemplified some of the problems experienced by faculty. The university year started one week early, on February 14; the first semester was shortened by a week; there was no study week before the exam period; only one week was allocated for faculty marking and preparation for the second semester, which was one week shorter than usual. Faculty were encouraged to take leave during the Games, since campuses were mostly taken over by Olympic staff, and were expected to resume their research activities in October. By July, Sydney's midwinter, the compressed timetable resulted in many faculty members reporting sickness and burnout.

At the modest end of the spectrum, the Human Movement Studies Unit at Charles Sturt University, Bathurst, 250k west of Sydney, promised international students "a once in a lifetime program" to coincide with the Olympics, with special courses on "The Olympics in Sydney" and "Outback Adventure." The program covered two six-week periods with a seven-week spring break during the Olympics and Paralympics. This campus was also host to the two-thousand-member marching bands for their pre-Olympic training, a move that some political observers saw as simply a Labor Party move to make a significant injection of funds to a marginal seat, particular in view of the timing of the announcement, which was kept secret until a few weeks before the 1999 election (M. Moore, 2000d). Other regional universities, including Newcastle and Wollongong, rented their aquatic centers to international teams, while those closer to the city entered into contracts that covered accommodation, catering, meeting rooms, and sport venues.

For the two universities located in or near the CBD—the University of Sydney and UTS—opportunities to reap Olympic-related benefits were extensive. Glossy color booklets titled "University of Sydney 2000" and "UTS and the Sydney 2000 Olympic Games" documented how these two institutions had been "touched by the Olympic spirit," as evident in their involvement in a wide range of Olympic activities. "The [Sydney] University's Olympic charter is being met through its people, facilities, research, knowledge and expertise," the booklet pronounced. University of Sydney faculty were responsible for advances in sports medicine, drug testing, weather forecasting, transport management, and other areas, as well as for the design of the two solar power plants at the Olympic site. Moreover, the publication boasted that the campus had been chosen "as the ideal location to house hundreds of officials and visitors"—while failing to mention the potential hardship to students who were asked to vacate the residences for the duration of the Games (see chapter 4).

UTS: In the Middle of the Olympic City

Despite the victories achieved by the housing committee and students' association, it was by no means "business as usual" in September 2000 for UTS students. In a decision-making process from which students claimed they were largely excluded, UTS administration closed some campuses, and restricted access to others, for a four-week period, either for "security reasons" or because the premises were to be used for Olympic purposes. Haymarket, the downtown campus adjacent to Darling Harbor Olympic venues, was rented to SOCOG as the headquarters for police and Olympic security, and the library was only open on a restricted timetable.

On the issue of student democracy and administration accountability, a controversy emerged in 1999 over the use of the yacht *Impulse*, which was purchased with student union funds. Ostensibly, its purpose was to provide a subsidized social activity, particularly for international students, but, as UTS Students' Association president Ryan Heath pointed out, there was no large-scale advertising of the yacht's availability and it was underutilized by students. The student newspaper *Vertigo* reported that SOCOG had rented the yacht at the subsidized student rate of twenty-five dollars at least six times in the preceding twelve months, including New Year's Eve, with IOC officials as SOCOG guests on one occasion (Corruption, 2000; Heath, 2000b; Level 7, 2000, 7).

In all of these transactions, SOCOG and the university administration were not accountable to students. Indeed, there was only one student representative out of thirty members of the University Senate, while, at the University Council level, the Students' Association president had no speaking rights, and, in Heath's experience, was generally ignored. Therefore, on the question of the university's Olympic involvement, Heath claimed that the "absolute lack of consultation of staff and students brings the legitimacy of the Olympic relationship into question" (Heath quoted in Brennan, 2000, 9).

Coordinating its Olympic ventures, the UTS Olympic Committee was set up in 1994 with Prof. Tony Veal as chair, and a part-time project manager was appointed in 1998. Its aims, according to the UTS Olympic Projects website, were "to capitalize on the opportunities for the university arising from the Olympic Games movement," to raise the profile of UTS nationally and internationally, and to promote the use of UTS facilities. In these initiatives, UTS collaborated with UNSW Center for Olympic Studies to promote interest in their various Olympic initiatives, and particularly to boost sales of their Olympic-related publications.

A monthly lecture series organized by the UTS Olympic Committee in 1999 and 2000 included a few Olympic critics—*Herald* reporter Matthew Moore and Colin Tatz, coauthor with Douglas Booth of "Swimming with the big boys" (Tatz & Booth, 1994) and author of *The Obstacle Race: Aborigines in Sport* (Tatz, 1995b), for example—as well as a longer list of Olympic athletes, government officials with Olympic portfolios, and Olympic industry employees. A new staff lounge at the UTS Broadway campus was offered as a meeting place for visiting Olympic researchers, writers, and academics, with telephone and computer access and free refreshments, for the duration of the Games.

Over ten courses in the UTS departments of computer sciences, management, journalism, sport management, leisure, sport and tourism, engineering, and general studies focused on Olympic topics. Significantly, a number of these courses required that students provide voluntary labor for some aspect of the Olympic industry—such as technology support, broadcast operations, volunteer recruitment, and promotional writing—in order to obtain a university credit.

Heath reported that there were student concerns about Olympic-related subjects that were compulsory for some degree programs, and about compulsory participation in Olympic-related projects within certain courses. While it might be argued that those who signed up for such programs or courses agreed to these requirements at the outset, students whose academic success depended on their performance as volunteers and their compliance with Olympic industry ideology were hardly in a position to develop a critique of Olympic industry practices. In other words, the function of the liberal university to promote free intellectual exchange was threatened by these kinds of arrangements.

University of New South Wales: A Real Olympic Partner

UNSW's complicity with the Olympic industry was front-page news in May 1999, when the Sydney media revealed that Vice-Chancellor John Niland had purchased a $245,000 corporate box (and an additional catering package) in the Olympic stadium for the duration of the Olympics and Paralympics (Porter, 1999; Uni's suite deal, 1999).

Academic staff reaction typified the outrage expressed by many university constituencies. The May 18 and May 26 general meetings of the UNSW Branch of the National Tertiary Education Union unanimously passed the following two resolutions:

- This meeting condemns UNSW management for paying exorbitant sums for a Stadium Australia suite for the Olympic Games 2000. This decision is particularly insulting given the failure by management to allocate adequate funding for salaries.

- That this meeting resolves to hold a stop work meeting of all members of Tuesday 1 June 1999 . . . for a protest at the Vice-Chancellor's forum over (a) the lack of an improved salary offer and failure to reach agreement in the current round of enterprise bargaining, despite seven months of bargaining, and (b) the low priority given to staff salaries in the University's spending as indicated by the recent purchase of an Olympic Suite. (UNSW Branch, 1999)

This kind of backlash forced Niland into a defensive position, still in evidence ten months later in his message in the Center for Olympic Studies magazine *Olympic Impact*. This publication, which had only appeared once before, in 1996, was revived in 2000 with the vice-chancellor's office providing the funds and ensuring its wide distribution in order to "showcase" the university's Olympic-related activities. As Niland explained,

> Some may consider it opportunistic, but I'm of the view that you take your chances when they arise . . . I intend to make the most of the unique opportunity of the Olympics being held in Sydney to advance the interests of UNSW. . . . By investing in a box at the main stadium we are in a position to recognize our major donors and enhance opportunities for future donor development. (Niland, 2000, 2)

He went on to promise that a "selected group" of staff and students would have access to the box (i.e., when it wasn't being used by more important university presidents, international researchers, and corporate donors); the process of choosing the forty staff members was to be open to suggestions. As a visiting scholar at UNSW at the time, I considered offering a "socialist alternative" suggestion—that those with the lowest salaries, probably female cleaning staff, should be issued the first invitations.

The UNSW Roundtable, Niland's other big Olympic project, invited eighteen leaders of top international universities to generate "a high-level exchange of ideas" on the following topics:

> development of new university paradigms in the wake of globalization, challenges facing university science, alternate resource models to support university growth, commercialization of university-developed intellectual property, and an attempt to assess the characteristics of leading universities in 2025. (McGuire, 2000, 2).

A not inconsiderable perk for conference participants and their partners was free access to the corporate box for their Olympic viewing enjoyment.

UNSW Center for Olympic Studies

The UNSW Center for Olympic Studies was established in 1996 at the initiative of Prof. Roger Layton, dean of the Faculty of Commerce and Economics; its director, Richard Cashman, and coordinator, Anthony Hughes, were specialists in sport history and sport sociology. The 1997 center directory listed sixty-five faculty affiliates, and boasted more than one hundred the next year (UNSW, 1998). Their expertise covered a range of Olympic-related topics such as solar heating, planning and design, waste management, tourism, communication, language services, sports medicine, and sport history.

The relationship between SOCOG and UNSW was firmly established by 1998, in part as a result of Vice-Chancellor Niland's initiatives. By March that year, both sides had discussed the recruitment of specialist media and information technology volunteers, the testing of interpreters, visual arts and festivals, and a scholarship for a Paralympian. Areas to be explored included the design of ceremonies, use of facilities, environmental research, and recruitment of other specialist volunteers in areas relevant to Olympic-related courses (e.g., the two then offered by the center). And by October, initial steps had been taken toward renting the corporate box.

In late 1998, the Center for Olympic Studies extended its outreach to the business community, by offering a membership package for officially recognized Olympic sponsors and providers, and "client and corporate briefing" sessions on the question of "Olympic property," in order to help participating companies "obtain greater leverage" from their Olympic sponsorships. Channel 7 was named the center's first corporate partner, an arrangement that the network saw, inexplicably, as part of its plans for "a broader community involvement in the Olympic Games" (UNSW, 1998). (In a conversation I had with a Channel 7 journalist in April 2000, I was told that, as the official Olympic network, it couldn't interview me or promote my book because it was critical of the Olympics.)

By early 1999, UNSW's formal Olympic involvement included the leasing of 320 beds in two residential colleges for SOCOG security staff during the Olympics and Paralympics. These arrangements, together with the rental of the gymnasium, pool, hockey oval, and campus meeting and convention venues to SOCOG, were expected to generate a revenue of about $750,000. SOCOG's use of the Australian Technology Park, in which UNSW held a one-third share, would also produce over $1.5m in rental income.

In 1999, in response to a SOCOG request, Vice-Chancellor Niland nominated the Center for Olympic Studies "to provide a common point of reference on matters Olympic for agencies such as SOCOG" as well as to inform the university at large about university-based Olympic activities, and to publicize its contributions to the Olympics (UNSW Center, 1999). This arrangement raises some obvious questions about academic freedom, when a university agrees to serve as an "information clearinghouse" for a private corporation.

As part of this role, the center accepted the invitation to help staff SOCOG's Research and Information Service for credentialed international media in the Main Press Center (MPC) throughout September and part of October. This arrangement required volunteer "scholars in residence" to work twelve-hour shifts and to provide research services through the MPC's database, hard copy resources, and links to "academic experts." Canadian and American media coverage in September, however, suggested that the assistance provided by these scholars was used only as background material—not too surprisingly, given credentialed journalists' priorities (see chapter 9).

By mid-2000, the center had hosted over five conferences and two local council forums, covering topics such as the environment, Aboriginal issues, Olympic history, sports medicine, and economic and tourism impacts. It offered three Olympic courses developed and taught by Cashman and/or Hughes: Staging the Olympics: The event and its impact; The modern Olympics; and Media, technology and the Olympics, the latter including a number of guest presentations by Sydney Olympic Broadcasting Organization staff. Largely self-funding, the center published, or copublished with UNSW Press or Walla Walla Press, over twelve books, reports, and monographs. It also organized the first annual Olympic Legends fundraising dinner for the UNSW Scholarship for Disadvantaged Elite Athletes.

University Volunteers: Another Hidden Cost

Since most Olympic volunteers had to be eighteen years of age or over, universities provided a more promising pool than high schools. The extensive recruitment of university students as volunteers, in a process involving at least eight NSW universities, incurred hidden costs in staff and administrative time—costs which, like the public servants' salaries discussed in chapter 5, were largely subsidized by taxpayers' money and absent from the official Olympic budget. Time-consuming background work for university staff included entering recruitment information on university websites, posting notices on campus, responding to telephone and e-mail inquiries, and distributing and processing application forms. The actual numbers of student volunteers in any given university ranged from 100 to 1,000 (Jacobsen, 1998).

In an initiative with direct benefits for SOCOG, the UTS School of Management course, "Volunteer Recruitment for Major Events," was designed "to incorporate the interviewing process of the 50,000 volunteers required by SOCOG," according to the UTS Olympic Projects webpage. Interestingly, the same webpage noted that UTS did not have "a sponsorship relationship with the Sydney 2000 Olympics Games."

In order to recruit senior media volunteers with some prior training and experience, SOCOG made direct approaches to communications students and academic staff in three Sydney universities and three other regional universities. Work in radio and television broadcasting, and in the print and electronic media included technology support, broadcast operations, promotional writing, typing, and copy-taking. For example, the Biography Collection Team, which began work in 1999, collected background data on Olympic athletes and their sports, while assistants in the area of "communication and recognition" produced a daily newsletter during the Games. This volunteer work usually counted toward a university credit in journalism or media studies, and SOCOG issued a certificate of completion.

UNSW Center for Olympic Studies coordinated the recruitment of UNSW student volunteers for SOCOG and for IBM, as well as organizing student internships and work experience. IBM's volunteer recruitment drive aimed at staffing its "Surf Shacks"—internet café facilities through which the public were encouraged to send fan mail to Olympic athletes. IBM first set up this program at the 1996 Olympics in Atlanta, and its promotional brochure promised volunteers the reward of interacting "directly with Olympic athletes and officials, VIPs and international visitors to Sydney." Apart from the free travel, meals, and uniform, volunteers could gain UNSW course credits from the experience.

The Other Side of the Coin: University Critics

As evident elsewhere in this discussion, some university-affiliated individuals, centers, and programs did attempt to challenge Olympic industry hegemony by working with community groups to organize conferences, conduct research projects, and/or write critical articles and reports. Some examples—by no means an exhaustive list—will be discussed in this section.

In 1994, the University of Western Sydney's Housing and Urban Studies group and Shelter NSW produced a research report titled *Olympics and Housing,* which recommended stronger legislation to protect tenants and control the private rental market, as well as an increased supply of low-cost housing (Cox, Darcy, & Bounds, 1994).

In August 1998, the Ian Buchan Fell Housing Research Center at the University of Sydney helped to organize a conference on *Homelessness: The Unfinished Agenda* and subsequently published conference proceedings of the same name (James et al., 1999). Sponsored by Mission Australia, Shelter NSW, the Law Foundation and Integrated Vision, it brought together elected representatives, government officials, academics, housing advocates, Indigenous representatives, and frontline service providers. Four homeless people presented moving accounts of their own experiences living on the streets, in shelters, or in jail. Anita Beaty, executive director of the Atlanta Task Force for the Homeless, spoke about the experiences of that city's homeless people during the 1996 Olympics. Included in the conference recommendations were calls for resources to match needs; coordination of policy, program, and service delivery; services to meet diverse and complex needs; protection of human rights; and legislation to reduce homelessness.

Similarly, some of the conferences sponsored by the UNSW Center for Olympic Studies—most notably "Green Games: A Golden Opportunity" in 1997 (see Lenskyj, 2000, chapter 8) and "Red, Black and Gold: Sydney Aboriginal People and the Olympics" (Cashman & Cashman, 2000)—as well as the Olympic forums with Auburn and Mosman municipal councils, facilitated productive discussions between community representatives, academics, and Olympic industry personnel.

Finally, UTS staff and students, including those working in the Community Law and Legal Research Center and the Students' Association, were among the key players in Olympic watchdog activism (see chapters 7 and 9), and the Australian Center for Independent Journalism, housed at UTS, published a special issue of *Reportage* in June 2000, titled "Housing Crisis in the Olympic City."

CONCLUSION

Some of the more sinister aspects of business arrangements between universities and corporations were documented by Naomi Klein in her groundbreaking book, *No Logo* (2000). Despite the secrecy surrounding these agreements, particularly the financial details—purportedly for commercial-in-confidence reasons—she was able to examine the conditions imposed by companies such as Coca-Cola, Reebok, and Nike on universities in Canada and the United States. Most relevant to the Olympic industry's attempted co-optation of Australian universities was the "nondisparagement" clause included in Reebok's and Nike's contracts. All persons affiliated with the university were prohibited from criticizing the corporate funder, and the university administration agreed to take necessary steps to silence such critics (Klein, 2000, 96–97).

With the widespread secrecy surrounding all the contracts between OCA/SOCOG and Sydney 2000 corporate sponsors and media rights-holders, it is impossible to ascertain whether or not nondisparagement clauses were included. The Canadian and American record of Olympic sponsors Coca-Cola and Nike, however, strongly suggests that such prohibitions may have been partly responsible for the relatively low level of public—or published—academic critique of Sydney 2000 in Australia. There is clear evidence of the chilly climate experienced by the small number of academics who did attempt to blow the whistle on universities' complicity in the Olympic industry. The "Olympic branding" of NSW universities was achieved through their exploitation of Olympic-related commercial opportunities, and through SOCOG's exploitation of "free" university labor, advertising, and goodwill. In this context, universities were obviously the weaker partner, and it was in university administrations' best interests to silence Olympic critics, just as they had gagged other "embarrassing" or "difficult" faculty members. These developments amply demonstrated the threat posed by transnational corporations—including those affiliated with the Olympic industry—to academic freedom.

7

"I'm Not Against the Olympics, But. . . ."

Local and Global Resistance

—————

Community organizations concerned with housing and homelessness, the environment, human rights, social services, and related issues, faced a formidable challenge when they confronted the Sydney 2000 Olympic industry. Some achieved limited success in raising public awareness of Olympic-related impacts, in influencing decision making at the local and state levels, and in slowing down the progress of the Olympic juggernaut. But, as the title of this chapter suggests, representatives of liberal community organizations often borrowed from "I'm not a feminist, but. . . ." rationalizations that women used in the 1970s and 1980s when they supported some principles of the women's movement, but wanted to avoid the radical *f* word.

By prefacing their Olympics critiques with assertions like "I'm not against the Olympics/I don't hate sport/I like the Olympics, but. . . ." many Olympic-related groups diluted their message significantly. And by implying a false separation between sport and politics, they effectively depoliticized the Olympics. On the other hand, the liberal strategy of avoiding the appearance of criticizing the actual Olympic sporting event was less likely to attract the "unAustralian" epithet, a label intended to blame and shame anyone who dared to cast a shadow over Australians' largely uncritical love of sport, or over Australia's largely unblemished national icons, an undifferentiated mass known as "the athletes."

From a different political front, some more radical member-groups of antipoverty and antiglobalization coalitions such as the Olympic Impact Coalition (OIC), later known as the Anti-Olympic Alliance (AOA), had well-developed analyses of the links between Olympic sport and global capitalism, most notably the complicity of national and multinational Olympic sponsors in environmental destruction and human rights abuses, and their contribution to the ever-growing gap between money-rich and money-poor people and countries. Their message was an unwelcome one in a climate saturated with "feel-good" Olympic rhetoric.

The Olympic industry has the power to suppress local dissent and to promote the illusion of unequivocal support on the part of host cities and countries; examples include the 1968 massacre of student protesters in Mexico City, the arrests of dissidents in Moscow in 1986 and Barcelona in 1992, and the criminalization of poverty in Atlanta prior to the 1996 Olympics (see Lenskyj, 2000, chapter 6 for an in-depth discussion of international Olympic resistance). Moreover, with the framework for Olympic debate already established by Olympic boosters, community-based critics often found themselves in a reactive rather than proactive position. Even under these conditions, groups such as the Toronto Bread Not Circuses Coalition, which opposed Toronto's bids for the 1996 and the 2008 Olympics, and the Berlin anti-Olympic (2000) group redirected public debate toward the potentially negative economic and social impact issues (Kidd, 1992; Lenskyj, 1996) and played an important role in the defeat of these three bids.

Challenges to Community Organizing

An early Sydney Olympic social impact report warned that people "will want to 'tag' issues . . . on to the Olympics and Paralympics, even if there is little objective connection" (Keys Young, 1995, i) and Olympic minister Michael Knight issued a similar warning at a community housing conference in 1997: "The Olympic Games should not be held hostage to those pushing a wider social agenda" (Knight quoted in M. Moore, 1997). Such pronouncements, heard regularly for seven years, had the required chilling effect in some circles. Many liberal community and social service leaders, as well as some Indigenous groups, were opposed to holding public protests during the actual Games, largely because they did not want to be seen as detracting from the event, or using it opportunistically. Some were concerned about appearing *unAustralian, antisport,* and/or *anti-Olympics*— three labels to be avoided if a group's credibility in mainstream Australian society was to remain unscathed.

The label *unAustralian* also resonated with Australians' entrenched ethnocentric, often racist, rejection of "whingers and whiners"—individuals, usually "outsiders," who allegedly complained too much about conditions in their adopted country. In the 1990s version, these "outsiders" were portrayed as troublemakers ("anarchists") from overseas, whose only goal was to initiate violence at S11-style antiglobalization protests; indeed, some politicians viewed the mere notion of questioning economic rationalism and corporate power as unAustralian. As Sydney activist Gabrielle Kuiper explained, at a time when it served conservative governments' interest to promote their own brand of nationalism, the unAustralian label would be applied to Olympic protesters of any color, who would also be called "radical, unrealistic, selfish, extreme, unreasonable, fanatical," and similar epithets (Kuiper, 2000a).

Throughout the last decades of the century, members of marginalized groups who organized public protests against systemic racism, misogyny, and homophobia, environmental destruction, global capitalism, nuclear testing, and other urgent social issues in Australia were frequently dismissed as "ratbags" and "unAustralian," particularly by the predominantly White, privileged politicians in both government and opposition parties. Knight applied the *ratbag* label to member-groups of the Olympic Impact Coalition (OIC) in February 2000 when they announced plans to protest during the Olympics ("Ratbags," 2000). The fact that these groups occupied vastly different positions on the political spectrum, from the mainstream Salvation Army and Red Cross, on the one hand, to the radical direct action groups, Reclaim the Streets and Critical Mass, on the other, apparently escaped Knight's attention.

By 2000, the "unAustralian" epithet was beginning to have more sinister connotations. The draconian acts initiated by the NSW government in the preceding years gave police virtually arbitrary powers, and suspended Australians' basic rights to freedom of assembly in Sydney, at least for the duration of the Olympics and Paralympics, and in some cases, for much longer periods. With police and security surveillance of several Olympic protest groups and environmental organizations, some civil liberties advocates were concerned that police could even arrest unauthorized protesters on the fabricated charge of "unAustralian activities" (Anderson, 2000).

RESIDENT GROUPS AND COMMUNITY ACTIVISM

Social Capital in the Olympic City, a report commissioned by Green Games Watch 2000 (Albany Consulting Group, 1997) provided a comprehensive and insightful analysis of the contribution made by social capital—most notably, trust, civic engagement, and shared values—to economic, social, and environmental performance ("sustainable prosperity"), and the necessity of incorporating public participation into policy-making processes in order to achieve societal goals. It noted, however, that the recent shift toward greater collaboration between communities, interest groups, and government agencies in NSW was threatened by the inflexible time lines of the Sydney 2000 Olympics.

Lauren Costello and Kevin Dunn's (1993) comprehensive analysis of resident action groups (RAGs) in Sydney provided relevant information at the local community level. They found that the lower socioeconomic areas of Sydney's west and southwest (including Homebush, in the Auburn local government area) were likely sites for dumping "urban nasties" such as waste disposal facilities, hazardous industry, and prisons. As a result, there had been rapid growth of community activism in these suburbs in the 1980s and 1990s, with a focus on industrial encroachment and urban development issues. Given the powerful influence of class privilege, however, citizens with the most pressing needs were often the least likely to influence local governments, and Costello and Dunn reported that councils in the west and southwest considered local RAGs to have had little effect on their decisions.

Conversely, there was evidence to support the claim that RAGs dominated by white-collar professionals were more effective because of their greater expertise in researching their position, using the media to good effect, and speaking the "language of the experts." However, since the organizing efforts of more privileged citizens were often directed toward classic NIMBY issues (not in my backyard)—for example, opposition to "noxious neighbors" such as community-based mental health facilities—their conservative political agenda did little to challenge existing power relations across class and ethnic boundaries.

In another analysis of power relationships between local governments and residents, Ritchie and Hall (2000) concluded that, in the context of megaprojects such as Sydney 2000, local authorities were likely to fear and avoid residents' reaction, with two consequences:

- an inability to listen, understand and respond to local needs, in other words, reinforcing the move away from serving towards political and economic control and power; and

- an open invitation to move further towards governance and away from government, in other words, away from accountability and towards implicit secrecy. (Ritchie & Hall, 2000, 8)

State and Olympic officials used shifting power dynamics and changing models of policy-making and regulation to good effect. The charge of NIMBYism—directed, for example, at opponents of the Bondi Beach volleyball stadium—played into class divisions by portraying Bondi residents as privileged and selfish, as discussed in chapter 8. But when Rupert Murdoch's Fox Studios objected to the triathlon passing by its "backyard," Olympic officials changed the route in a backflip that many observers viewed as a speedy response to corporate pressure. In a different Olympic-related example, innercity residents and retail businesses were increasingly employing private security guards to move "noxious neighbors"—homeless people, youth, and Aborigines—out of the CBD in time for the big event.

Throughout the parliamentary debates on Olympic-related legislation, discussed in chapter 2, Greens MLAs Lee Rhiannon and Ian Cohen were among the very small number of politicians who supported citizens' rights to free speech and peaceful assembly, while, at the federal level, Greens Sen. Bob Brown was one of the few to oppose the *Defence Legislation Amendment*. Rhiannon and Cohen regularly joined in protest rallies and marches, and Rhiannon's office assisted in OIC activities and planning. The Green Party, like green politics generally in Australia, did not limit itself to narrow environmental issues, but worked toward developing alliances with Indigenous groups, the trade union movement, and other social justice organizations, with varying degrees of success. As Australian environmentalists Drew Hutton and Libby Connors explained in their comprehensive history of the Australian environmental movement, by the end of the 1990s, international alliances were discussing the overarching problem of free trade and globalization, and examining how key social justice issues could be addressed in the context of "debilitating pressures for deregulated trade and investment regimes, increased power of multinational corporations, dismantling of social infrastructure, and rapid economic growth that was largely reliant on exploitation of non-renewable resources and increased pollution" (Hutton & Connors, 1999, 261). As this chapter will demonstrate, for many progressive people, the Olympic industry symbolized the convergence of key social justice and environmental issues in the context of globalization.

COMMUNITY CONSULTATION: OLYMPIC INDUSTRY-STYLE

Excessive secrecy, withholding of information, and exclusion from real decision making were the hallmarks of Sydney Olympic organizers' relationships with the community representatives who volunteered up to four years of their time and energy to serve on advisory committees, most notably the Social Impact Advisory Committee (SIAC), the National Indigenous Advisory Committee (NIAC), and the Homebush Bay Environmental Reference Group (HomBERG). Of course, experienced activists were fully aware that the "advisory" role occupied a low rung on the citizen participation ladder, and when the bodies to be "advised" were the NSW government and the global Olympic industry, community influence was minimal. The following discussion will focus on the experiences of community representatives in two of these advisory groups: SIAC and HomBERG.

Social Impact Advisory Committee

SIAC was established in 1996, following lengthy lobbying by the NSW Council of Social Services (NCOSS), the Public Interest Advocacy Center (PIAC), Shelter NSW and the NSW Ecumenical Council. Its purpose was to provide advice on social impacts through the Olympic Coordination Authority (OCA) to the Olympic minister, who in turn reported to the premier every six months. Chaired by the Reverend Harry Herbert, executive director of the NSW Uniting Church's Board for Social Responsibility, SIAC was composed of community representatives and government departmental representatives, with the latter group changing so often that the stability of the committee was jeopardized.

SIAC's political position, according to Herbert, was pro-Olympic: "Members of the Committee are not opponents of the Olympics. They have never argued that the money spent on the Olympics would be better spent on other things." He went on to explain that their goal was "to maximize the good and minimize the bad" (Herbert, 2000a).

Herbert, like NCOSS director Gary Moore and PIAC senior policy advisor Amanda Cornwall, reported frustration at OCA's general attitude of secrecy, as evident in its repeated failure to consult with them or even to share basic information. For example, SIAC did not receive a copy of the Department of Fair Trading's report on residential tenancy until after the government had announced its response, which was to reject about half of the recommendations (Herbert, 1999). In an attempt to improve communication and transparency, SIAC proposed that the committee's six-monthly reports should be made available to the public and to parliamentarians, but this recommendation was not implemented.

In 1997 SIAC's housing subcommittee commissioned consultants Elton and Associates to review progress on social impact management issues. The Elton report recommended that four key government agencies (Fair Trading, Housing, Community Services, and Urban Affairs and Planning) should issue status reports every six months, with OCA taking responsibility for compiling summaries for SIAC and the general public. But, by September 1999, although four government reports had been completed, none had been made available to the public, and not all SIAC members had access to them. Furthermore, as noted in the Shelter NSW 1999 report on housing and homelessness, the government had failed to initiate the full range of "finely tuned and targeted measures" as recommended in the Elton report, while the inclusion of general government initiatives in the six monthly status reports gave a false impression of action (Cox, 1999, 11).

Homebush Bay Environmental Reference Group

Two community-based environmental groups, Greenpeace Australia and Green Games Watch 2000 (GGW) were key players during Olympic preparations in Sydney. GGW was established with state and federal funding in 1996 as an environmental watchdog, for the purpose of reporting on the implementation of Sydney 2000's environmental guidelines; in keeping with its policy, Greenpeace did not accept government funding.

In their interactions with Olympic organizers, both groups generally found the Sydney Organizing Committee for the Olympic Games (SOCOG) to be more responsive to their concerns than OCA (at least until February 2000 when SOCOG's environmental unit fell victim to budget cuts and its functions were taken over by OCA). With OCA responsible for the construction of all the Olympic venues over a seven-year period, it was of course more likely to lock horns with environmental groups.

Greenpeace, for its part, tried to convey to OCA that disagreements over certain issues did not mean that the group was not interested in publicly promoting OCA's successful environmental initiatives, but it became increasingly difficult for Greenpeace to perform that function in the face of OCA's frequent obfuscation and hostility. Furthermore, Greenpeace was left out of the information loop on a number of important issues, and routinely waited months for OCA responses to their letters requesting information or action (Greenpeace, 2000a; Luscombe, 1999; Millais & Palese, 2000).

The 1997 GGW report identified serious problems with OCA's attempts at public participation and community consultation, and concluded that the process was in danger of becoming ineffective, tokenistic, and superficial (Albany Consulting Group, 1997, 64). And, as GGW coordinator Bob Symington reiterated just six months before the Olympics, OCA "must reverse their entrenched culture of secrecy and its resulting non-accountability and start delivering best practice community consultation and dissemination of information" (GGW, 2000b). Even the annual reports by the liberal Earth Council, the official environmental monitor of Sydney 2000, cited lack of transparency as one of OCA's most serious shortcomings.

In March 1998, in response to the ongoing controversy over contamination at the Homebush Bay Olympic site, Olympic minister Michael Knight announced a $12m program to "guarantee ongoing monitoring and management" of the remediated lands. One of the provisions of the program was the establishment of HomBERG to review the monitoring process and ensuring a voice for community, scientific, and environment groups. Two years after its inception, Greenpeace expressed concern that, despite regular meetings and participation by stakeholders, HomBERG's effectiveness was seriously impeded by OCA practices: "information requests have in general been dealt with slowly and there has been little or no detailed feedback on achievements or outcomes from the range of programs, despite discussions and requests for more detailed information" (Greenpeace, 2000a, 2).

The Greenpeace report went on to point out that delays and problems with specific projects had not been reported to the committee until eighteen months later; OCA appeared to believe that such issues were not relevant to HomBERG. In Greenpeace's experience, "The OCA has often been difficult to communicate with, unwilling to provide information requested by watchdog groups and obstructionist in exploring some environmental solutions." Greenpeace demanded that OCA "be more proactive in community participation and consultation" (Greenpeace, 2000a, 2, 6). Similarly, GGW blamed OCA for its contribution to "the appalling mismanagement" of the $12m program (GGW, 2000b).

The independent chair of HomBERG, Australian National University professor emeritus Dr. Ben Salinger, who resigned in 2000, had also expressed serious concerns about the program's viability, and supported the goal of increased transparency and disclosure. Salinger was well known for his book, *Chemistry in the Marketplace,* in continuous print for twenty-five years. The new chair, Dr. Michael Knight (not to be confused with the Olympic minister of the same name), was a hydrogeology specialist from the University of Technology Sydney (UTS). He had extensive research experience regarding water, land, and soil contamination in the Newington Army Depot (Homebush Bay) area, having been retained by the Department of Defence as the main review consultant; his numerous coauthored publications on those topics were dated from April 1992 to May 1995, according to the UTS Olympic website. It is interesting to note that a 1996 report prepared for GGW by Kate Short (later known as Kate Hughes, and from 1999 employed as OCA's special advisor for the environment), found that several scientific analyses of the Homebush site and detailed remediation plans had been commissioned by the government between 1990 and 1992, but that a decision had been made to take no action before the bid was submitted in 1993 in order not to "jeopardize" its success (Short, 1996).

In addition to Greenpeace and GGW 2000, members of resident action groups in Auburn, Rhodes, and Meadowbank, representatives from the National Toxics Network, National Parks Association, Waste Crisis Network, and others, were invited to participate in HomBERG. Some of the resident group representatives had little experience as environmental activists; they were community members with an obvious interest in environmental issues in their neighborhoods, but did not necessarily speak the "language of the experts" or espouse Greenpeace's or GGW's more radical politics.

Greenpeace and GGW generally viewed the reference group rather cynically as "window dressing": a six-weekly social event that often proved a waste of time. And, as Greenpeace campaigners Corrin Millais and Blair Palese explained, the community groups found the experience frustrating; they wanted to see practical results and benefits, and were not participating just to complain. An examination of Greenpeace and GGW media releases, Olympic reports, and newsletters amply demonstrated that both groups publicly applauded OCA's and the government's environmental success stories at every opportunity. However, with no structures in place to require accountability in delivering results, Greenpeace eventually saw HomBERG meetings as occasions for community representatives to witness OCA failures, rather than as opportunities to engage in genuine community consultation.

On May 11, 2000, when OCA granted me permission to attend a meeting as an observer, I perceived the general climate as friendly, even jovial, although most of the community representatives, wearing visitor security IDs, sat in a highly visible cluster at one end of the table. Much of OCA's information was presented in technical language, replete with acronyms and shorthand terminology; admittedly, those present had followed the issues for years, but it seemed likely that some (including myself) found these methods of information-sharing inaccessible. In another example of OCA communication style the local newspaper, *Parramatta Advertiser,* carried an announcement on treatment of chemical waste. "After-hours noise levels are expected to be below sleep disturbance levels" was not the clearest way of conveying the news that residents would probably not be kept awake by noise of the "modified Base Catalyzed Decomposition plant" that would operate twenty-four hours a day for the next three months (OCA, 2000).

Confrontations appeared unlikely in the superficially congenial atmosphere of this particular meeting, despite the often defensive and unsatisfactory responses offered by OCA staff. However, in a rare moment, during his presentation of GGW's report on the Lidcombe liquid waste plant, GGW coordinator Bob Symington stated unequivocally that GGW's interactions with Waste NSW, the state government department responsible for the plant's operations, were better than those his group had with OCA.

NO GREEN MEDAL FOR SYDNEY 2000

Environmentalists' involvement in issues related to the Homebush Bay contamination and remediation up to about 1998 have been relatively well publicized and documented (see Cashman & Hughes, 1998; James, 1998; Lenskyj, 2000, chapter 8). Less well-known were community-organizing efforts around environmental and urban development issues unrelated to the cleanup. This activism, often initiated by local groups and supported by Greenpeace, GGW, Friends of the Earth, and other environmental organizations, was generally prompted by Olympic-related encroachment on Sydney communities, with the Bondi Beach volleyball stadium the best-known example (as discussed in detail in chapter 8).

A 1998 GGW press release titled "Global vs. Local: Communities Feel Olympic Onslaught" (1998c) summarized a wide range of issues that had prompted local action, including the Ryde water polo venue, the Rushcutters Bay sailing venue, the Bankstown cycling track site, the Sydney Harbor sewage tunnel, temporary use of a St. Marys site for the Olympic village, and SOCOG's use of the Department of Defence site at Regents Park. A common theme in all of these examples, like the Bondi Beach construction, was the alienation of public land for Olympic use, and in some instances, the potential for permanent alienation. GGW representatives met with International Olympic Committee (IOC) environment committee chair, Pal Schmidt, in April 1998 to discuss these problems and to seek better communication with the IOC. Again in April 1999, Greenpeace and GGW met with IOC Sport and Environment Commission member Olav Myrholt to discuss ongoing problems, including the use of ozone-depleting chemicals, environmental guidelines for sponsors, the Homebush Bay cleanup, the Bankstown cycling track, and community consultation.

Olympic Cycling Track vs. Endangered Species

In February 1999, in preparation for construction of the Olympic velodrome and cycling track in the southwest suburb of Bankstown, the council put a drain adjoining the velodrome—what GGW termed *a gross pollutant trap and drain* through an endangered fragment of Cumberland Plain Woodland. Furthermore, the drain construction destroyed $28,000 worth of native bush regeneration carried out by the Bankstown Bushland Society (BBS) to serve as a buffer to the woodland, which was protected by the *Threatened Species Conservation Act* (1995). About fifty residents attended a public rally organized by BBS on August 23; OCA declined to send a representative. In June 2000, overriding the two environmental groups' objections, the NSW government approved OCA's development application for a criterium cycling warm-up track through a *second* endangered (and protected) woodland, one of the three remaining examples of Cooks River clay plain scrub forest on the planet (Bondi—latest victim, 1999, 1; Latham, 2000, 4-5).

OCA's statement of environmental effects included plans for limited native (not indigenous to the area) bushland regeneration that critics claimed would not successfully replicate the original ecological community of 220 species. Despite more than a year of campaigning against the track, BBS's and GGW's efforts were unsuccessful. In a sequence of events similar to those at Bondi Beach, the fencing of the site was completed while the statement of environmental effects was still open for public comment, the project was approved, the two environmental groups were denied access during construction and "blocked from monitoring the project"; GGW reported that the entire debacle looked like "mutual collaborative noncompliance" with threatened species legislation on the part of the local and state governments (Latham, 2000, 4-5).

Greenpeace vs. OCA, McDonalds, and Coca-Cola

The biggest challenge taken on by Greenpeace concerned OCA's failure to meet the original environmental guidelines in relation to refrigeration and air-conditioning. The guidelines mandated the use of environmentally friendly refrigerants and processes, otherwise known as "greenfreeze" technologies. The prohibited hydrofluorocarbons (HFCs) in conventional refrigerants contributed significantly to ozone depletion and global warming. Greenpeace's July 1999 *Briefing on Refrigeration & Air Conditioning* exposed OCA's systematic failure to follow greenfreeze guidelines in twenty major Olympic venues and facilities. OCA's use of the ozone-depleting refrigerants was revealed in a confidential document obtained by Greenpeace following a Freedom of Information application. By 2000, Greenpeace reported that the problem extended to several thousand units of sponsors' equipment, including Coca-Cola vending machines, and refrigeration and air-conditioning in seven new McDonalds' stores, and 2,000 bar refrigerators in the athletes' village and media center. Coca-Cola alone had 1,700 HFC-cooled refrigeration units (Greenpeace, 2000b).

McDonalds, a Team Millennium Olympic sponsor, had been targeted by GGW in 1998 for its "recalcitrance against the spirit of the Green Games." In Newcastle, about 160km north of Sydney, McDonalds had challenged a local council's waste management policy that required reusable plates and cutlery in one of its outlets. But, wearing its "environmentally friendly" hat, the company proudly announced in its "McDonald's and the Environment leaflet," "as a global leader we have a responsibility to be an environmental leader as well. We are constantly taking steps that move us closer to doing all we can to preserve and protect our earth for you and your family" (cited in Greenpeace, 2000b, 13). Of course, it could be argued that "taking steps that move us closer. . . ." was simply a "weasel" clause, similar to those found in the Sydney 2000 environmental guidelines, which were sprinkled with phrases such as "wherever practicable" and "where possible." And, as Greenpeace pointed out, the fact that the guidelines were not legally binding was a serious shortcoming.

In 1999, Coca-Cola became the target of a global Greenpeace campaign, organized through the website cokespotlight.com, which generated thousands of supporters around the world. In June 2000, Greenpeace announced a victory: Coca-Cola had met the group's demands by agreeing to phase out HFCs by the 2004 Athens Olympics, to expand its research into refrigeration alternatives, and to require suppliers to install HFC-free refrigerants in all new equipment by 2004.

In December 1998, Greenpeace took OCA and its consultant, Environment Planning, to the Australian Federal Court on charges that OCA was misleading the public by claiming that its choice of an ozone-depleting air-conditioning system in the SuperDome was the best environmental choice. This was not an accusation that OCA was violating Sydney 2000's environmental guidelines, but rather a charge of making misleading public statements; as a result, it failed to capture much media or public interest. After all, by this time, an Olympic organization that misled the public wasn't exactly newsworthy.

In a classic example of Olympic industry arrogance, OCA first attempted to claim Crown immunity from prosecution because it was an instrument for the state, and immunity from the Australian Trade Practices Act because it was not a trade organization (Ozone showdown, 1999). In other words, OCA saw itself as outside (or possibly above) the law of the land. But this was not the end of the story. By 2000, it became clear that OCA was prepared to stall indefinitely, and had significantly greater financial resources to do so than a nonprofit organization such as Greenpeace. As a result, the case was settled out of court, with Environment Planning agreeing not to repeat the misrepresentation that it was using green-friendly refrigeration products.

Dangerous Dust: An Olympic Legacy

By September 1999, there were serious concerns about possible links between contaminated dust fallout from Olympic remediation works, and the increase in asthma, bronchitis, and skin rashes among residents of Ryde, Melrose Park, and Meadowbank; earlier health problems among prisoners and staff at Silverwater Prison were also believed to be related to Auburn landfill remediation works. According to one anecdotal report, when a local resident phoned OCA to report dust floating in his swimming pool, he was simply advised not to swim. Earlier in 1999, OCA had responded to community pressure by installing dust monitors (GGW, 1999). In July 2000, concerned residents, prompted by medical evidence of chromosomal damage in Homebush Bay residents, approached Greenpeace to request environmental testing. And in August, GGW and the Total Environment Center called on the NSW health minister and Olympic organizers to hold an independent inquiry into residents' health concerns.

Greenpeace Toxics campaigner Mark Oakwood summed up the ongoing problems of air, water, and soil contamination in the Homebush Bay area:

It's about time the NSW government honored its commitments. Greenpeace has actively campaigned for the full clean-up of toxic waste in and around Homebush Bay for years. The Government promised in 1997 to completely remediate this area in time for the Olympics, and yet residents still live on the shores of one of the most polluted waterways in the world. (Greenpeace, 2000c)

Just weeks after his statement, most of the international media were reporting that Sydney 2000 was an environmental success story. However, when Greenpeace issued its August report card, giving Sydney 2000 a bronze medal and a score of six out of ten, stories of this significant downgrading found their way into some international media (e.g., Barkham, 2000a; Young, 2000a)

POLICE AND PROTEST IN THE OLYMPIC CITY

Violent police intervention in peaceful protests reached its peak in NSW in the 1960s and 1970s, most notably during anti-Vietnam War demonstrations and gay and lesbian rights marches. Overall, the 1980s and early 1990s were marked by a more enlightened police approach, but legislation passed in 1997 and 1998 marked the beginning of a new era in terms of police power over public behavior and peaceful protest, as discussed in detail in chapter 2. These trends were part of a global pattern of change in policing of mass protest, directed primarily at the huge antiglobalization rallies that followed the Seattle model. Accompanying legislation in many Canadian and American cities banned marching without a permit, hanging banners, blocking traffic, altering billboards, carrying plastic tubing (to protect protesters' linked arms during direct action blockades), and even the wearing of satirical face masks or balaclavas (Mackinnon, 2000).

In May 1998, a peaceful protest and party was organized in Sydney Town Hall Square by Justice for Young People to protest the *Police and Public Safety Act*. Participants reported that police waited until dark, and then between thirty and forty officers on foot, four on horseback, members of the police rescue squad, council officers, eight police cars including three paddy wagons, and some plainclothes officers shut down the party and roughed up the young people, although they did not manage to confiscate the sound equipment (O'Gorman, 2000; Sentas, 1998).

By 1999, increasing numbers of citizens were experiencing the impact of state power over public assemblies, beginning with the police commissioner's refusal to authorize several weekday protests in the city. In an unprecedented move in March 2000, police refused to approve the route that had been taken by the International Women's Day march for decades (Rhiannon, 2000a).

In June 1999, in what protesters termed *practice exercises* for the Olympics, four hundred police officers were rostered to control the relatively small June 18 anticorporate demonstration in Sydney. The J18 organizing collective had been under surveillance earlier that year, with undercover police attending its meetings in a Sydney café (Boon-Kuo, 2000). (The same café was used for planning meetings of PISSOFF [People Ingeniously Subverting the Sydney Olympic Farce] and the Independent Media Center in the first half of 2000, and again it was suspected that the venue was under surveillance.) Also in 1999, an anti-GST (goods and services tax) protest resulted in twenty-eight arrests, and protesters reported that the police gave them the "choice" of surrendering and arrest, or capsicum spray and arrest (Boon-Kuo, 2000).

By 2000, overzealous policing of peaceful demonstrations was the norm. During the March 20 visit of Queen Elizabeth II to Sydney, a number of Australian Aid for Ireland protesters gathered with signs protesting British actions in Ireland. Police destroyed the placards and confiscated the banners before the Queen passed by. It was significant that, just one day earlier, St. Patrick's Day marchers had carried similar messages without any police intervention (Rhiannon, 2000a). At a rally I attended on the evening of April 10 to protest mandatory sentencing in the NT, the small crowd that marched to the prime minister's closed Sydney office was met by a phalanx of police on horseback (a scenario that lent itself well to the image in the next day's paper of a young Aboriginal child, in her mother's arms, patting one of the horses).

In March 2000, a protest organized by the group Reclaim the Streets had resulted in police violence, including baton and capsicum spray attacks. Prompted by these events, and in preparation for May Day demonstrations, UTS Community Law and Legal Research Center held a well-attended training session for activists on April 26 to discuss police powers, demonstrators' rights, the complaint process, and other issues and strategies in light of recent Olympic-related legislation. The UTS center subsequently published a ten-page Activists' Rights Guide, which outlined successful tactics and provided legal information, and held a second training workshop. Activists were advised to demonstrate in large, well-organized groups; to look out for their own safety and the safety of others; and to witness, record, and photograph any police violence during demonstrations. As the guide stressed, it was not critical that activists "obey the law"; citizens' assertion of basic rights, as set out in the *International Covenant on Civil and Political Rights,* to which Australia was a signatory in 1980, "does not require the permission of police or governments." However, it went on to state, "the repression of resistance and dissent in Australia is often backed by police intimidation, fabrication of evidence and violence" (UTS, 2000, 2).

On May 1, sixteen mounted police and dozens of officers on foot dispersed a May Day protest against global corporate power, in what participants saw as clear evidence of escalating police intervention in peaceful protest. One of the targets of the 2000 May Day march, Westpac Bank, was not only involved in financing the Jabiluka uranium mine—a project that threatened an environmentally vulnerable area of the NT— but was also an official sponsor of Sydney's so-called Green Games; thus, critics claimed that Westpac was in breach of its own and international environmental policies.

CACTUS (Campaign Against Corporate Tyranny with Unity and Solidarity) was a UTS-based group formed in early 2000 to organize May Day protests outside the Australian Stock Exchange. It subsequently held protests against Olympic sponsors Shell, Nike, McDonalds, and Westpac, as well as SOCOG and the World Economic Forum. Meeting weekly at the UTS Broadway campus, CACTUS sought "to support a cross-section of people, unions and issues in combating the common foe of corporate power," as their flyer explained. A teach-in held on July 29 included sessions on the WEF and the Olympics; globalization and women; and racism, imperialism, and the Third World.

ALTERNATIVE MEDIA AS RESISTANCE

Anti-Olympic and Olympic watchdog organizations made very effective use of the electronic media in the lead-up to the Sydney Olympics. Activist groups with websites included the Anti-Olympic Alliance at cat.org.au/aoa, PISSOFF at cat.org.au/pissoff, Rentwatchers at rw.apana.org.au, Greenpeace at greenpeace.org.au, and Green Games Watch 2000 at nccnsw.org.au/member/ggw, and many of these had links to similar overseas groups such as Toronto's Bread Not Circuses Coalition at breadnotcircuses.org.

Activists and supporters could also join the olympic-link list, which provided an invaluable link both locally and internationally for most of 2000. Unfortunately, it was repeatedly spammed with hundreds of unsolicited commercial messages in late September, and again in November, with the result that most people unsubscribed by that time. Although some people believed that the spamming was a deliberate attempt to close down this anti-Olympic list, it operated without interference in the crucial organizing period up to and during the Olympics.

The Sydney Alternative Media Center (SAMC) and the Sydney Independent Media Center (IMC) were the two major alternative news sources before and during the Sydney Olympics. They differed from other alternative media in that they operated not only a website but also an office/ studio space. SAMC was staffed by media professionals and aimed at providing international journalists with an alternative information source to SOCOG or the various government trade and tourism agencies. With about half of these journalists looking for nonsport stories, SAMC offered them contacts and information about issues such as Australia's environmental successes and failures, and the history and culture of Indigenous people. The IMC, on the other hand, was an interactive website and a physical space organized by volunteers from a wide range of backgrounds; like its counterparts in other countries, it operated on the principle, "Everyone is a witness. Everyone is a journalist."

The extensive antiglobalization protests at the World Trade Organization meeting in Seattle in November 1999 helped to put independent media centers on the map. After the success of seattle.indymedia.org in presenting the world with an insider's view of the protest, similar centers emerged in nine countries on three continents, in three languages, by mid-2000. However, with the majority located in English-speaking, money-rich countries, most notably the United States and Canada, organizers acknowledged that there was work to be done to make the global IMC network accessible to all.

In Australia, planning for both the September 11 antiglobalization protests at the World Economic Forum, and the anti-Olympic protests later that month, included the establishment of independent media centers in Melbourne at melbourne.indymedia.org and in Sydney at sydney.indymedia.org. The Sydney IMC website began operating in mid-June 2000, for the purpose of providing an unfiltered online forum for discussion and debate.

National and international mainstream media's highly selective and often distorted coverage of Olympic-related events and protests in 2000 amply demonstrated the need for alternative, grassroots media. In addition to the important news function, the IMC provided "a permanent record of our experience of protesting the many social injustices highlighted and/or exacerbated by the Olympics, an alternative, activist record of events and experiences" (Sydney IMC, 2000). For sociologists or historians interested in chronicling grassroots protests and social change movements, as well as for community activists in other cities or countries, IMC archives were an invaluable resource.

Finally, although this was not a major function, the IMC site facilitated the organization of (publicly advertised) Olympic-related protest events by serving as an electronic notice board. Like other protest groups, the IMC did not escape police attention. In one example reported to the IMC e-list, police in an unmarked car interrogated IMC volunteers who were unloading used computers from a van on a Newtown street in August 2000. The police officers' major (stated) interest was in the computers, which they suspected were stolen.

The IMC was organized by a diverse collective of media activists. As the announcement of the September 2 launch explained, "As activists we are weary of having our actions trivialized and our views marginalized by the mainstream corporate-owned press." Operating a technology-based enterprise such as this on a shoestring budget posed a challenge, which the collective met with a variety of creative approaches: fund-raising events such as film evenings, slide shows, and concerts; calls for loans or donations of everything from video cameras to office supplies; and a team of volunteers able to repair and upgrade old computers. The collective, about thirty members, welcomed all volunteers, and offered training for newcomers in the technical aspects of running an interactive website, which included stories, images, videos, and sound recordings.

The active (automatic publishing) software used in Seattle, Sydney, and elsewhere originated in Australia; it had been developed by a team of media activists that included Matthew Arnison, a member of the Sydney community activist technology collective, Cat@lyst. The Sydney IMC was designed so that any individual could independently post a contribution, or add comments to existing material, by following the simple publishing instructions or getting help through the tutorial page.

The commitment to democratic principles meant that there was no screening of materials, although as the Sydney IMC guidelines explained, the collective would correct obvious mistakes, and, on rare occasions, when a story was "way outside" the purpose of the website, it would be deleted. There was extensive debate in electronic activist circles over the extent to which any kind of screening constituted censorship. The open policy allowed mindless pro-Olympic rhetoric to be published; in the case of the AOA website (which served a different purpose to the IMC), this resulted in a large number of Olympic supporters swamping the interactive page and organizers removing these messages each day. Conversely, in the Melbourne Indymedia site, the policy permitted equally mindless and often offensive attempts at anti-Olympic satire. Organizers generally saw these as relatively minor and inevitable problems associated with an IMC—the price to be paid if this was to serve as a real forum for public debate. By September, hundreds of articles, and dozens of photos, sound recordings, and videos, mostly on Olympic-related issues, were accessible on the Sydney IMC site. Topics and issues included the Tent Embassy, Walk for Peace, Broadway squats, Torch Relay protests, Bondi Beach volleyball stadium, and policing practices.

The IOC Cyberpolice and Alternative Media Sites

In August 2000, in keeping with its zealous guardianship of the O word, the IOC extended its jurisdiction to cyberspace. A team of software experts was hired to search the Internet for unauthorized domain names that used "Olympic properties" in order to protect their value in the multinational marketplace. On July 13, taking advantage of the 1999 American Anti-cybersquatting Consumer Protection Act, the IOC, US Olympic Committee, and the Salt Lake City Organizing Committee filed a lawsuit against more than eighteen hundred registered Internet domain names for alleged infringement of property rights—in other words, an electronic version of ambush marketing. The IOC's July 13 press release claimed that the lawsuit was intended to protect the interests of corporate sponsors, consumers, and athletes. IOC marketing commissioner Richard Pound added "the values of the Olympic movement" to this list—presumably a refererence to the fifteen pornography and forty-three gambling websites named in the lawsuit (IOC, 2000a).

The two main targets of the IOC action were commercial sites perceived as a threat to the value of "Olympic properties" and unauthorized sites that planned to stream live Olympic coverage, thereby threatening NBC's $1.2b (time-delayed) broadcast rights to the United States. Even athletes who wanted to post their daily journals to a Canadian newspaper website were prohibited from doing so on the grounds that this was an IOC copyright violation, and, of course, a perceived threat to NBC's monopoly (Woolsey, 2000).

The FBI National Infrastructure Protection Center's report on hacking alleged that anti-Olympic hackers ("hactivists"), such as the IMC collective, would try to close down official Olympic sites, even though it was clear that IMCs were organized for completely different, and totally legal and legitimate purposes. (In what Ray Jackson [2001, 6] described as "capitalist/corporate paranoia," the FBI report also identified the Anti-Olympic Alliance as a potential security threat.) Members of anti-Olympic protest groups were also concerned that they would fall under IOC scrutiny if an Olympic-related word, even spelled incorrectly, appeared in their domain name. One anti-Olympic site, for example, was called <olympisc.org>. On September 25, the concerns proved valid, when the nonprofit organization Unolympics.com received a threat of legal action from the IOC for alleged unauthorized use of the Olympic rings and Sydney 2000 logo on its home page. The group was given twenty-four hours to remove the symbols.

The Unolympics home page "SHAME 2000: Official Site of Australia's UnOlympic Performance in Events that Matter" identified Indigenous justice, human rights, environment, reconciliation, and foreign policy as five key issues, and showed an image of five collapsed rings ("ovals") representing Australia's failure in these areas. The Shame 2000 logo combined these "ovals" and an image of a person on a toilet throwing toilet paper in the air, in a manner reminiscent of the IOC rings and Sydney 2000's logo, with its Opera House peaks and boomerang. (An earlier variation on the logo, used by opponents of the Bondi Beach volleyball stadium in their 1999 newspaper the *Bondi Guardian*, converted the boomerang and dots into a female volleyball player and ball, but this version escaped Olympic copyright police detection because it was not distributed electronically.)

Unolympics.com fought back with humor—and won. Its spokespeople argued that the resemblance to the official Sydney 2000 site was "purely intentional." "We wanted to build a site that was visually unattractive and very difficult to navigate. The Sydney 2000 site was an inspiration," they claimed (Unolympics.com, 2000). They went on to explain their symbolism, as well as the obvious differences between these images and the official logo and site, which "anyone with half a brain" could see. Within two days, the IOC lawyers had withdrawn their threat.

An article in the *Guardian* (UK) in September was critical of the IOC's "obsessive suppression" of companies that were not official Olympic sponsors. Barkham reported that twenty Internet sites were ordered to remove audio and video clips, and, according to this account, even the "reputable" *Herald* website was told not to publish sound from interviews recorded inside the official press area (Barkham, 2000b).

ANOTHER KIND OF RESISTANCE: HUMOR AND SATIRE

By the end of September 2000, thanks to television and the Internet, what has developed as a distinctly Australian sense of humor (i.e., among the Anglo-Celtic majority) had become at least more familiar to the rest of the world—although not necessarily better understood by anyone outside the country. Many aspects of Australian humor and satire, whether in the entertainment industry or everyday interaction, follow the British rather than the American model. Irreverence, cynicism, and unrestrained language are essential components, along with the "larrikin" (rowdy) and antihierarchical elements that challenge authority, ridicule officiousness and obsequiousness, and cut "tall poppies" down to size.

Frontline and *The Games*: Reality Television

Two popular television shows of the 1990s—*Frontline* and *The Games*—exemplified the Australian approach to satire. *Frontline*, which was later aired in Canada with the title *Breaking News*, was first produced in 1994. It showed, without apology, the manipulation and distortion of news stories by a (fictional) television news and public affairs program. In this moral abyss, any and all deceptions were justified in the ratings war, and, as the (real) scriptwriting team explained, "Whenever we thought our ideas for *Frontline* plots might be a little far-fetched, we would meet someone in the industry who convinced us we had not, in fact, gone far enough" (Cilauro et al., 1995, vii). The "checkbook journalism" that they satirized in 1995 was reflected in real life in 2000 when the whistle was finally blown on right-wing radio talk show hosts' "cash for comment" practices, which were subsequently investigated by the Australian Broadcasting Authority.

The Games shared a similar history of life imitating art. This series of "sandpaper-dry satire" started in 1998–1999 on the Australian Broadcasting Commission (ABC), and by May 2000 was available to American and Canadian television viewers in over fifteen cities. According to an inside source, SOCOG staff initially joked that the show's plots were not as outrageous as the daily dramas within the organization; or, as a Herald journalist put it, the Games team was "struggling to rival the real-life absurdity of our Olympic preparations." And, according to its producer, Mark Ruse, "The beauty of this series is that real events are our promos. Reality is our publicity" (Ruse quoted in Enker, 2000, 5).

As the series developed a sharper edge, it was rumored that scriptwriters were getting ideas directly from Olympic insiders. By the 1999 season, some of the plots were foreshadowing real events, and by 2000, Olympic industry figures like Kevan Gosper were inadvertently providing lines that The Games team simply borrowed verbatim. In much the same way as the executive producer of the real public affairs program Sixty Minutes mildly complained that their Tuesday morning news conferences were "starting to sound like last night's Frontline" (Cilauro et al., 1995, 11), Olympic organizers' public statements were increasingly difficult to distinguish from actor-writer John Clarke's fictitious ones—that is, when he wasn't actually quoting Olympic industry personalities, whose pronouncements provided ample material for satire. Except for the characters who occasionally spoke as the voice of conscience, Sydney's Olympic officials were usually portrayed as cynical pragmatists.

Topics on The Games included budget shortfalls, control and manipulation of the mass media, the privatization of publicly funded sport facilities, dodgy sponsorships, visiting IOC members' sexual proclivities, and cover-ups of Olympic organizers' mismanagement and general gaffes. The discovery, in April 2000, that SOCOG's "souvenir" tickets were too big for the turnstiles provided Clarke's character with a great line. Defending the oversize tickets, he pointed out that they were the right size—it was the turnstile machine that was too small. SOCOG's defense was almost as funny: they claimed that "souvenir" tickets were meant to be kept, not to be put through the machine. And the popular episode titled "The 100 Meters Track"—which focused on the problem of the stadium's running track measuring only "approximately" 100m—had a real life counterpart in 2000 when it was reported that a triathlon route in Western Australia was somewhat shorter than the required length.

Clarke provided helpful Olympic advice in a *Herald* sidebar called "Make Syd-e-nee a Winner" (2000). The first tip was prompted by a proposed ban (later modified as a result of community opposition) on bringing food into Olympic venues and thereby threatening McDonalds's monopoly: "If attending Olympic events, visitors should be advised to eat before leaving home." The second suggestion advised locals to conceal the fact that Sydney suffered chronic traffic congestion: "If you are with a visitor in a traffic jam in Sydney, say: 'This is very unusual—a truck must have tipped over.'"

It was difficult to find any Australian viewer who did not praise *The Games* as excellent satire—one critic termed it "the most brilliant and biting piece of postmodern satire Australian television is ever likely to see" (Manne, 2000a)—and this reputation was well deserved. However, in analyzing humor, it is important to consider the extent to which persuading an audience to laugh at a serious social issue actually dilutes its impact, thereby making it more palatable and less threatening. Indeed, this is a key dimension of what many see as a distinctively Australian sense of humor: any topic, no matter how serious, is fair game for humor. (I was once told that I didn't understand "the Australian sense of humor"—by someone who didn't realize I was Australian—when I expressed outrage that the moderator of a panel discussion, based on the television "hypothetical" format, at a women's sport conference viewed anorexia as an amusing and entertaining topic.)

The reported enjoyment that Olympic insiders derived from the series is interesting, since a genuinely effective political satire should cause defensiveness, even outrage, on the part of those being lampooned. It is clearly not unAustralian to laugh at dishonesty and incompetence within the Olympic industry. On the contrary, it is quite in character for "real" Australians to laugh at themselves, and quite in keeping with the larrikin element to cut officious and self-important individuals down to size. Therefore, despite the fact that *The Games* focused attention on many of the major controversies in which Olympic organizers were embroiled in the late 1990s, the series evoked amusement and admiration rather than community outrage and political action. One of its very few critics, Friends of the Earth policy officer and former Waverley councillor Tom McLoughlin (2000), called the show a "satirical TV sitcom" and not "serious political comment."

In the same irreverent vein, as part of Channel 7's twenty-four-hour Olympic coverage in September 2000, a nightly program titled *The Dream* mocked Olympic personalities and sports. Olympic organizers were unamused, however, when the program's (anti)mascot, Fatso the Fat-arsed Wombat, proved more popular than the official souvenirs.

Street Theater and Mock Olympics

The idea of a mock Olympics was a popular community group response, aimed at drawing public attention to social issues while making fun of "serious" Olympic rituals and events. While OCA was having a meeting on housing in June 1998, Rentwatchers performed a "Housing Medals Ceremony" in Sydney's business district. The bronze medal was awarded to landlords for "opportunism and self-gain," the silver to real estate agents for "ingenuity and greed" and the gold to developers for "world record profits in these hard times." Tenants received the Wooden Spoon award for coming last, and the Zero Tolerance Award went to "The Capsicum Spray for the Homeless" (Olympics, 1998). Again in September 1999, while Olympic organizers were holding one-year-to-go celebrations at Darling Harbor, Rentwatchers held a medal ceremony for the "Greed, Grief and Gain Olympics" and then unfurled a banner from the overpass above the performance site bearing the slogan, Olympic Dream—Tenants' *Knight*mare (Protesters shake Olympic celebrations, 1999).

Shortly after the UNSW vice-chancellor's plans to purchase a corporate box became publicly known, students responded by organizing a mock Olympics. Academic staff came up with a list of mock events that reflected their frustration over months of unsuccessful bargaining and management's prioritizing of the box over adequate funding for staff salaries: "See How Far You Can Fall Performance Pay High Dive (No water in the pool—one try only, ladder back to the tower removed at the VC's discretion)"; "The 70 Hour Work Week Marathon—winner gets to do it again next week, so do the losers"; the "Swallow the Managerialist Hype Iron Person Race"; and the "Shaft a Recalcitrant Staff Member Javelin Throw" (UNSW Branch, 1999).

Cyber-humor: A New Subversive Activity

In 2000, some alternative websites were set up specifically to present Olympic critique and/or satire: for example, realgames.org.au, the unolympics.com, sillyolympics, and the olympisc.org. The Unolympics website carried a combination of satire, news items, and critical social commentary; a typical satirical piece lampooned Prime Minister Howard for his refusal to apologize to Indigenous people, claiming that he had a "problem area" near his mouth that made it impossible for him to say the word *sorry.*

A September newspaper item reported that residents of a small country town in Australia had declared it an "Olympics-Free Zone" and promised on-the-spot fines for any visitors who discussed Olympic sport or doping scandals (No fans here, 2000). The same kind of humor was evident in a September posting to the IMC—a mock news item that described how a man had been jailed for "telling friends that he wasn't all that interested in the forthcoming Games." He was sentenced to "two weeks of hard labor Olympic viewing" and "under NSW Olympic laws, he could also be forced to undergo a 'reeducation process.'" Issuing a statement from jail—one that sounded remarkably like a SOCOG press release—the man said that

> he passionately and fervently hopes that this is Australia's best ever Games . . . and that all Australians should get behind the Games and the truly great work of the organizing committee, and that his only wish was that Sydney could host the Games every four years, instead of just this once-in-a-lifetime opportunity. (Gould, 2000)

Even the official Sydney 2000 website olympics.com provided humor by inviting queries from overseas visitors planning to attend the Games. Apparently unconcerned about alienating potential tourists, the website posted some of the most humorous (or most idiotic) questions (and their country of origin), along with classic Australian put-downs: for example: "Will I be able to see kangaroos on the street? (USA). (Depends on how much beer you've consumed. . . .); Can I bring cutlery into Australia? (UK); (Why bother? Use your fingers like the rest of us. . . .)."

Humor in Print

The University of Technology Sydney Students' Association orientation handbook for 2000 provided further examples of satiric commentary on the Olympic industry. An article titled "How They're Sharing the Spirit in Three Easy Steps" began with a serious critique:

> The Olympics is not about sport. It is an unprecedented opportunity for the mass accumulation of private profit through a deliberate social and urban restructuring of the city as an economic tool. . . . The casting of the Olympics as a "spectacle" produces the necessary social relations/hysteria for Sydney to undergo an evident urban transformation. (UTS, 2000, 38)

It went on to provide a three-step "recipe": escalate rents, conduct urban cleansing, and patrol the streets. The text was accompanied by graphics and two words (*fuse* and *detonator*) that suggested the making of a mock bomb, with names of the "ingredients" blocked out. This satirical piece proved to be a legal problem, since material of this (allegedly) dangerous nature, when distributed on a large scale, had to be approved by the classification board. No doubt, business relationships between UTS and SOCOG played some part in prompting this overreaction to material that could in no way be read (even with a magnifying glass) as an actual bomb-making recipe.

The *Herald*'s front-page cartoons and weekly columns, particular in Saturday editions, provided a good supply of anti-Olympic satire. Richard Hinds's June 10 column attacked SOCOG for instructing Australians to forget the "small problems" ("incompetence, greed and campaigns of misinformation") and to get "all goose-pimply and feelgood about its jumped-up school sports carnival." He presented a list of demands for SOCOG to meet, including the requirement that "a selection of worthy community workers occupy Kevan Gosper's VIP seats at all Olympic events, while Kev gets one D-class ticket to the preliminaries of the Greco Roman wrestling" (Hinds, 2000).

No discussion of Australian satire would be complete without reference to Dame Edna Etheridge (actor Barry Humphries's alter ego). Dame Edna was on tour overseas at the time of the Olympics and could not participate in the opening or closing ceremonies as many Australians had hoped. In an *International Express* (U.K.) piece published in August 2000, she expressed disappointment that she wouldn't be able to run "a lap of honor around the stadium." But, she explained, "a pushy official chose his own ghastly daughter to perform the honors." She went on to describe the "uniquely Australian sports" that would be included in the Olympics, most notably "immigrant-bashing" where "a bronzed, muscular Australian surfer will pour scorn on some hapless immigrant" and "Pommie-baiting" where "a weedy Englishman wearing a string vest . . . will also be subjected to considerable ridicule" (Callan, 2000, 2).

THE CHALLENGES OF COALITION-BUILDING

The Olympic Impact Coalition (OIC) announced its formation early in February 2000. An eclectic group of over thirty community organizations—from the Salvation Army and the Red Cross, at one end of the political spectrum, to Reclaim the Streets and Copwatch NSW, at the other—supported the coalition's position statement. Other member groups included the NSW Greens, the Bankstown Bushland Society, Shelter NSW, NCOSS, and the National Union of Students. OIC demands included rights for Indigenous Australians, protection for the homeless and tenants, and the right to free movement—all rights guaranteed under UN conventions to which Australia was a signatory. On financial issues, it called for SOCOG and OCA to stay within their budgets (with the IOC and AOC reducing their share of revenues), and to offer concession tickets and disability access at all venues. And, for the post-Olympic period, its recommendations included an IOC charter of civil, social, and environmental principles, a post-Olympic host city report for Sydney, and the public release of the Sydney Olympics contracts, management, pricing, and financing arrangements.

Among the first OIC initiatives was a week-long series of protests targeting the February visit to Sydney of the IOC coordination team, which included President Samaranch, Vice President Richard Pound, Coordination Commissioner Jacques Rogge, and Director-General Francois Carrard. Events included a protest calling for housing justice that greeted the IOC at Sydney Airport, a vigil outside IOC members' hotel, and a meeting with members of the IOC team. Their most widely publicized activity was a demonstration held outside SOCOG headquarters on February 16, with speakers representing tenants, social services, students, and others.

Members of Reclaim the Streets wearing orange boiler suits, balaclavas, and gorilla masks received more media attention than some of the speakers, an outcome that provoked extensive criticism. However, it was Reclaim the Streets's tactics, rather than the media coverage, that came under fire. One of the speakers, Green Party member Ian Cohen, issued a public rebuke to the masked protesters. Unfortunately, Cohen was not the only person on the political left to find the masks problematic. Over the next few months, when I was introducing myself as a member of OIC in order to invite representatives from environmental, Aboriginal, and other community groups to the May 14 OIC planning day, I often received a rather negative reception, along with the comment, "Oh, the group with the gorilla masks." My standard response was to explain that the coalition represented a wide range of political positions, and that the street theater approach was just one of many.

Even the radical U.S.-based Direct Action Network considered bandannas and masks to be inappropriate protest attire, on the grounds that they intimidated the public (Brown, 2000). However, protesters in the United States were increasingly wearing face-covering to prevent police from filming them for identification purposes; conversely, police at mass protests were alleged to have removed their badges for the same reasons—to avoid being identified (Barrett, 2000). Interestingly, in a different Sydney context, a man wearing a full-body gorilla suit—"Kevin Kong"—to advertise the *Sun-Herald*-sponsored City to Surf Run in July 2000 was not accused of intimidating or inappropriate behavior.

In February 2000, shortly after the OIC had announced its presence and platform, City Central police inspector David Darcy, a protest liaison person, expressed his views on the OIC's planned actions, specifically their intentions not to communicate with the police, in a letter to Green Party member Lee Rhiannon: "silence is a form of violence. Even if the intentions of the group are non-violent, the environment is more unpredictable and the potential for negative, unintended outcomes, be they initiated by police or activists, is raised significantly" (Darcy cited in Bacon, 2000)

Rhiannon and others viewed Darcy's "silence is violence" statement as a veiled threat against citizens who had "a legitimate right to protest." Darcy did, however, express concern that some police commanders lacked experience in dealing with nonviolent activists and needed training in negotiation roles, a task that he was prepared to take on. Groups such as PIAC had been meeting with Darcy and others from the police service to discuss police training and the discretionary powers of nonpolice personnel.

In light of Police Commissioner Ryan's reported crackdown on officers who leaked unflattering stories to the media, Darcy's whistle-blowing about alleged inadequacies in police training may have been unwise. Indeed, by June, despite continued coverage of these issues in the mass media, Darcy told organizers of the Sydney University Institute of Criminology's panel on Olympic security that he was not allowed to speak (even though he had originally agreed to do so) because it was inappropriate to talk publicly about security. However, Darcy continued to liaise with protest groups in what some viewed as the "velvet glove" approach adopted by police in the city that was soon to be the focus of world media attention. He engaged in extensive conversations with activists, gave out his mobile phone number, and by September was even participating in IMC online discussions— purportedly in a proactive attempt to avoid further confrontations between police and protesters.

On February 10, just before the arrival of the IOC coordination team, Olympic Security Command Center head Paul McKinnon revealed that the IOC's week-long visit would be used as a security "test event" for the Olympics, with undercover police and special uniformed response groups keeping "a close and intense watch" on anti-Olympic lobby groups (Kennedy & Connolly, 2000). Since the OIC did not plan to ask permission to protest, it is not surprising that there were police complaints about the lack of communication—which probably put a damper on their "test event" planning.

By that time, members of Sydney community groups mobilizing around Olympic issues were voicing concerns about phone taps, surveillance, and infiltration of meetings and workplaces by intelligence agents. In reality, most of the community groups' activities did not require sophisticated spying methods. Although they did not always go through the often futile process of applying for police permits, meetings and rallies were widely advertised, held in public venues, and open to all comers, and the mass media were informed of upcoming events such as the planned protests against the Bondi beach volleyball stadium, to be discussed in chapter 8.

On February 15, three OIC representatives—Greens MLA Rhiannon, NCOSS director Gary Moore, and Shelter NSW executive director Rod

Plant met with Carrard to discuss their concerns about the negative social impacts. Carrard was given a copy of the Shelter NSW report on Olympic-related impacts on housing and homelessness, *Ready, Set, Go*, before the meeting, and came well prepared to discuss substantive issues. One outcome was his assurance that he would speak with the premier and monitor the situation when the committee visited Sydney again in June. Although OIC representatives were heartened by the official response, the irony of the situation was obvious: two leaders of social service organizations and an elected representative were asking the IOC to advocate on behalf of disadvantaged people to the premier, despite the fact that the premier himself was a democratically elected representative and therefore someone who should be both accessible and accountable to his constituents.

On March 1, PIAC, represented by its Olympic spokesperson Amanda Cornwall, together with John North, president of the NSW Law Society, Kevin O'Rourke, Council for Civil Liberties, Lyall Munro, Metro Aboriginal Lands Council, and others, held a media briefing to call for a repeal of Olympic public order legislation. At that time, it was still possible for a disallowance motion to stop passage of the *Sydney Harbor Foreshore Authority Act*. North warned that new laws could increase the likelihood of violent Aboriginal protests by making protest more difficult and giving excessive power to "the wrong people"—people with minimal training authorized by OCA. On April 5, Greens MLA Ian Cohen moved the disallowance motion in an eloquent and thorough documentation of existing police powers and public order offenses, as well as evidence of the discriminatory implementation of such regulations to date, but the motion was not passed.

OIC/AOA Activities: May to September

OIC organized a one-day planning meeting of its member groups and other interested parties on May 14, 2000. Speakers representing Indigenous, environmental, global justice, antipoverty, housing advocacy, human rights, and other groups gave brief overviews of their platforms and planned Olympic-related activities; a detailed protest time line was then developed and circulated to all participants, with dozens of events listed up to the end of September. Discussion then focused on mass protests to be mounted during the Olympics, including the rather ambitious plan of one protest per day. The biggest protest was planned for the opening day, September 15, in support of Indigenous rights and social justice issues. At this meeting, various anti-Olympic and Olympic watchdog organizations agreed to form a new coalition to replace OIC: the Anti-Olympic Alliance.

On June 10, the first day of the state ALP conference, AOA and their supporters held a demonstration against Olympic-related legislation at

Sydney Town Hall Square, demanding that politicians repeal all Olympic laws, ban capsicum spray, and remove arbitrary move on powers for police. Among the banners was one expressing the view that the Olympic Games itself was "annoying and inconvenient"—in other words, the same (prohibited) behavior named in Olympic-related public order legislation.

The issue of "inconvenient" behavior is worth examining. Most court activities were to be suspended for the duration of the Olympics, as were the normal business operations of most CBD institutions, because of street closures, Olympic live site events, and tourist crowds. The full deployment of police officers on Olympic-related duties meant that police witnesses would not be available for court hearings, district and supreme courts were closed, local courts were open, and new or urgent cases and those involving foreign nationals would be heard. Even normal hospital functions were curtailed, with elective surgery suspended for two weeks to allow for Olympic-related emergencies. The Sydney Stock Exchange, however, was one of the few to carry on business as usual, the rationale being that it would be inconvenient and confusing for international stock exchanges if Sydney were to close down for two weeks. While the capitalist imperative dictated stock exchange timetables, the continued delivery of normal hospital and community services was obviously lower down the list of Olympic organizers' and state officials' priorities.

In July and August, Justice Action and the Australian Cannabis Law Reform Movement organized the Freedom Riders, a group that traveled to NSW maximum security prisons to draw public attention to the failure of drug prohibition policies, and the 8 percent rise in the NSW prison population in the last year. Justice Action, also an AOA member organization, called for a pre-Olympics amnesty for "prisoners of the drug war." The Freedom Ride planned to arrive in Sydney just before the Games for the Sydney 2000 Hemp Olympix. On Monday September 11, a Reclaim the Streets rally assembled at Victoria Park and proceeded to the Town Hall, accompanied by "a large contingent of police including the 'cavalry'" as one participant described it. After dancing and partying there, they returned to the park to join in the Hemp Olympix, which included two gold medal events: the speed roll and the art roll, all using legal herbal products (Hollywell, 2000).

During the torch relay through the north coast of NSW, two "assaults" on the torch were made within two days. On August 24, a teenager sprayed the torch with a fire extinguisher, and the next day, a teenager tried to grab it, was caught and taken into custody (Teenager, 2000). In Canberra, several young men standing on a rooftop pulled down their pants as the torch passed by. A different kind of torch-related incident took place the next week when it passed through Liverpool, southwest of Sydney. With the entire complement from the Liverpool police station on duty for the torch relay, a summons could not be served on a wife-beater due to lack of staff (Jewell, 2000b).

OLYMPIC SPONSOR NIKE: JUST DO IT BADLY

The sporting goods transnational corporation, Nike, has important Olympic industry links on a number of fronts. In relation to the Sydney Olympics, it was a major sponsor, while, throughout Australia, it was an employer of about three hundred thousand grossly exploited outworkers (homeworkers).

International protests targeting labor practices in Nike's Asian sporting goods factories are well-known and extensively documented, and the Nike transnational advocacy network has been called "one of the most vigorous international collective actions of the past decade" (Sage, 1999, 207). Like other corporations that exported work to Third World countries in order to maximize profit, Nike benefited from the cheap labor, nonunionized workforce (predominantly women and children), minimal safety and environmental standards, repressive political climates, and favorable tax breaks available in Asian countries.

Throughout the 1990s, Nike was arguably one of the most scrutinized companies of its kind, with academic, religious, labor, human rights, and development organizations producing over sixteen major reports into length of work week, wages (in relation to cost of living), sexual harassment, corporal punishment, and other human rights abuses. The company was also the topic of hundreds of news articles and opinion pieces, mostly critical (Klein, 2000). By 1998, as a result of the extensive advocacy campaigns, Nike agreed to raise the minimum age of workers and to improve working conditions; at the same time, it continued to put a lot of money into image-enhancing public relations campaigns.

The television satire, *The Games,* tackled Nike (which of course remained unnamed, but readily identifiable) in its 1998 series. In one of its most biting critiques of a commercial sponsor, John Clarke complained about "a billboard advertising an athletic shoe that tells me there's no second prize." When Bryan Dawe, his second-in-command, protested, calling the message "inspirational," John let fly,

> It must be enormously inspirational to people who made the actual shoe, stuck in a sauna somewhere up in Asia getting about five cents a year . . . to the woman on the production line, Bryan, trying to work out whether her one remaining lung allows her sufficient aerobic capacity to rugby-tackle a rat at some stage of the day so that she can lug it home and feed her family. (*The Games,* 1998).

The Nike Image and Celebrity Athletes

Nike made extensive use of celebrity athletes, most notably Black basketball player Michael Jordan, to endorse its products, and its advertising routinely presented an image of a company interested in promoting racial/ ethnic and gender equality. But as Varda Burstyn (1999, 207) explained in her incisive analysis of sport and masculinity, by marketing the Black celebrity athlete as "corporate culture hero," Nike helped to develop a "market morality" with narcissistic, consumerist values that eroded a sense of community and solidarity, particularly in Black communities in the United States. The consumerist impact was particularly obvious—not just in the United States but globally—among children and adolescents, whose ideas of status and popularity were powerfully shaped by brand-name clothing.

Furthering its image as woman-friendly, Nike entered into a two-year partnership with the Canadian Association for the Advancement of Women and Sport (CAAWS) in 1999 to promote girls' sporting participation; one of its initiatives, as advertised on a CAAWS flyer distributed in 2000, involved grants of $100–$200 weekly for two years to female athletes, coaches, officials, and organizations. The chasm between Nike's public relations efforts to promote female sporting participation and empowerment in Canada, the United States and Australia, on the one hand, and the everyday experiences of the disempowered, sexually harassed, and abused female workers in Asia, on the other, provided ample evidence of the company's hypocrisy (Cole & Hribar, 1995; McKay, 1995). And on the issue of money, the $.16 per hour *wages* (about $13.00 per week) that Nike paid its factory workers in China to support themselves and their families (Klein, 2000, 474) stands in stark contrast to the $100.00 *grant* paid to a Canadian girl or woman to "help make their sporting dreams come true," in the words of the CAAWS flyer.

When challenged about this "partnership" by two Bread Not Circuses members (Jan Borowy and I), CAAWS justified their position and forwarded Nike's Code of Conduct, which, it claimed, had satisfied any concerns they had about Nike's labor practices. But, as Naomi Klein explains in her indictment of Nike and other multinationals, these codes of conduct were not legally enforceable; they were drafted in response to embarrassing media investigations by public relations companies in the United States, rather than in cooperation with local factory managers representing employees' demands and needs (Klein, 2000, 430).

With the Olympics coming to Sydney in 2000, Nike extended its advertising scope to Australian celebrity athletes. A controversial television advertisement aired in Australia in June 2000 featured twenty athletes, most of whom had contracts with Nike, saying they were "sorry" for a number of small, presumably amusing, shortcomings (on the grounds that they were in training). Unlike all the other athletes in the ad, Aboriginal runner Cathy Freeman says "Can I get back to you later?" As *Herald* journalist Louise Evans (2000) explained, Nike, like Benetton, was using "sensitive social issues"—the stolen generation of Aboriginal children and the national "sorry" campaign—to generate its sales pitch. With its over-use of the highly emotive word *sorry* in these trivial contexts, the ad was justifiably viewed as "distasteful," insensitive, and offensive by many Indigenous and non-Indigenous Australians, who unsuccessfully called for it to be withdrawn. Predictably but unconvincingly, a Nike spokeswoman was reported to have stated that the ad had "nothing to do whatsoever with reconciliation" (Magnay & Hornery, 2000). Indeed!

Nike Protest in Australia

Nike's Australian operations were less widely known internationally. Unlike their counterparts in Asian factories, the most exploited Australian workers in the textile, clothing, and footwear industries were home-based outworkers, estimated at over 300,000—that is, 15 outworkers to every one factory worker. In order to make a living wage, these workers, helped by their spouses and children, worked 14–18 hours a day, 7 days a week (Fairwear, 2000a). The Nike Code of Conduct maximum of a 60-hour workweek in its overseas factories (or lower to comply with local limits), as well as provisions for overtime and days off, did not apply to Australian outworkers. With Olympic rhetoric celebrating Sydney 2000 as a festival of the world's youth, the exploitation of young outworkers (and their parents) by an Olympic sponsor was yet another example of blatant Olympic industry hypocrisy.

The Australian Nike activist group Fairwear, launched in 1996, used lobbying, letter-writing, consumer awareness campaigns, and protest actions targeting Nike retailers to draw public attention to Nike's labor practices domestically as well as internationally. In April 2000, Fairwear and the Textile, Clothing and Footwear Union of Australia (TCFUA) launched an eight-week "Nike—Slavery Just Stop It" campaign to end the exploitation of Nike outworkers in Australia and to pressure Nike to sign the TCFUA Australian Homeworkers' Code of Practice. The code set out criteria for participating retailers and manufacturers, the latter including fair pay rates for homeworkers, full documentation of work and income, and minimum and maximum workloads (Fairwear, 2000b).

On June 6, for the first time in its history, Nike appeared in court, charged by TCFUA with exploitative labor practices. To mark the event, Fairwear organized protests outside the Melbourne court and Sydney's downtown Nike shop. Nike subsequently admitted breaching three sections of the Clothing Trades award, including failure to provide TCFUA with a list of subcontractors and other workers so that their wages and conditions could be monitored. With Nike's 1998 Annual Report listing revenues of $US9.6b, the fine of $15,000 constituted little more than a moral victory for workers (Sage, 1999). June was also a bad month for Nike's cyber-advertising, when hackers allegedly diverted visitors from the Nike website to the antiglobalization s11.org (Potter, 2000).

Fairwear correctly viewed the Olympics as one of the best opportunities available to draw world media attention to Nike's continued record of human rights abuses domestically and internationally; its September 2000 campaign will be discussed in detail in chapter 9.

CONCLUSION

AOA member Vicki Sentas (2000) neatly summarized anti-Olympic activism in the UTS student paper, *Vertigo:* "What brings these groups together under a common umbrella . . . is that the Olympics is the cause and the effect of mass social and urban change and the shrinking of public space . . . there is an increase in social divisions, with the rich getting richer and the poor getting poorer" (Sentas quoted in Henschke, 2000, 26). On the same theme, an AOA announcement ended with the quip, "The Olympics: making the world safe for global capital."

Unfortunately, while the more radical Olympic watchdog groups made the links between the Olympic industry and the growing power of global corporations to subvert domestic labor and environmental standards for their own ends, other groups succumbed to the "Olympic spirit" rhetoric that posited a false distinction between what happens on the playing field or in the swimming pool—"Olympic sport"—and the organization and commercial support behind the bigger Olympic enterprise. Their often-stated position, "We're not against the Olympics, but. . . ." effectively served Olympic industry ends.

8

Bondi Beach Volleyball Stadium

The Battlers Lose the Beach

Bondi is arguably the most famous of Sydney's beaches, both locally and internationally—a fact that did not escape the notice of NBC's Olympic head, Dick Ebersol, on his 1996 visit to Sydney. At that time, according to many reports (e.g., M. Moore, 1999b), he insisted that Bondi should be the venue for beach volleyball, thereby setting in motion a series of events that culminated in the construction of a 10,000-seat, $20m temporary stadium on the sands of Bondi Beach in 2000.

Bondi's unique appeal was captured in the April 1999 editorial of the *Bondi Guardian,* a joint publication of Bondi Olympic Watch (BOW), an antistadium community group, and Green Games Watch 2000 (GGW), an environmental organization that monitored the Sydney 2000 Olympics:

> The OCA [Olympic Coordination Authority] is trying to capitalize on what most people familiar with Bondi Beach already recognize: that not only is the area significant in its heritage and environment, but that its iconic status represents an Australian ideal of public space and access. It is this very thing that the OCA is endeavoring to package and market to the media, but [it] sullies the icon by promoting the belief that any and all construction represent progress. (Editorial, 1999, 2).

In other words, OCA was attempting what Atlanta urban anthropologist Charles Rutheiser (1996) termed *imagineering:* that is, the social engineering and marketing processes used by corporate elites to commodify the image of a city (or a beach), often through the judicious use of slogans and symbols, in order to boost tourism and attract global capital.

In light of frequent accusations of NIMBYism (not in my backyard) leveled at the Waverley Council, where Bondi Beach is located, and at antistadium community groups, it is important to establish that Bondi was the site of more annual festivals and cultural and recreational events than any other NSW beach. It hosted the City to Surf Fun Run, Festival of the Winds (kite-flying), Pacific Festival, South American Festival and Sculpture by the Sea, and other events, all of which attracted over five hundred thousand people in 1998 (Pearce, 1999b). Many of these activities had to be rescheduled or canceled in 2000, at a time when, as the council, businesspeople, and residents pointed out, they would have been more than happy to organize such events to give Olympic visitors an authentic view of the beach and its culture—in the words of the mayor Paul Pearce, "a slice of Australia."

On the question of ball games, however, the council had consistently rejected applications for beach volleyball tournaments from 1992 until August 1997, when it first gave approval in principle to the OCA's beach volleyball proposal (Quinlan, 1999a). At that point in time, more than a year before various local, national, and international scandals had tarnished the Olympic brand name at home and abroad, the decision to use the beach for this purpose had originally generated little or no opposition.

Bondi: The Beach, The Park, and the Suburb

For many, Bondi's international reputation is richly deserved: the beach is a long stretch of yellow sand, framed by sandstone headlands, rolling breakers, and a wide promenade, with the adjoining beach pavilion characterized by a distinctive facade of archways. Throughout the twentieth century, Bondi has evolved as an icon of Australian beach culture. Ironically, it was this status that played a major part in its selection for Olympic beach volleyball, even though, as many opponents pointed out, there were other Sydney beaches, as well as parks or even a purpose-built venue at Homebush Bay, which would have served equally well. Moreover, many argued, it was already a major tourist attraction and needed no further advertising to put it on the world map.

For over ninety years, the Bondi surf life-saving club, established in the early 1900s, has provided a voluntary community service (like all such clubs in Australia) by patroling the beach and educating the public about safe surfing. And the heritage-listed seventy-year-old Bondi Pavilion, with its open-air theater, gallery, meeting rooms, and craft rooms, currently serves as an arts and cultural center for about forty community organizations—a particularly important function in a municipality that lacks a town hall or similar facility.

The park and beach comprise a 13.1 hectare area of Crown Reserve land designated for public recreation, with Waverley Council having managed the Bondi Park Reserve Trust since 1885. For most of this period, the area was accessible both geographically and socioeconomically; originally a working-class suburb, it was characterized as the home of the mythical "Bondi battler"—a resident (usually a man) who struggled against the odds to better himself economically.

Located only 7km from the CBD, the beach was served by the famous Bondi trams until the 1950s, when these were replaced by buses. In terms of accommodation, there were modest brick bungalows and semidetached houses, and affordable flats for rent, either for short-term vacationers or long-term tenants. Cheap fish and chip shops, snack bars, pubs and souvenir shops served local and tourist needs until their gradual replacement by the 1980s with more upscale cafés, boutiques, restaurants, and apartment buildings, as well as the occasional luxury hotel, one of which occupied a block of prime real estate overlooking the beach.

However, even in the new millennium, Bondi Beach and promenade continued to attract a diverse group of people, in terms of age, ethnic background, social class, body size, and fitness level—the last two factors particularly significant when contrasted with some of Sydney's other suburban beaches, which were by now dominated by a fashion-conscious, thin, and fit youth culture, including a sizable component of young British and European backpackers. Many of those opposed to the stadium made reference to the needs of a wide range of people, including elderly people, parents with babies, wheelchair users, in-line skaters, joggers, walkers, and tourists, who use the promenade and park every day of the year.

Beach Volleyball: The Sporting Spectacle

When beach volleyball made its debut as an Olympic event in Atlanta in 1996, sixteen hundred tonnes of sand were trucked in and poured over a park to create volleyball courts that were some distance from the nearest beach. The success of this type of venue demonstrated that there was indeed a viable alternative to the Sydney 2000 plan, which subjected an ocean beach to possible environmental damage, as well as the negative social, cultural, and economic impacts resulting from the construction of a 10,000-seat temporary stadium, a 400-seat competition court, and five warm-up courts. This event was only granted Olympic status in 1993, and was therefore a late addition to the Atlanta 1996 Games. No beach volleyball venue was identified in the original Sydney bid materials; more importantly, the bid's twenty-three-page environmental guidelines, although extensive by the standards of the time, failed to address the complex issues that would inevitably arise if a beach were chosen for the event.

The 1997 agreement between OCA and Waverley Council was signed in the absence of detailed sketches or site plans to show its exact dimensions and location. There were conflicting reports about the proposed capacity: from 1,500 seats to the eventual number of 15,000. Initial estimates and discussions led Waverley mayor Paul Pearce and others to believe that the structure would be in place for only three months, and that no seating would be constructed around the secondary court (M. Evans, 1999b; M. Moore, 1999b; Pearce, 1999d).

An early sign of trouble appeared in April 1998, when a brief *Herald* news item mentioned that the powerful International Volleyball Federation (FIVB) president had expressed his desire—in other words, insisted—that the stadium should be located directly in front of the Bondi Pavilion, rather than the existing plan to position it toward the south end of the beach, well away from the heritage-listed building. Equally significant, the article noted FIVB's plans to raise the sport's profile internationally, a goal that was later achieved, in part, by the controversial decision to impose *maximum* measurements for the form-fitting uniforms to be worn by female players: two-piece outfits no more than 6cm wide at the hips, and one-piece outfits with an open back and upper chest. Typical of the sexual double standard, men were not made to wear form-fitting clothing—although maximum lengths were specified for their shorts—and a proposal to have men play topless was rejected because sponsors did not want to lose valuable advertising space on men's tank tops (Armstrong, 2000; Cockerill, 1998).

Not surprisingly, many Bondi stadium opponents could not resist critiquing beach volleyball as an Olympic sport, as well as OCA's selection of Bondi Beach as an Olympic venue. Some correctly noted the sexploitation of female players' bodies, as exemplified by the new uniform requirements, while others viewed it as an American import that only achieved Olympic status because Atlanta had hosted the 1996 Games. It was also argued that international television cameras would focus on the sport (or, in a variation of this, on the women) rather than on the beach; therefore, one could probably hold the event in a parking lot without loss of television viewership.

In hindsight, it is clear that, while democracy suffered a serious blow, FIVB's and NBC's purposes were optimally served by the selection of Bondi as the beach volleyball site. Although it was true, as the *Bondi Guardian* pointed out in 1999, that this was "not exactly a flagship Olympic sport," by the end of the Olympics, the "Bondi = beach volleyball babes" equation was firmly entrenched in Canadian and American viewers' minds, thanks to NBC's and CBC's extensive film coverage and commentary, which focused not only on the players, but also on the beach, harbor, and coastline. And, unlike other lower-profile Olympic events, there were beach volleyball events on ten out of the fifteen days of Olympic competition.

Struggles over Public Land in Waverley

In 1998, as stadium plans were being developed behind-the-scenes, Bondi residents and Waverley Council were occupied in a struggle against a different threat to public land: a proposed heavy rail link from Bondi Junction 3.2km to Bondi Beach, with a tunnel and station to be built on parkland. In an April 1998 media release, Mayor Pearce claimed that the Rail Access Corporation had deliberately misled local residents about the council's alleged agreement to the proposal, which "would lead to massive disruption and alienation of the Bondi Beach park." Furthermore, the council demanded a full assessment that examined "the genuine environmental, social, economic and transport implications . . . rather than just thinking of the financial returns for the Lend Lease/Macquarie Bank consortium" (Pearce, 1998a). With widespread resident opposition and the emerging volleyball stadium debate, the environmental impact statement experienced three major delays (Wainwright, 1999).

Since Lend Lease was one of the major developers at the Homebush Bay Olympic site, Bondi's successful resistance to the railway proposal struck an indirect blow to the Olympic industry, as well as symbolizing a victory of municipal over state government—although complicated by the fact that both the mayor and the government in power were Labor. But only a year later, Pearce and the council agreed to an Olympic project that would alienate 30 percent of public parkland for six months, and one that clearly bypassed "genuine" assessment of environmental, social, economic, and transport implications—namely, the beach volleyball stadium. Opponents feared that this decision would create a precedent to be exploited by the NSW government in future railway discussions.

The Mayor and the Stadium

Pearce played a prominent role in the stadium debates, with his actions culminating in what most antistadium protesters saw as an obvious "backflip." In October 1998, before there was much public scrutiny of the proposal, his "Olympic Update" report to the council presented Waverley's involvement in three Olympic events—beach volleyball, road cycling, and Paralympic Road cycling—as a *fait accompli*. He did note, however, that planning control for all events rested, not with the council, but with a group comprising representatives from the council, the Sydney Organizing Committee for the Olympic Games (SOCOG), and OCA (Pearce, 1998b).

In February 1999, a few months after the formation of BOW, Pearce stated publicly that no venue agreements between OCA and the council would be signed until residents had the chance to discuss the contents and air their concerns at a public meeting (Pearce, 1999a). In March, and again

(a) is of minimal environmental impact, and

(b) is consistent with an operational plan, and

(c) is removed and the building or land reinstated to its previous use and condition or to a better condition by 30 June 2001, or such later date as agreed by the Director-General of the Department of Urban Affairs and Planning.

(d) Minor development which is of minimal environmental impact and is (or is part of) an Olympic Games project, an OCA project. . . . (SEPP 38, Schedule 1)

These less-than-stringent conditions for exemption were easily met by the proposed stadium, as long as its environmental impact could be classified as "minimal." It was still necessary for OCA to complete a Statement of Environmental Effects (SEE), but approval was fast-tracked thanks to the SEPP amendment.

OCA's consultation process included a meeting with the Bondi and District Chamber of Commerce, a group that might have been expected to support the project. Its members, however, were unconvinced by predictions of increased business opportunities during the Olympics, and a resolution was passed to take "the strongest possible action to protect its membership from the inevitable disruption to their businesses both in the immediate area and traffic routes to and from the venue" (Bondi brush-off, 1999). Members argued that any small economic benefit would not compensate for nine months of losses caused by construction and facility closures.

Resistance to the Olympic Juggernaut

Bondi Olympic Watch formed the first organized opposition to the stadium in late 1998, when concerned residents began meeting weekly to discuss the issues and to develop lobbying and public awareness strategies. Meetings were usually attended by up to fifty people from across the left's political spectrum: Greens, environmentalists, even paid-up Labor Party members. The group faced the usual obstacles arising from coalition and consensus politics, particularly in relation to strategies: for example, while liberals wanted to mount legal challenges, anarchists planned civil disobedience. The campaign had considerable success in keeping public attention on the issue during 1999 and 2000, right up to the time when it was no longer possible to delay or stop the excavation of the beach and construction of the stadium.

BOW invited OCA to a public meeting in December to listen to their concerns. OCA's response was reported to have been "vague and noncommittal" and it declined to take part in the February 1999 community meeting (Caution, 1999). The Green Party was also alert to the potential problems, and in December 1998 Greens pressured OCA to release details of its plans, which revealed some of the obvious negative impacts on the community. Greens MLA Lee Rhiannon, who was also a Bondi resident, predicted that with one third of the beach inaccessible, local residents would be shut out, and local businesses would lose money. She also expressed concern that Waverley ratepayers might experience financial repercussions (Greens want Bondi, 1998). Significantly, these developments were taking place around the same time that the International Olympic Committee (IOC) was facing allegations of bribery and corruption in its host city selection process, while, closer to home, the actions of the Sydney bid committee were under extensive scrutiny. Moreover, the undue secrecy surrounding all SOCOG and OCA business had been attacked by *Herald* Olympic editor Matthew Moore only a few months before (M. Moore, 1998b).

On April 8, 1999, when OCA finally made public its draft SEE—the first such document with full details of the project—it evoked widespread community outrage. One of the requirements was the fencing off of 10 percent of the beach for construction from March 2000, and an additional 10 percent from August on, with the park behind the pavilion closed in May, and the pavilion, surf club, and areas of Park Drive, in June; normal operations would not resume until about November. The stadium would cover an area of sand about 60m x 90m, and about 300 steel piles 7m–11m in length were to be screwed into the sand to anchor the structure, which at some points was 16m high, dwarfing the adjacent two-story pavilion. Of particular concern, in light of major winter storms of the preceding three years, was the positioning of the stadium leaving a corridor of only 5m between the perimeter fence and the high tide mark. It was predicted that in heavy seas the beach would be cut in half by the stadium and fence, with serious implications for public safety and life-saving functions. The transport plan requiring seventy buses to bring crowds from Bondi Junction station was viewed as totally inadequate, given the configuration of roads near the beach and past experience with events of this size (e.g., City to Surf Run). In a related construction project, a test event planned for October 1999 would require a temporary stand to be constructed for three thousand spectators, with a beach closure for about six weeks.

A public meeting was called for Sunday April 18 to discuss the issues and develop strategies for resistance. BOW and Green Games Watch 2000 produced a joint publication, a four-page newspaper titled *Bondi Guardian,* which documented the serious flaws in OCA's plans for the Bondi stadium, as well as problems with the Bankstown criterium cycling track, the Ryde Aquatic Center, and the Rushcutters Bay marina. In addition to environmental, social, and cultural concerns, the publication identified OCA's blatant disregard for the needs of beach, promenade, and pavilion users for up to nine months in 2000. It was noted that OCA refused to post a bond against damages to the area, or to agree to a community legacy or compensation for pavilion users, despite a projected $16–$20m revenue from ticket sales, and an estimated $200m from the total $1.3b in TV rights (Kovner, 2000).

A feature of the original plan that caused the most community resentment was the proposed construction of a bridge from the stadium to the upper story of the pavilion, where an area would be refurbished to serve as the entertainment center and lounge for the "Olympic Family" and sponsors, so that VIPs would not have to negotiate any stairs. This would necessitate closing the pavilion to regular users as early as June 2000. In this postscandal era, special privileges for "Olympic Family" members were unlikely to be looked upon kindly. "The buggers can walk down" was one of the pithier recommendations heard at the April 18 meeting.

A major shortcoming of OCA's stadium project was its almost total failure to provide for genuine public consultation. The fact that there were only three copies of the very lengthy environmental impact document on public display in the municipality of Waverley (with a fourth copy 20km away at Homebush Bay), and only a two-week time frame available for public comment, reflected a glaringly inadequate process. As BOW member Peter Winkler pointed out, the proposed stadium and fenced-off area of 5.9 hectares was close to half the area of the beach and park, and not the deceptive 20 percent figure given in OCA's April newsletter (OCA, 1999).

OCA sent Stuart McCreery to the April meeting to face a crowd of about one thousand people, the vast majority of whom vehemently opposed the entire plan. For his part, McCreery answered most questions with equanimity, if not information, and his responses were consistently met with outright jeers, or worse. Asked about alternative sites under consideration, he consistently maintained, "There is no Plan B." His habit of addressing the audience as "You people. . . ." several times in the course of the meeting did little to challenge public perceptions of OCA staff as arrogant and indifferent to local community concerns.

The final outcome of the meeting was a notice of motion that read, "This meeting rejects outright the proposal to erect a stadium at Bondi Beach and to commandeer Bondi Beach and Park for the year 2000 Olympic beach volleyball event." It called on the council to vote against proceeding with the stadium. Most dramatically, the majority of those present indicated their willingness to begin a campaign of civil disobedience, which would include chaining themselves to fences and sitting in the path of bulldozers when the construction project began. Volunteers were signed up to distribute twenty thousand copies of the *Bondi Guardian* to local residents, and to join in future organizing efforts to block the stadium. The campaign to collect signatures on an antistadium petition to Parliament was revitalized, and twelve thousand people had signed by December 1999.

An independent study from the University of Sydney Coastal Studies Unit dated April 19—too late to support BOW's position at the public meeting—substantiated protesters' concerns about possible wave impact on the perimeter fence and revetments, and the resulting hazard for those walking along the beach (Short & Cowell, 1999). The report's public safety recommendations included setting up two temporary lifeguard stands, which were included as OCA responsibilities in the May 11 agreement. Procedures for managing pedestrian traffic along the fence and increasing beach monitoring and maintenance were also listed.

This report was one of the few official sources to recognize Aboriginal ownership, by noting that material brought to the surface during excavation may contain Aboriginal archaeological material, which, under NSW law, must be reported to the authorities. In his letter to the UN high commissioner for human rights, Aboriginal councillor Dominic WYkanak also drew attention to the ceremonial rock carvings overlooking the beach, and noted that Aboriginal shell middens had been uncovered during construction of Queen Elizabeth Drive (the main promenade) (WYkanak, 2000).

Different Suburb, Same Fight: Ryde Pool Action Group

In addition to the unifying influence of larger environmental organizations such as Greenpeace and GGW on Bondi residents' organizing, there was evidence of solidarity with other community organizations such as the Ryde Pool Action Group and the Rushcutters Bay group, both of which sent letters of support and representatives to BOW meetings. At that time, Ryde residents were facing some similar concerns to their Bondi counterparts, with their six-pool municipal swimming center—on land that had been specifically designated in 1954 as a public park or recreation area—slated for demolition to make way for a new Olympic water polo facility and a privately operated leisure center. As Ryde spokesperson Mark Burnside explained, "Reclassification of public land to allow for the water polo development to proceed leaves the community with an insidious long term legacy. It is the first step in the chronic, long-term alienation and commercialization of public land that must be stopped immediately" (Burnside quoted in GGW, 1998a)

The Ryde Pool Action Group engaged in a lengthy legal battle with Ryde Council over the construction of the new pools and leisure complex. It achieved one victory in April 1999, when the NSW Land and Environment Court found that it was in the public interest for the action group to call for an investigation of the council's procedures regarding "the removal of public land from council's control and delegation of its management and operation to the private operator" (*Ryde Pool Action Group Inc. vs. Ryde City Council,* 1999). The court therefore rejected Ryde Council's application requiring the action group to deposit about $40,000 as security for costs.

Residents were without a pool for almost two years, the new Ryde Aquatic Leisure Center only had three pools, and half of the new center was to be operated as a private club with yearly fees of about $1,600 per couple. The NSW legislation exempting Olympic construction from the usual approval processes was abused, in Ryde Pool Action Group's view, by the private operator, whose development application for "Olympic facilities" was speedily approved despite the fact that construction of the private club section of the new center would not be started until December 2000, that is, after the Olympics (Boccabella, 1999). Moreover, in typical OCA fashion, initial estimates of construction costs—$7.1m—increased to $24m in less than two years, largely because of SOCOG's requirement that the 51m pool be enclosed and the water filtration plant upgraded (Jamieson, 1999). And, in another manifestation of Olympic industry arrogance during the official opening of the water polo venue in April 2000, Michael Knight acknowledged that some politicians had been opposed: "there were some elements in the council and some in the community . . . so here you see that things that don't come easily are very worthwhile" (Knight quoted in M. Evans, 2000c).

The Olympic Industry Responds: "No Bully-Boy Tactics" at Bondi

Within a week, in a somewhat surprising move, Knight and SOCOG vice president John Coates both responded to the widely publicized outcomes of the April 18 protest meeting at the Bondi Pavilion by stating that they had no intention of forcing Bondi to host the event. Knight explained that the government's powers were "to ensure the safe staging of events" and that "bully-boy tactics" would not be used to secure the venue, while Coates acknowledged the "groundswell of opposition" and noted that compensation was a crucial factor in future negotiations (Beach volleyball, 1999; M. Moore, 1999c). As GGW's Brett Hoare explained, it appeared that OCA, if faced with an intolerable domestic political situation, was even prepared to say no to the IOC and NBC. At the same time, the scenario provided a convenient opportunity for SOCOG, having just cut $75m from its budget, to save money by choosing a cheaper alternative, and save face by appearing to be responsive to local community concerns. For example, the use of an existing sports field, such as Cronulla's rugby league venue, which was already equipped with grandstands and toilets, would only incur the cost of transporting sand.

BOW members continued their campaign: attending council meetings, gathering signatures, and consulting with lawyers about challenging the agreement. Lenny Kovner reported that, according to their legal advice, there was "a huge discrepancy" between the 1997 agreement-in-principle and OCA's final agreement that the council could have readily used to challenge the contract. However, he said, the mayor publicly hinted at a possible $4m penalty if the council tried to break the contract (Kovner, 2000).

Large numbers of protesters attended the May 11 council meeting, at which the council voted 7 to 5 in favor of the principles of agreement. Not coincidentally, OCA director-general David Richmond was waiting off-stage, ready to put his signature on the document. Kovner described how "it was close to riots" that night, with protesters achieving a minor victory by talking to television reporters themselves, while successfully disrupting a television interview that Richmond attempted to give outside the council.

Stadium opponents made a few small gains in the May 11 agreement. The unpopular "VIP bridge" was eliminated, and the construction start date was put forward two months, thereby considerably shortening the period that the beach and pavilion would be closed to the public in 2000, and the October 1999 test event was canceled so that there would be no closures in 1999. A new stadium design announced later that year called for 700 thinner and shorter screw piles instead of 300, a change that was said to reduce construction time and installation noise; there would also be a 6m reduction in the height of the roof (M. Evans, 1999e). The final design, however, was reported to be using only 320 screw piles, supporting 275 tonnes of prefabricated steel scaffolding (Magnay & Ho, 2000).

Another public meeting held at the pavilion on Sunday June 20 attracted about one thousand protesters. Winkler reiterated community concerns about the negative impacts on users of the promenade, pavilion, and beach, while Pearce repeated his decision to "moderate the impact" (Verghis, 1999). BOW found it difficult to maintain a presence on the beach over the winter and lost some momentum at that stage.

In September, with the council now comprising four Labor, three Greens, and four Liberal members after municipal elections, the Greens put forward a motion calling for rescission of the agreement with OCA. Although this motion failed, the majority voted in favor of Liberal councillor Sally Betts's motion to seek urgent legal advice about rescission.

Speaking to the Greens' motion, former councillor and local resident Tom McLoughlin claimed that the threat of councillors facing a hefty surcharge for misconduct if they broke contract was "a political and legal bluff" and a "threat to democracy" (McLoughlin, 1999). This was probably true, but his proposed counterclaim for damages against OCA for alleged misleading and incomplete information, including failure to exhibit all the relevant development application documents, would have been a futile exercise. After all, past history had shown that Olympic organizers were well practiced in skirting the normal requirements of planning, environmental, and freedom of information legislation.

An Olympic Legacy: True or False?

In all of these negotiations, OCA's and Pearce's understanding of the concept of a *legacy* appeared markedly different from that of the antistadium protesters. At the end of the day, the weight of evidence lay with the protest group's position: they would not be duped into believing that *compensation* constituted a legacy. Furthermore, OCA was "double-dipping" when it called the $1m spent on renovations—which it needed for its own purposes—a community benefit.

As Kovner explained, there were three essential items required by OCA at the outset to equip the pavilion for use by media, staff, and VIPs: new washrooms, an elevator, and a paint job. The public showers and toilets clearly needed upgrading, and since the pavilion was to be featured in international television coverage, painting was necessary. On the question of the elevator, Kovner believed that OCA needed it for VIPs, but conveniently presented it as a "legacy" for future pavilion users with disabilities. He estimated that the elevator would cost about $400,000, close to half the so-called legacy. Rewiring to increase the building's electronic facility for the international media was also on OCA's list, but Kovner claimed that regular pavilion users—pottery, craft, and drama classes—would not reap a great benefit from this. Repainting and rewiring had appeared in the original package that OCA representative McCreery discussed on April 18 and in OCA's *Waverley Update* publication (OCA, 1999). And, as Kovner pointed out, four years earlier the council had hired an architect to estimate the cost of a complete refurbishment of the pavilion, and $7m was the figure given at that time (Kovner, 2000).

The May 11 agreement devoted four pages to what it grandly called "Lasting Community Benefit." In addition to these items, it threw in a disabled access podium and ramp (but with a completion date of December 15, 2000, well after the Games were over), and highlighted the fact that the refurbished toilets would be accessible. Finally, it announced a social legacy of $30,000, which Pearce later promised to direct toward services for youth and homeless people (Pearce, 1999e). In real terms, however, this amount would have minimal impact in a municipality characterized by Olympic-related gentrification, increasing rents, evictions, and homelessness.

Predictably, the agreement focused on the financial and commercial issues arising from OCA's use of Waverley Council property. Both parties, it stated, were concerned with ensuring "that the corporate and commercial interests and statutory functions of Council and the interests of parties with a commercial interest in Bondi Pavilion . . . are protected. . . ." (OCA, 1999, part E). On the question of actual compensation, the pavilion's four commercial tenants were closed down for up to seventeen weeks and compensated accordingly, although the major restaurateur was given the catering contract for the Games. The council was compensated for commercial revenue shortfalls as a result of park, beach, and road closures. Since it was impossible to quantify negative social or cultural impacts, and difficult to measure long-term environmental damage, neither of these potential problem areas was addressed in the agreement.

The Fight on the Sand, May 2000

As the May 1 starting date for stadium construction neared, BOW gained its second wind. A surprise early morning move on April 1 mobilized protesters earlier than expected, when OCA brought in heavy machinery, accompanied by plainclothes police, to conduct a test drilling of the beach. BOW immediately set up an information phone line, and organized volunteers to watch the beach around-the-clock from a nearby apartment.

Events on Monday May 1 were short and dramatic: in an action organized by BOW and the Greens, about two hundred protesters gathered on the beach at 6:30 A.M. to await the 7:00 A.M. arrival of OCA construction workers. Faced with the potential embarrassment of international media coverage of a confrontation with protesters, OCA then delayed the start of construction until May 8.

Protesters assembled on the beach once again in the early morning of May 8, but by the end of the day, the Olympic Goliath had emerged victorious—not too surprisingly, in view of the three Black Hawk helicopters, two police launches, fifteen mounted police officers, and one hundred and fifty SWAT team police on foot, all poised to take on about one hundred and fifty men, women, and children who comprised the protest.

The action began when about twenty workers employed by OCA attempted to enclose the area of the beach in front of the pavilion with stakes and plastic ribbon, thereby designating the area for OCA-authorized access only within the meaning of the NSW *Inclosed Lands Protection Act 1901* (updated July 19, 1999). This act defined "inclosed land" as "any land, either public or private, inclosed or surrounded by any fence, wall or erection. . . ." and prohibited unauthorized entry. The key provision of this antiquated act, from the perspective of OCA and the police, was the following notice, subsequently posted on the perimeter fence:

> Any person who without lawful excuse enters into inclosed lands without consent of OCA or who remains on inclosed lands when requested by

OCA to leave, and while remaining on the land conducts himself or herself in an offensive manner will be committing an offence or a trespass and may be arrested. *(Inclosed Lands Protection Act, 1901).*

These behaviors incurred a potentially heavier penalty (up to twenty penalty units) than protesters' planned civil disobedience actions of sitting in the path of the earthmoving equipment. Undeterred, BOW members and supporters proceeded to pull out the stakes that marked the "inclosed land," and were quickly arrested. The first group—about thirty protesters—was detained for "breaching the peace," taken to Bondi Junction by paddy wagon, and released with instructions not to return to the beach. The protesters did, of course, return to the beach, and for the next several hours, as Kovner described it, there was a stalemate. Although small in number, protesters were "quite resilient" and dug themselves into the sand in front of the tractor. Memorable images of a small number of peaceful resisters sitting on the sand, and six buried up to their armpits, surrounded by dozens of police officers, appeared in the mass media as a vivid reminder of police and Olympic industry power (Peatling, 2000c; 21 arrested, 2000).

An effective sit-in, in Kovner's experience, would have required about fifteen hundred people, but even with the small BOW numbers, the tractor couldn't move, and for several hours media reports were presenting the protesters as the winners. In the afternoon edition of the usually rightwing *Daily Telegraph,* for example, the front-page story gave protesters' voices more space than police (Connolly, 2000). Protest leaders engaged in discussion with the workers, many of whom were young men working at their first job after a long stretch of unemployment. In a surprise move in the early afternoon, a union representative intervened to stop the driver of the bulldozer from continuing work because he was not covered by workers' compensation.

As Kovner pointed out, a "Protesters stop the stadium" story couldn't go to the evening news, and Michael Knight was believed to have been involved in the police decision to move in and make the twenty-one arrests, thereby ending the standoff. And so the day's story read the way OCA wanted: the protesters made their point, democracy was served, then they were arrested, and the stadium could proceed. Moreover, with OCA's huge media budget—contrasted with BOW's maximum bank balance of $400—the Olympic industry had a host of professional media people capable of controlling the timing of news releases and shaping the final story for the evening news (Kovner, 2000).

Police guarded the site overnight, and removed about fifty protesters who tried to block access to the site the next morning. A private security company subsequently took over twenty-four-hour guard duties, and the perimeter fence was highly illuminated every night to deter trespassers. An incident that typified the overzealous behavior of security guards occurred in May when busloads of senior citizens were arriving for a special seniors' music day at the pavilion. When the guard saw that one of the buses had temporarily stopped in a no parking zone (obviously because the seniors, many using walkers, could not be dropped off 100m away as directed), he gave the driver a $120 parking ticket. When a television crew covering the protest showed up to film the confrontation between the guard and pavilion staff, the guard retreated (Kovner, 2000).

A new problem emerged in the second week of May, as discolored liquid began seeping from the excavation site on the beach. The following Sunday, several hundred protesters entered the restricted area inside the plastic fence to assess the damage, but no arrests were made. On Monday, May 15, the Environmental Protection Agency (EPA) reported finding low level fecal coliform contamination—levels about 1/400 of coliforms in raw sewage (P. Pearce, 2000). Meanwhile, fifty construction workers were instructed to have hepatitis A shots, and OCA reported that work had been delayed by about a week (M. Evans, 2000d).

By late May, as many critics had predicted, heavy seas, strong winds, and higher-than-usual tides cut the beach in two, and seawater entered the site until workers built a sand levee and installed additional sandbags. Warning signs and even orange and red warning lights were erected so that beach users would not be trapped against the fence. By this time, many protesters were understandably upset and demoralized at the sight of the beautiful beach fenced off and torn up by heavy machinery—a feeling that I shared when I first I saw the construction site on May 27—and, for them, this particular battle was over.

The Media: Trivializing Dissent

With FIVB's stated interest in boosting the sport, the *Herald* made a number of attempts to generate interest in beach volleyball, or, rather, in female volleyball players, beginning with an October 1998 article subtitled "Can the 'Perv Factor' Fill the Stands at Bondi's Olympic Beach Volleyball Events?" The issue was whether the sport's sex appeal would attract sufficient ticket sales in Australia, where it had a relatively low profile; in Atlanta, seats had sold out nine months before the Games (L. Evans, 1998). A few months later, an article in the *Herald*'s sport section (Quinlan, 1999a) presented Volleyball Australia's (unconvincing) claim that this was "the 100 percent gender-perfect sport" simply because both sexes participated and officiated. Again, in May 1999, Heather Quinlan's article on medal hopes reported that players blamed antistadium protesters and Waverley Council for "eroding Australia's home-ground advantage"—in other words, for being unAustralian—by prohibiting any training or competition on the beach prior to the Olympics (1999b). And later in 1999, at the start of summer competition, another of Quinlan's articles (1999c) repeated the same refrain.

In April 1999, as details of the planned stadium came to light, newspapers and television stations provided extensive but not always unbiased coverage of the event. The right-wing *Daily Telegraph* carried a predictable editorial, titled "Throwing Sand in Our Faces" (1999), which accused protesters of "selfish and dangerous" plans that would jeopardize the financial success of the Games and cause international embarrassment for Australia—more unAustralian activities. The same paper, however, included a less partisan account in its news section (McDougall, 1999).

Although the *Herald's* coverage was generally comprehensive and balanced, some organizers were disappointed that its accounts failed to mention GGW2000 or the *Bondi Guardian* newspaper. Ten days before the April 1999 public meeting, the *Herald* had published a scathing editorial that accused the Waverley mayor of NIMBYism. Admitting "some inconvenience" during construction, the editorial concluded, in typical Olympic industry rhetoric, that the "small pain" is "worth the great gain of having a Games event at the superb location of Bondi Beach" (Nimbyism, 1999). Paul Pearce responded with a strongly worded letter to the editor on April 16 challenging the charges and listing some of the numerous public festivals and events hosted by the council on the beach every year (Pearce, 1999b). Debate on the *Herald's* letters page continued sporadically in the next few months, and again in 2000 when construction began. While *Herald* Olympic editor Matthew Moore and journalist Michael Evans provided balanced coverage, Louise Evans reverted to patronizing NIMBYism and "spoilsport" arguments in a July 1999 opinion piece, where she called Olympic excitement "life-defining" and proclaimed that "what the outraged residents of Bondi seem to forget is that the Olympics will be the biggest and most exhilarating event in their sad lives" (L. Evans, 1999).

Of the local community newspapers, the *Southern Courier* (South Sydney) carried a promotional piece—accompanied by the prerequisite images of female volleyball players' bodies—that appeared to be based largely on OCA news releases (Wilkinson, 1999). In contrast, the alternative publication *City Hub* published a critical cover story titled "Stopping the Olympic Juggernaut" following the April 18 meeting (Banham, 1999); the women in the cover illustration were wearing T-shirts and cycling shorts, and the "volleyball" was a ticking bomb embellished with the five Olympic rings. And, in May 2000, the *Eastern Suburbs Messenger* carried a relatively balanced account of the arrests, together with a graphic photo of peaceful protesters surround by armed police officers (21 arrested, 2000). Also in May, a short *Herald* news item, "Only Dealing in Fax" (2000) announced that many of the media people covering the protest had received a "mysterious" fax from another antistadium group, which went to some lengths to point out that it had no connection to the "militant" protest group Bondi Olympic Watch. Assuming this was not a hoax, it was certainly a counterproductive strategy to announce this rift to the mass media in Sydney, which by this time were largely unsupportive of the stadium opponents. In June, a *Herald* editorial titled "An Australian Olympic Flame" (2000), told "resisters" to "consider the bigger picture," including the restoration of the pavilion. "More important," it continued, "Bondi Beach's iconic status will be conveyed to hundreds of millions of people as the stunning pictures of the Olympic beach volleyball contests go out to the world."

In September 2000, when world media began covering the Olympic beach volleyball event, the preceding two years of community struggle were routinely trivialized or rendered invisible. In the Olympic bid city of Toronto, for example, the two major newspapers reduced the fight to whining and NIMBYism. A front-page *Globe and Mail* story titled "Surfboard Guerillas Fight Olympic Hoopla" (Cernetig, 2000) repeated an unidentified Sydney newspaper's view that protesters were "killjoys" and that their planned disruption—"flashing mirrors into the lenses of NBC cameras"—was "pathetic." While this article at least made an attempt to cover the debate, a *Toronto Star* sports journalist reduced the protest to a snide sound bite: "A few locals whinged about their precious patch of vanilla sand being disrupted and threatened to disrupt back" (C. Young, 2000). Another *Star* story asserted that the whole struggle evoked nothing more than a yawn now, and a *Washington Post* article cited in the *Globe* claimed (erroneously) that, although residents opposed the stadium, "now that it's here, most just smile and shrug" (Kesterton, 2000).

CONCLUSION

A September 26 *Herald* item confirmed stadium opponents' fears: FIVB was already working on plans to include the Bondi site, even without the stadium, in its 2001 world tour, although FIVB leaders said they would postpone seeking council approval until "things settle down" (K. Jackson, 2000). It is possible, however, that the power that international federations wield over Olympic host cities will be somewhat diminished in FIVB's future dealings with the politically mobilized Bondi residents.

The Bondi case study provides a classic example of the worst abuses of power on the part of the Olympic industry over a range of social, environmental, and Indigenous issues. Moreover, in hindsight, it appears that the FIVB, NBC, OCA, and some Waverley council members were determined not to be swayed by public opinion or protest, whatever the cost. As events unfolded, culminating in scenes of nonviolent protesters surrounded by police and military muscle, it was clear that democracy was the final victim in the Bondi stadium battle.

9

September 2000 in Melbourne and Sydney

Democracy at Risk

———=◦◇◦=———

There were three events of international significance in Australia during September 2000: the protests against the World Economic Forum, the Olympic Games, and the anti-Olympic protests. The links between the three events, and their relationship to the ongoing issue of reconciliation between Black and White Australians, will be examined in this chapter.

S11: Against Corporate Globalization

The World Economic Forum (WEF) held its Asia-Pacific Economic Summit at Melbourne's Crown Casino, on September 11-13, 2000. The timing was intentional: the eight hundred delegates were reminded that world media attention would be on Australia the week before the Olympics, and were encouraged to attend the Games after the summit. Conveniently, antiglobalization protesters could do the same—although their travel and accommodation would not be covered by expense accounts.

Within the WEF membership, it was not difficult to identify transnational corporations with a well-deserved reputation for environmental destruction, human rights infringements, inhumane labor standards, and other practices that threatened the welfare of individuals, communities, and natural environments: Nike, Coca-Cola, Monsanto, Rio Tinto Mining, Dupont, Western Mining, and Exxon-Mobil. Not coincidentally, many of these were also Olympic sponsors.

The WEF event was targeted by the S11 Alliance, a network of groups and individuals concerned about corporate power and globalization, whose goal was to close down the summit. At the same time, a program of forums, workshops, and networking opportunities was organized to help build the international antiglobalization movement. Like other international networks, organizers made extensive use of Internet communication, a practice which, according to a *Chicago Tribune* journalist, involved "some of the very tools that have made the globalization of world trade such a controversial issue" (Schmetzer, 2000). And, one might add, the same tools that facilitated electronic surveillance by national intelligence agencies.

By August 2000, rumors were circulating that a roving band of British anarchists planned to join in both the S11 and the Olympic protests, with the latter including blocking stadium entrances and "ambushing" wives of corporate leaders. This information was reported to have been obtained from police surveillance of websites and e-mails (Clennell, 2000; Connolly, 2000). Despite the fact that the rumors appeared to be largely the product of a media beat-up that originated in a British tabloid, as discussed in chapter 1, they lent legitimacy to aggressive police intervention. Indeed, on August 6, the NSW police service issued a statement that it "would not tolerate violent or unlawful activity and will take all appropriate measures to ensure the Olympics are as safe and enjoyable as possible for everyone concerned." It went on to explain that "peaceful and law-abiding demonstrations in public areas" would not be impeded, a somewhat empty gesture given the fact that Olympic legislation made it impossible to conduct a "law-abiding" demonstration in most areas of the city.

Groups comprising the S11 Alliance represented a range of political positions—from elected representatives to anarchists. Police in Victoria's Protective Service Division were reported to have been meeting with S11 organizers throughout 2000 in an attempt to "stage manage" the protest (Connolly, 2000). Subsequent events, however, suggested that Melbourne police were better suited to aggressive policing than to behind-the-scenes negotiating. In one Olympic-related example, plainclothes officers were reported to have harassed a man and a woman who were awaiting the July 30 arrival of the torch relay in Melbourne. The police recognized Marcus Brumer and Melainie Neofitou as antinuclear protesters and members of the radical environmental group Earth First! and attempted to search Brumer's bag. When Neofitou tried to get the attention of nearby media, she was thrown to the ground by an unidentified man, who said she was under arrest. He released her when the media arrived, but press photographers were threatened with removal of their Olympic accreditation if they published any photos of this incident. The *Australian* carried a report of the incident but, like other newspapers, did not include pictures. Earth First! (Melbourne) reported that, twenty minutes later, their members successfully blocked the path of torch-bearer Sir Gustav Nossal, who had received money to promote a nuclear waste dump in Australia, with a banner declaring Nuclear Industry, a Flaming Disgrace (Earth First! 2000).

The overwhelming majority of individuals and groups within the S11 alliance planned a nonviolent protest. A human chain blocked entrances and delayed the start by one hour, and organizers had to transport some delegates by boat and helicopter. In one highly publicized incident, the car carrying Western Australia's premier Richard Court was surrounded and damaged, and he was trapped for some time. Court was later reported to have labeled the action *unAustralian* (Schmetzer, 2000). What was not widely reported, however, was the fact that all delegates had been warned not to use private cars (Barrett, 2000).

On the second day, the police changed their tactics, removed their identity badges, and charged the crowd. About 200 protesters were injured, with about 30 requiring hospital treatment for injuries, including some serious fractures. A small number of police officers were also injured. The Victorian ombudsman subsequently announced an inquiry into police behavior, and about 50 protesters engaged a law firm to prepare civil actions, alleging that police used excessive force—kicking, stamping, hitting with batons, and charging on horseback—during attempts to break up groups of protesters who were passively blocking a driveway (*Law Report*, 2000). The S11 Legal Support Team called for the resignations of the officers responsible for calling the baton charge; as they pointed out, the charge constituted an infringement of the Victorian Police Procedures Manual, which allowed baton use only as a last resort to overcome "violent opposition to lawful arrest" (Dwyer, 2000).

Overall, S11 organizers concluded that the blockade and protests were successful in "taking a stand against the right of global capital to rule the world." At the same time, activists were urged to develop a framework that respected the diversity of the movement for radical change in Australia. S11 groups planned to continue their attempts to unite diverse interests, and to build on existing campaigns and trade union struggles against targeted global corporations.

S11: Lessons for Sydney

Events in Melbourne had significant implications for subsequent protest in Sydney. Antiglobalization activists demonstrated the strength of their numbers and the effectiveness of their generally nonviolent protest, which received international media attention for several days, and the event contributed to the ongoing struggle to promote public debate about global inequality, free trade, human rights, and transnational corporations. For their part, the Victorian police engaged in a show of force presumably intended to deter similar protests in Sydney during the Olympics, since there was some overlap in the groups and individuals involved in Melbourne and Sydney resistance movements.

The S11 Alliance, while not without its internal rifts, had the advantage of a clear, single focus on global justice, a manageable three-day time frame, and successful precedents, most notably the Seattle demonstrations of 1999. In contrast, the groups organizing protests in Sydney had (at least) two distinct agendas that often proved incompatible: first, to use the opportunity provided by the Olympics to draw world attention to the government's history of oppression of Indigenous people, while not detracting from or criticizing the Olympic sporting event or its participants; and second, to mount a critique of the Olympic Games in terms of the government's misguided spending priorities, the unfettered power of multinational corporations, and the commercialization and corruption of high performance sport. With various protest actions taking place for at least six months before the Games, it was difficult to maintain momentum and energy. Finally, the diverse groups involved in the general Olympic-related protest efforts held markedly different positions, not only in their political analyses, but also in their preferred modes of protest. In short, as many progressive voices in Australia have observed, the notion of solidarity within the Australian left is laughable.

SYDNEY IN SEPTEMBER: OLYMPIC RESISTANCE

The Olympic activists' calendar of events, which was widely circulated the week before the Games began, included Fairwear and Nikewatch's Alternative Opening Ceremony, Anti-Olympic Alliance's (AOA) "Protest the Olympic Torch" demonstration, Metropolitan Aboriginal Land Council's march to Howard's office, AOA's opening ceremony protest, AOA's and Rentwatchers' "Live Site" action, Refugee Action Collective's solidarity action in Parramatta, CACTUS's Carnival for Global Justice, and MALC's closing ceremony march. The announcement advised participants to wear protective eye wear, to avoid wearing contact lenses, and asthma sufferers were reminded to carry prescribed medication, in order to protect themselves against police capsicum spray attacks. Fortunately, there were few confrontations with police; unfortunately, many of the proposed protest actions failed to materialize.

Like many activist organizations, Nikewatch, a campaign associated with Community Aid Abroad/Oxfam Australia, recognized that the Olympics, and the fifteen thousand international journalists expected in Sydney in September, represented "the best chance we'll every have to put pressure on Nike to lift their game." In early September, Nikewatch organized a national tour by a fired Nike union organizer from Indonesia (whose name was withheld) and Jim Keady, a former soccer player and coach at St. John's University in the USA. Keady had challenged the university's pending deal with Nike as exclusive provider of clothing for its sport teams, thereby becoming the only known professional athlete who publicly refused to endorse Nike and quit his job in protest. In August 2000, he spent four weeks living in Indonesia to see factory conditions for himself and to find out if he could survive on Nike-level wages of two dollars per day (Connor, 2000b; Robinson, 2000).

On September 4, Nikewatch began its pre-Olympic actions in Sydney with the public release of a new report on conditions in Indonesian Nike factories prepared by Oxfam researcher Tim Connor. Titled "Like Cutting Cane," the report documented previously unknown examples of human rights abuses including management's violent suppression of union organizing activity, and humiliation and harassment of female workers who claimed menstrual leave (a provision provided under Indonesian law). The same day, Nikewatch organized a public debate on the question, "Do conditions in Nike factories meet the Olympic ideal of respect for human dignity?" with Jim Keady and the Indonesian worker in the NSW Parliament House. Perhaps strategically, the framing of the question implicitly accepted the so-called Olympic ideal as a reality, and failed to consider the extent to which the "human dignity" of homeless people and other disadvantaged populations was damaged by the hosting of the Olympics in Atlanta in 1996, Seoul in 1988, and other host cities over the last two decades (see Lenskyj, 2000). Predictably, Nike refused to send a representative to the debate, claiming that staff were too busy "being utilized to ensure that the Sydney Games are a success" (Connor, 2000b). Nike's "moral high ground" approach was no doubt intended to convey the message that the timing of Nikewatch's protests was both anti-Olympic and unAustralian.

On September 1, the Socialist youth group Resistance held a protest against the Olympics and their corporate sponsors near Auburn Station, with a march to the Nike warehouse and the Auburn McDonalds. Speakers addressed Indigenous issues, globalization, environmental concerns, government spending priorities, rent increases, and restrictions on civil liberties during the Olympics. And on September 11, the same day as the WEF protest in Melbourne, Nikewatch and Fairwear held an alternative Olympic opening ceremony in Victoria Park, Sydney. It featured a march of workers pulling a giant Nike shoe, chased by Fairwear's giant pink pencils, challenging Nike to sign the Homeworkers' Code of Practice.

In Newtown, AOA organized a September 14 "Protest the Olympic Torch" event, advertised as a "public laughing at Samaranch's cigar." About two hundred protesters greeted the hallowed flame with jeers and laugher, chanting "More drugs in sport" as it passed by—actions that surprised torchbearers who were expecting the usual cheering response to this pseudoreligious Olympic icon. Other protesters called for an end to Olympic corruption and for government funds to be spent on social services rather than the Olympics (Dwyer, 2000). The *Herald* account reported "ugly scenes" and noted that one protester wore a mask and a swastika—but failed to explain that it was a John Howard mask, and hence a statement about the Howard government's racist politics (Protesters greet torch, 2000). Later that day, twenty cyclists from Critical Mass, an international procycling and sustainable transport group, held a special Olympic ride in the suburb of Parramatta, close to the Homebush Bay Olympic site.

MALC planned to hold a protest near Sydney airport on Sunday September 10, with Aborigines and supporters forming a human chain to draw visitors' attention to Indigenous issues. This was one of the few protests that received police approval—probably because it was some distance from the CBD and Olympic venues, and was organized by a powerful Aboriginal group—but it failed to attract the expected numbers. As discussed in chapter 3, original plans for a mass protest march assembling at the Tent Embassy were dropped at embassy organizers' demand just before the Games began.

September 15: The Big Day

Around noon on Friday, September 15, two Aboriginal groups and their supporters, totaling about five hundred, marched from Redfern and the Tent Embassy to Hyde Park, and then on to John Howard's office "to ask how sorry he really is." Protesters chanted "Always was, always will be, Aboriginal land" and carried signs saying Bad Sport John Howard, while speakers called for justice and recognition of Aboriginal sovereignty. According to an IMC report (Kuiper, 2000b), police cars stopped traffic and cycle police rode beside the marchers.

Earlier that day, Police Commissioner Peter Ryan and another police officer who had been liaising with the Tent Embassy organizers Isobell Coe and others for some time, were among the guests at the corroboree. A traditional smoking ceremony was performed for Ryan's benefit, he made a statement about new beginnings, and received a hug from Coe. Calling for peace and reconciliation, Coe and Kevin Buzzacott, who had led the Walk for Peace from central Australia, drew attention to the plight of Aboriginal peoples, and urged John Howard to issue an official apology. Many subsequent speakers, visibly angry, targeted Howard, as well as voicing their criticism of highly paid Aboriginal bureaucrats who, they alleged, had sold out. Overall, little was said about the actual Olympics—in Coe's words, "what we are going to start here is bigger than the Olympics"—but it was hoped that the global scrutiny generated by the Olympics would force the Howard government to act on Aboriginal demands.

Reviewing these events in the October ISJA newsletter, Dan Clark took a more radical perspective, and one that was shared by Ray Jackson, Trevor Close, and many other Indigenous people who were frustrated by the endless compromises and sellouts: for example, the "galling" sight of the police commissioner at the smoking ceremony, when the same police "constantly harass, verbal, imprison, bash and intimidate Indigenous people" (Clark, 2000, 11).

A public meeting called by *Green Left Weekly* was held the following Wednesday, September 20, to discuss Indigenous rights and activism. Speakers represented the Indigenous Students' Network (Joel Bray), Democratic Socialist Party (Kim Bullimore), Aboriginal Government of Australia (Clarrie Isaacs), and ISJA (Ray Jackson), and, according to the IMC report, all the speakers were disheartened by the September 15 rally. Jackson called the Olympics "a missed opportunity" to campaign for Indigenous rights, although the international media's pre-Olympic coverage of the Tent Embassy and Peace Walk had been quite extensive. On the general issue of reconciliation, it was suggested that many non-Indigenous people who participated in the May 28 Harbor Bridge walk for reconciliation may have believed they had made their statement to the Howard government—in unprecedented numbers by Australian standards—and that no more protest marches were needed, especially during the Olympics. Several speakers called for a return to mass direct action strategies, similar to the S11 demonstrations of the previous week. They also identified the need for goals and vision, strong leadership, and alliances rather than divisions between groups (Dreher, 2000). It was clear that coalition-building had been hampered, on the one hand, by racism within non-Indigenous groups, and on the other hand, by Indigenous groups' internal political differences.

A member of the Un- and Underemployed People's Movement against Poverty, Monika Baker, posted a message to the IMC in solidarity with Indigenous protesters, calling for a broader, united front of national protest involving Aboriginal people, refugees, unemployed, and poor people. She, too, was critical of people in the "Aboriginal industry" who had sold out, along with those in peak social service organizations who had failed to protect the rights of low-income people. But, like Jackson and others, Baker recognized the barriers to organizing such alliances: those working in the "industry" or in community groups funded by the government did not want to take risks, while other Indigenous people were so traumatized by daily emergencies that they could not participate at all (Baker, 2000).

Other analyses noted problems underlying both Indigenous organizing and coalition-building with non-Indigenous organizations. Although the 1988 Bicentennial protests, often held up as the example to follow, were successful in both numbers and impact, the social and political context at that time was markedly different from the situation in the Olympic city twelve years later. The date January 1, 2001 marked the centenary of Confederation (when the six states joined to form Australia), and again, according to some Indigenous sources, their people had been "bought off" in order to avoid major protests and international embarrassment. Uluru, a sacred Aboriginal site, was again used as the symbolic beginning of the "celebrations," and the *Sydney Harbor Foreshores Act* conveniently remained in place to ensure that protesters stayed away from the center of the festivities.

The Protests Continue

On September 27, members of the Tent Embassy and the Walk for Peace marched to the Block in Redfern, then on to Hyde Park and the Town Hall. The same day, CACTUS and other protesters assembled at the George Street Nike store (or, according to some accounts, a sports store that sold Nike products); staff quickly closed the shop. The group then marched down George Street through peak hour traffic to Martin Place, where they protested outside the Westpac Bank, a major financier of the Jabiluka uranium mine.

About a hundred twenty protesters subsequently gathered in the Domain, in solidarity with the September 26 global day of action against the International Monetary Fund and World Bank, at that time meeting in Prague. In a peaceful protest action, they sat down on the grass to form the shape "S26." Proceeding through city streets to the front steps of Parliament House, members of this "unauthorized assembly" were moved on by police. As the IMC report noted, by this time a rapidly growing contingent of police and security was accompanying the protesters, and there were "minor scuffles" when protesters tried to enter the building where John Howard's Sydney office was located. "With police jogging alongside, trying to catch up," they marched through another Olympic live site, shouting, "We have the right to demonstrate, this is not a police state" (Dusk & John, 2000). In an IMC exchange the next day, Inspector David Darcy and a CACTUS representative each claimed that the other side was responsible for starting the minor confrontation between police and protesters.

It is interesting to note that Darcy had begun posting messages to the IMC a few days earlier, and continued to do so on a variety of issues and debates, including police action at the Broadway squats and Reclaim the Streets protests later in the year. Following IMC's open publishing principles, the collective welcomed any and all contributions, including those from members of the NSW police. Although rebuttals to Darcy's postings ranged from reasonable to rude, many saw this as an opportunity for potentially productive dialogue, and not a subversion of IMC goals. However, on this issue, I would argue that Olympic and state officials, who represent institutions with huge public relations budgets, should not exploit the few opportunities that are financially accessible to grassroots activists—for example, community meetings, public hearings, and independent media of various kinds—to get their message out.

On September 29, near Kirribilli House, Howard's Sydney residence, Kevin Buzzacott delivered a statement to Australia and the world, indicting Howard and his government for their failure to recognize Aboriginal human rights issues, and, in the case of Howard, "even to say sorry for the crimes your ancestors have done." He called for "all Black people, leaders and elders to support this ancient request for peace" and for the world to support the statement. Finally, he called on Howard to resign and to dismantle his government. Commenting on Howard's lack of response to the invitation to the peace fire, he said: "Whilst the Prime Minister is busy entertaining international guests, he has failed to recognize the real people of Australia, who are still suffering under the abuses of a 212 year war. If the Prime Minister won't come to the peace fire, the peace fire and all its elements will come to him" (Buzzacott, 2000).

Environmental Protest: The Struggle Goes On

The Australian government's Environment Department organized an "Environment Theme Day" on September 15 at the Sydney Media Center. International media were offered presentations on "Australia's unique environment and approaches to protect it," and the event was chaired by the prerequisite former "Olympian"—in this case, Robert de Castella. Protesters led by Greens MLA Lee Rhiannon and Wilderness Society members entered the foyer and unfurled a large banner with the words Forests Too Precious to Woodchip. Security forced them outside after about twenty minutes—after all, they were infringing the *Darling Harbor Authority Act,* the *Sydney Harbor Foreshores Act,* the *Olympic Arrangements Act,* and no doubt a few others—but they continued to distribute literature on Australia's record as the worst per-capita greenhouse gas polluter, and on the destruction of Tasmania's ancient hardwood trees, the tallest in the world, which were being logged at the fastest rate in history (Oquist, 2000).

Greenpeace activists developed a creative solution to the suppression of public protest with a "crop circle" in a field under the Sydney airport flight path: the word *TOXIC* was spelled out, with an arrow pointing toward the Homebush Bay Olympic site, where soil, sediment, and water were still not fully remediated.

AOA Protests = Subversive Activities

On Sunday September 17, AOA activists challenged the *Olympic Arrangements Act* at one of the CBD live sites, Martin Place. They displayed banners, made speeches on a microphone, and handed out leaflets to the crowds, warning them, "DANGER! You have just been handed an illegal LEAFLET containing unAustralian sentiments, from an Olympics criminal . . . fulfil your national duty as a patriotic citizen—dob in (report) an Olympic criminal today. . . . "

It went on to explain the repressive new Olympic-related laws, the housing and homelessness crisis in Sydney, the government's denial of Aboriginal sovereignty, gentrification of Aboriginal and working-class neighborhoods, and the $2.5b of public money directed to the Olympics. "The Olympics—keeping Sydney safe for global capital," it concluded.

Needless to say, there was a heavy presence of security guards, Olympic Coordination Authority (OCA) officers, and police who were quick to act when AOA began the action. As the IMC account pointed out, the lunchtime crowd "witnessed firsthand the application of the new laws as dozens of heavy-handed security guards and police descended and harassed the protesters." They were threatened with arrest and fines if they didn't stop their activities, even though the *Police and Public Safety Act* specifically exempted public protest and assembly.

Calling for participants to join in a second "subversive stunt," the AOA website cat.org.au/aoa borrowed some Olympic legislation language by asking, "Do you have what it takes to be an Olympics criminal? . . . a not-to-be-missed opportunity to come along and publicly indulge yerself in a bit of well-intentioned but illicit *annoying and inconvenient* behavior!" (emphasis in original).

The second action, watched by police, security, and a large number of media, took place the following Friday at Circular Quay, another Olympic live site. Some AOA members considered these actions more successful in raising public awareness and gaining media attention than the mass marches, most of which failed to draw large numbers.

On September 29, Critical Mass invited Olympic athletes, particularly cycling teams, to join other cyclists and skaters in a ride over the Harbor Bridge and a gathering, with food and music, at Bradfield Park on the north side. This was part of Critical Mass' "global celebration of nonmotorized transport" that takes place on the last Friday of every month in over one hundred cities around the world. Demonstrators called on the NSW and Commonwealth governments to "change the balance from cars" to alternative environmentally friendly modes of transport, and to fund and implement the National Cycling Strategy. As their media release explained, the ride was planned with the approval of the NSW police and the Olympic Roads and Transport Authority (Critical Mass, 2000). About one thousand cyclists participated, stopping traffic for thirty minutes in a peaceful demonstration.

Hands Across the Pacific: International Resistance

Toronto's Bread Not Circuses Coalition organized an international media event on Wednesday, September 13 to draw attention to the negative social impacts on Olympic host cities. A telephone hookup between Sydney,

Atlanta, and Toronto allowed activists and journalists in the three cities to discuss current issues, with a focus on events in Sydney. Beth Jewell, Rentwatchers, Louise Boon-Kuo, University of Technology Sydney (UTS) Community Law and Legal Research Center, and Dominic WYkanak, representing Indigenous and Torres Strait Islander issues, participated from Sydney. In Toronto, the speakers were Anna Willats of the Committee to Stop Targeted Policing, David Hulchanski, University of Toronto housing specialist, and Jan Borowy and I, representing Bread Not Circuses; from Atlanta, Anita Beaty, director of the Atlanta Task Force for the Homeless participated in the event.

Jewell and Boon-Kuo discussed problems of rent increases, boarding-house closures, and harassment of homeless people, all exacerbated by the Olympics, and the threat to public protest imposed by Olympic-related legislation. Discussing Indigenous issues and pending native title claims on Bondi Beach, WYkanak reported that Olympic organizers and Michael Knight had continued to display "ignorance and racism" on this matter. Toronto participants drew attention to housing and related social issues, as well as to recent trends in targeted policing of street homeless people.

Speaking from a city that hosted the Games four years earlier, Beaty explained what Atlanta's Olympic "legacy" really looked like: the continued existence of laws that criminalized poverty and homelessness, and the almost complete privatization of urban public space. She described how a big downtown park, formerly a haven for homeless people, was now taken over by Georgia State University and aggressively patrolled by its security staff, to the extent that drivers of vans distributing food to homeless people in the park were ticketed.

On September 22, Jewell participated in the Pacifica Radio (publicly funded radio) program, *Democracy Now,* with two Aboriginal women; I was the fourth guest on the show. Nancy de Vries and Lola Edwards, who were members of the stolen generation, also took part in a second program in the series. They spoke eloquently and movingly about their childhood experiences and called on the Howard government to apologize, just as one would say "I'm sorry" if a member of one's family were hurt. As de Vries explained, "the soul of this country will never be at rest" until that day.

Disadvantaged People: A Long Sixteen Days

As discussed earlier, the Homeless Protocol that was eventually put in place represented an attempt to protect homeless people from being moved on against their will, unless they were a danger to themselves or others, and required police and security to contact the Sydney City Council outreach team before moving a homeless person. From September 8 to 30,

Redfern Legal Center (RLC) operated a twenty-four-hour legal advice hotline for homeless people, youth, protesters, or anyone asked to move on by police security guards or other Olympic personnel. In a proactive step that proved very effective, RLC notified all local police commanders, NSW government ministers, and the premier that its volunteers would be monitoring the situation and would legally assist anyone whom police or OCA security moved on or arrested under the new Olympic-related laws. They also distributed hundreds of wallet-size cards to homeless people, informing them of the protocol provisions, the hotline, and RLC's services.

Despite traffic restrictions, street closures, transport problems, and other changes during the Olympic period, most social service agencies attempted to maintain their services. For example, the Public Interest Advocacy Center was open for limited hours, and People with Disabilities NSW operated an Olympic and Paralympic Disability Advocacy Service to provide advice for locals and visitors adversely affected by the Games.

Shelter NSW conducted surveys of homeless people in Sydney during the first and second weeks of September (Vinson, 2000). On the night of September 4, interviewers visited six sites where charitable organizations provided food for homeless people, in order to administer questionnaires on respondents' accommodations, their awareness of any (unspecified) changes in authorities' treatment of street homeless people, and their familiarity with the homeless protocol and/or the legal assistance phone line. The service providers had contact with 537 homeless people, of whom 110 agreed to be interviewed (103 men and 7 women). More than half the men anticipated that they would "sleep rough" that night, and about three quarters of the total group were regular users of the meal service.

On the question of authorities' treatment, about 47% of the men noticed changes for the worse; in the under-30 age group, 75% of male respondents (27/36) reported negative changes. These men described how recent actions of police, council rangers, and security guards had become rougher and more harassing; examples included public searching and strip-searching, for no reason; treating homeless people in a "degrading" way; intimidation, threats, and discrimination (Vinson, 2000, 5–6).

The second week's survey—conducted on September 11—involved 15 service providers and 1,260 clients; 189 men and 11 women participated in the interview. The same patterns emerged, with over 42% reporting changes. Six women also mentioned increased police harassment, including bag searches and strip searches. Younger men, in particular, reported being moved on, harassed, searched, strip-searched, charged with loitering, or stopped for "walking too fast." A few specified that police did not physically move them on, but were continually "picking on people" verbally, ordering them to move, asking them questions, and so forth. About 10% of those who did not experience any change made positive comments about authorities' behavior.

Overall, the Shelter NSW survey documented an Olympic-related escalation of police and other authorities' harassment of homeless people, but the figures—with roughly half providing examples of negative changes and the other half reporting no changes—did not support claims of dramatic increases. On the other hand, the findings point to the indisputable fact that hundreds of street homeless people suffered increased harassment at the hands of the authorities in the weeks before the Games began.

As the RLC report later observed, the government probably wanted to avoid being seen—particularly by the international media—as implementing an "Atlanta-style policy" of street sweeps during the actual Games, and only nine incidents were recorded by volunteer staff. Overall, it appeared that police targeted homeless people "in places where they congregate, for the purpose of checking out their IDs and for any outstanding warrants" (Blunden, 2000, 8). For example, a few days before the Games, police conducted an ID and warrant check, as well as searching five homeless men who were waiting in a park near Central Railway for the food van; one had no ID and was detained for four hours. In another example at Circular Quay, an area covered by the *Harbor Foreshore Authority Act,* a seventy-two-year-old homeless woman was moved on from her regular spot near the wharves, and on a later occasion was roused by a police officer, who kicked her foot to wake her up. RLC responded to the woman's complaint about the officer's degrading behavior by writing a letter to the police commander.

The Homeless Protocol only covered Sydney's CBD; in the western suburb of Parramatta, close to Olympic Park, the council had adopted a homeless protocol that bound council workers, but the Parramatta police were not signatories. The most serious incidents of police harassment of homeless people occurred in Parramatta between September 29 and October 1. Because the local Church Street mall was in use as an Olympic live site, the council and church-based agencies had been operating a shelter called "Safe Haven" in the Parramatta Mission Hall. Open for most of the Olympic period, it provided food, showers, and entertainment for homeless people. However, by September 29, "Safe Haven" had to close because of a prior hall booking, and it was at this time, according to agency workers, that the police allegedly increased their patrols, pursued a particular group of about seven homeless men, continually asked for IDs and checked for outstanding warrants, and finally arrested them for relatively petty offenses.

According to the RLC report, when one of the arrested men produced the RLC card, "the police officer ripped it up in front of him and said words to the effect that it (the Protocol) wouldn't apply here (in Parramatta)" (Blunden, 2000, 16)—an action that conveyed a clear message about this officer's insulting attitude to homeless people and their advocates. This was not an isolated incident. One respondent to the Shelter

NSW survey discussed earlier, a young man in his twenties, made this statement on September 11: "I've had four checks today in the street. I've been strip-searched in a toilet. 'If you show us that piece of paper (a Shelter handout) again, you'll be arrested'" (cited in Vinson, 2000, 11). Such attitudes and actions on the part of Sydney and Parramatta police stood in stark contrast to the "velvet glove" public image that Inspector Darcy and others attempted to convey in the Olympic city.

"PEOPLE WILL FORGET": THE OLYMPICS BEGIN

The "people will forget" refrain had been a staple of Olympic rhetoric throughout the worst of the International Olympic Committee (IOC) bribery investigations, and during the scandals that Sydney Olympic organizers had generated without IOC help: the premium ticket scheme, the marching band controversy, Gosper and the torch relay fiasco, and budget blowouts that by 2000 were following a lunar cycle. According to this prediction, the combined effects of Olympic magic and a short collective memory would produce public amnesia the minute the opening ceremony began.

Other observers predicted that the euphoria would begin with the torch relay—or more accurately, with the Australian torch relay's starting point at Uluru, since Gosper's poor judgment and arrogance had already cast a cloud over the Greek part of the event. From government and Olympic officials to academics, journalists, and "people on the street," significant numbers of Australians, either jaded or hopeful, shared this view. According to politics professor Robert Manne, writing in the *Herald*, "With the coming of the torch relay [to Australia] all previous Olympic disillusion simply melted away" (Manne, 2000b). And communications professor John Sinclair argued that the Sydney Organizing Committee for the Olympic Games (SOCOG's) efforts to invest the torch and relay with "socially inclusive symbolism" should not be seen as either "benign altruism" or "mere cynical ideological manipulation." Despite the excesses of the media coverage, Sinclair claimed, it symbolically provided "at least a glimpse of egalitarian values asserting themselves when challenged and images of Indigenous people which powerfully legitimized their special status and belonging in this country. . . ." (Sinclair, 2000, 38, 44). Certainly, the choice of Uluru and Indigenous athletes Nova Peris-Kneebone and Evonne Goolagong-Cawley as the first torchbearers, conveyed these messages.

The mass media played a key role in controlling the timing and extent of the amnesia and euphoria phenomena. Popular wisdom among journalists held that for several weeks before the Games began, there would be an (unwritten) editorial blackout on negative Olympic stories. In my own experience promoting a book critical of the Olympic industry at precisely this time, I found there was some truth to the rumor, which I heard from a number of journalists. The alternative media—for example, Pacifica Radio and the *Village Voice*—and progressive publications such as the *Guardian* (UK), were markedly more receptive than the mainstream media during the pre-Olympic period.

In one notable exception to the "good news" stories that dominated the mainstream press before and during the Olympics, the *Vancouver Sun* published an incisive critique of corporate sponsorships and environmental rhetoric by a former Canadian water polo team member, Kaliya Young. Titled "Why I'm Not Game for the Olympics," the article explained why Young had retired from the team rather than participating in the Olympic culture, which she termed *nationalist, ethnocentric, imperialist,* and *consumerist* (K. Young, 2000).

Olympic Mythmaking

In keeping with the spirit of Olympics past and, no doubt, Olympics to come, the media reveled in stories of personal triumph over adversity. The struggle to become a high-performance athlete, and then to qualify for Olympic competition, invariably lent itself to this kind of mythmaking, which NBC perfected in 1996 with its "human interest" approach to covering the Atlanta Games, later dubbed the "feminine Olympics." It was partly as a result of its market research on women that NBC focused on individual athletes' stories as a way of increasing the numbers of female viewers, who, it was discovered, were interested in the full background of Olympic athletes, and not just the results of Olympic competition (Borcila, 2000). This was of personal interest, since in my earlier research on female participation in sport, I had documented gender-related differences in values and priorities, with social aspects, including fun and friendship, generally valued more highly by females than males; therefore, female viewers' interest in background stories was not surprising (Lenskyj, 1994). But as David Andrews (1998, 16) aptly observed, although NBC's Olympic coverage established a central place for female sport in "the inventory of American cultural practices and experiences," the network's "stereotypical and demeaning models of women as both the objects of production . . . and subjects of consumption" had the effect of neutralizing any positive political impacts of the increased female presence.

Broadcasters and print media embraced the human interest model in their coverage of Sydney 2000. One story that emerged as a mass media favorite focused on Eric Moussambani from Equatorial Guinea, whose 100m swimming performance took longer than Olympic-level swimmers in the 200m event. Subsequent accounts revealed that he had never swum that distance since he began training in January 2000. With a mixture of admiration, condescension, and plain racism, media reports treated the event as "proof of the enduring Olympic spirit"—a glaring contradiction in light of the Olympics' unequivocal "faster, higher, stronger" ethos. The tone of media coverage at times resembled the old and insulting adage about the dog walking on its hind legs: it's not done well, but you are surprised to find it done at all. In a variation on this theme, one Toronto journalist reduced the incident to "the sporting equivalent of having his pants pulled down in public," but concluded with the predictable "Olympic spirit" clichés (P. Young, 2000b). The *Guardian* (UK) was one of the few sources to show any interest in Equatorial Guinea's reputation as "Africa's most abject and bloodthirsty dictatorship" (Engel, 2000).

Some accounts of Moussambani's performance noted that similar stories of "successful failures" had emerged from other recent Olympics— perhaps as a form of resistance to the unrelenting emphasis on gold-medal performances (D. Clark, 2000; Keating, 2000). In Toronto, a less successful media attempt to generate a "successful failure" focused on Canada's synchronized swim team (including four University of Toronto students), who, according to *Star* writer Rosie DiManno's endlessly glowing accounts (e.g., DiManno, 2000b), had been penalized for their "courageous" and "creative" approach. Inexplicably, in view of the team's stated goal of making synchro more of a "spectator sport," the duet team performed a routine titled "Madness." Its inappropriate and offensive characterization of mental illness, which the swimmers described as entertaining and pioneering (Risky routine, 2000), not only deserved the judges' low scores, in my view, but, had it been performed on the University of Toronto campus, would arguably have contravened the university's antidiscrimination policy by ridiculing this form of disability.

By the end of the Games, Australian journalists felt freer to criticize, and *Herald* reporter Malcolm Knox listed a "dirty dozen" Olympic athletes whom he labeled *bad sports* and *major-league assholes*. Knox was not only critical of individuals' foul play, but also directed some barbs toward Nike ads, the U.S. track and field executive, overzealous officials, and self-indulgent professional athletes. And, describing an incident in which one runner was disqualified for shouldering his opponent, Knox concluded cynically, "To confirm his adherence to the Olympic ideal, he appeals" (Knox, 2000)

On a somewhat different plane, the Australian Bureau of Statistics (ABS) quietly offered its own critique of countries that considered themselves the top medal winners by publishing a medal tally by population, to which the *Herald* website provided a link. As it noted, "A number of factors will influence the medals won by athletes from a [particular] country . . . one fact could be the size of the population." This kind of medal tally, calculated on October 1, shed a different light on the notion of winners and losers, with the Bahamas heading the list, followed by Barbados, Iceland, Australia, Jamaica, and Cuba. Canada ranked 40th, the United States, 46th, and China, 75th (ABS, 2000). Using some of the same logic, two Wellesley College researchers, whose work was reported in *The Economist* in September, found that most of the differences in medal counts between countries were attributable to population and gross domestic product (To the rich, 2000). And in June, a study published in the *Journal of Science and Medicine in Sport* briefly captured media attention with its finding that every gold medal won by an Australian athlete since 1996 cost the federal government about $40m (Gittins, 2000; Hogan & Norton, 2000). By September 2000, however, most Australians were celebrating the country's medal tally, and mere monetary considerations were unlikely to detract from the excitement.

Packaging Black and White: The Opening Ceremony

Images of the highly anticipated opening ceremony reached Canadian and American viewers at 3:00 A.M. on Friday, September 15. One of its most salient features, as Robert Manne (2000b) observed, was "the extent to which creative Australians are now reliant on motifs borrowed from Aboriginal culture for their sense of what makes this country distinctive, of what lends it timelessness, mystery and depth." He failed to recognize the fine line between this "creative borrowing" and appropriating or stealing Indigenous culture. And, as Darren Godwell (1999c, 11) warned, "The Sydney 2000 Games cannot fabricate some happy native sideshow" for international tourists, while ignoring two centuries of colonization and human rights abuses.

This is not to suggest that Aboriginal performers were unwilling participants in Olympic-related cultural activities. As I explained in chapter 3, the Indigenous community is not monolithic, politically or culturally, and many viewed the central position of Aboriginal dance, theater, and art in the Olympic cultural program as a promising step toward reconciliation. Rhoda Roberts, artistic director for *The Festival of the Dreaming,* a series of four Olympic arts festivals held from 1997 to 2000, saw this as an opportunity to reject the usual tokenistic images of Indigenous culture and to move away from the usual "anthropological gaze" to which Indigenous artists and performers were subjected. The vision developed by Roberts and her colleagues included both a celebration of Indigenous identity as "a living and adapting culture" and its inclusion in the contemporary Australian arts and cultural industry. (Roberts, 1999; 11)

Discussing the representation of White Australia's identity in the opening ceremony, Manne claimed that Australian "intelligentsia have liberated themselves from the old colonial cultural cringe": "In placing the suburban motor mower and the outdoor dunny at the center of our national myth, those who choreographed the opening ceremony declined to feed their vast global audience with the familiar stereotypes and invited it, instead, to take an interest in a nation they did not yet understand" (Manne, 2000b).

Canadian and American media coverage confirmed that many international audiences and media were indeed bewildered by symbols such as lawn mowers, outdoor toilets, and zinc cream, and a Japanese viewer complained that parts of the ceremony were "a complete mystery" (*Daily Telegraph,* 2000). But few audiences failed to recognize the symbolism (if not the tokenism) of the highly visible Aboriginal participation in the opening ceremony. In fact, in conversations with Canadian friends and colleagues who understood issues of race and racism, I discovered that many viewed the Aboriginal performers and Cathy Freeman's lighting of the cauldron unproblematically as evidence of progress in Australia's race relations. These were people who would not have assumed any parallel connection between Black boxer Mohammed Ali's cauldron-lighting role in the 1996 Atlanta Olympics and improved race relations in the United States. Not too surprisingly, Olympic organizers claimed that Freeman had been deliberately chosen to light the cauldron in order to make a strong statement about reconciliation (Hill, 2000), and her role, together with the Indigenous cultural performances, probably achieved this symbolic goal.

On the other hand, it could be argued that the Australian government and Olympic organizers were hoping to capitalize on the widespread lack of knowledge and understanding of Australian politics and Indigenous issues on the part of overseas media and audiences. Many observers outside Australia and New Zealand would probably be unaware of the common, often tokenistic practice, in liberal White Australian circles, of including Aboriginal dance performances in cultural and other public events, and inviting an Aboriginal elder to extend a traditional "welcome to land." MALC chair Jenny Munro, for example, was to welcome Samaranch on behalf of the traditional owners of the land at Homebush Bay, but she also organized Aboriginal protests.

For his part, Samaranch presumptuously thanked his "friends from the Aboriginal and Torres Strait Islander communities . . . you have helped to write a glorious chapter in the history of Australia" (Samaranch quoted in M. Moore, 2000f). During this "glorious chapter" while Aboriginal dancers were performing for mostly White audiences, Black men continued to die in police custody. In a seven-week period in May and June 2000, eight Aborigines died in custody in Western Australia alone (Ridgway, 2000).

In a Melbourne *Age* article, "Bitter Olympic ironies," Manne (2000a) pointed out that overseas Olympic visitors would probably be unaware of Freeman's background, most notably the fact that her grandmother was one of the stolen generation. Manne went on to provide evidence that the struggle was not over, by focusing on the example of the conservative magazine, *Quadrant*—a favorite of the prime minister—that had been conducting a three-year campaign to discredit the fact of the stolen generation as Aborigines' so-called "collective false memory syndrome." In a final flourish on the eve of the Olympics, *Quadrant* had held a conference in Melbourne to celebrate the Howard government's legal victory over two Aboriginal members of the stolen generation who had sued for damages, and had lost.

Responses to the opening ceremony were, of course, mixed. Some applauded the highly visible Aboriginal presence in the arena (if not in the stands), and in the imagery of the Captain Cook segment. Some drew attention to the injustices of paying prominent performers thousands of dollars for their appearance, while others were told they should consider themselves "privileged" to be volunteers. The image of the thirteen-year-old White vocalist Nikki Webster singing about dreams coming true with God watching you, and walking hand-in-hand with traditional Aboriginal dancer Djakapurra evoked cynicism in many quarters as schmaltzy and tear-jerking. The heavy-handed symbolism was, of course, intended to suggest reconciliation between Black and White Australians, and that was precisely the message that overseas media and viewers picked up. At best, the symbolic bridging of the gap between Black and White, traditional and contemporary, and young and old, might have raised White Australians' awareness of potential ways in which racial, cultural, and social differences could be celebrated, rather than exploited as a means of maintaining the status quo.

One of the (non-Aboriginal) dance performances was choreographed in the style of Tap Dogs, an internationally recognized tap dance troupe that had its origins in (White) male, working-class Newcastle, and used welding equipment and scaffolding as props. One observer saw this as a "crude and cruel" image that glorified "the construction of the 'Australian' culture in concrete and metal, with what looked like thousands of Howard Youth dancing their face off" (Lewis, 2000). And the segment on the post-Captain Cook period included, as one Toronto reporter interpreted it, "everything that served to tame the land"—including Ned Kelly as yet another gesture towards Australia's larrikinism (Campbell, 2000).

"Sorry": The Closing Ceremony

The band Midnight Oil, whose members had a long history of political involvement in Indigenous and environmental issues, used the closing ceremony to make an unequivocal statement in support of reconciliation, seen by millions of international television viewers. Peter Garrett and the other band members were dressed entirely in black, with the word *SORRY* clearly visible in white on their shirts. As Garrett explained, although recognition of Indigenous culture was "one of the essential themes" of these Olympics, the question of the apology hadn't yet been raised, so "we figured we would do it" (Garrett quoted in C. Jones, 2000).

Meanwhile, in Toronto, the Canadian band Blue Rodeo came under fire in a community newspaper for performing at the Olympics. Critics pointed out that this group, which had a record of supporting Native rights in North America, should not be seen as cheerleading for the Olympics and the racist Australian government. It was suggested that the group follow the example of another band with a social conscience, Rage Against the Machine, which had given a free concert for protesters at the Los Angeles Republican convention a few months before; similarly, Blue Rodeo could perform for the S11 protesters to demonstrate their political commitment (Jefferson-Lenskyj, 2000).

Midnight Oil's "sorry" statement not only publicly embarrassed the prime minister, who was present at the ceremony, for his refusal to apologize to Indigenous people, but also flouted the IOC rule prohibiting "political" or "propaganda" messages inside Olympic venues. In an earlier gesture, a member of another band, Savage Garden, had appeared wearing a shirt with an Aboriginal flag on it. One observer described what she saw as the "supreme moments" of the closing ceremony: the Aboriginal band Yothu Yindi's call for reconciliation in the song, *Treaty*, and Midnight Oil's powerful message in *Beds are Burning*: the land belongs to the Indigenous people. In her post to the *Daily Telegraph* website, she stated, "These two bands made a statement, with joy, that from both White and Black Australians there is so much good will and good grace to reconcile the wrongs of the past."

There was not, of course, unanimous support for Midnight Oil, and it appeared that some spectators and journalists misunderstood their actions. Despite the fact that their intent was both genuine and serious, a British commentator (McGillion, 2000) described the band as the "larrikin" element in the ceremony, as did an Australian journalist, who claimed that the group's statement "seemed to be in keeping with the overall larrikin ethos of the show" (Burning issue, 2000). This reduction of political action to a childish flouting of authority was both inaccurate and insulting.

On radio talk shows and the *Daily Telegraph* website, the tone was more scathing. A post from a Western Australian woman, typical of the backlash, asked why Midnight Oil felt "they had to ram their sorry message into everyone's home." She went on to make the dubious claim that "Most Aussies totally agree with the Prime Minister on this and it's just the minority that make it look like ALL Aussies want the government to apologize. . . . Definitely not the place for political messages. . . ." An angry NSW woman claimed that Midnight Oil "ruined a fun evening," while an American viewer accused the bands of being "stuck somewhere in the 1970s in terms of political correctness . . . Music is not the medium of the political message any more: the Internet is." Of course, critics of both the government and the Olympic industry had been making excellent use of the Internet for a long time.

Reported reactions from politicians were at times surprising; Liberal Peter Nugent, described as a supporter of Aboriginal rights, condemned Garrett for "introducing domestic politics into the Olympics" although he said he was "sympathetic to the message" (It was politics, 2000). Nugent's position paralleled one published in a letter to the University of Toronto *Bulletin,* in response to an article I wrote about Sydney 2000. Taking issue with my critique of Australian legislation that suppressed public protest during the Olympics, the letter-writer claimed that it was "only good manners," when people had guests, to put aside "domestic squabbles" and to stop behaving like "spoiled children" (DiMarco, 2000). Unlike Nugent, who at least understood the full context, John DiMarco reduced the complex reconciliation issue in Australia to a "domestic squabble" in a manner that many would consider patronizing and offensive.

Some Australian responses to the closing ceremony called for greater recognition of the *real* multicultural Australia, for example, immigrants dancing in their "native costumes" rather than "tacky floats"; some of these suggestions clearly implied that there was an overemphasis on Indigenous Australians. "So-called Aussie icons who live overseas" (e.g., Olivia Newton-John)—presumably the epitome of unAustralian behavior—were as unpopular as Midnight Oil on the *Telegraph* readers' website. The inclusion of the drag queens made famous by the movie *Priscilla, Queen of the Desert* offended fundamentalist Christians, who were vocal in their opposition as soon as the program was made public. Grasping at straws, one website post claimed that the drag queens were an "embarrassment— nothing to do with sport"—not a particularly cogent argument in light of the fact that very little of the content in the ceremonies met that requirement. Moreover, the sight of Australian men in dresses was not new to international audiences: the August 2000 *National Geographic* had published a photograph of men in white tutus, beer bottles in hand, taking part in Australia Day celebrations on Sydney Harbor—inexplicably, to illustrate Bill Bryson's cover story on Sydney, The Olympic City (Bryson, 2000).

Mainstream Media: Sydney, Toronto, New York

There was extensive international media interest in the plight of Australian Aborigines in the weeks before the Games, and many important stories were told with sympathy and understanding. Even the *Toronto Star*'s Rosie DiManno and Royson James, neither of whom had a reputation for progressive politics, produced insightful articles on Indigenous issues. James was less successful in his other role as relentless Toronto 2008 Olympic bid booster, manifest in his desperate attempts to draw parallels between Sydney and Toronto. Gushing over every aspect of Sydney in general and Olympic venues in particular, he devoted an entire column to the beauties of Blacktown, with new baseball and softball facilities that the mayor, Alan Pendleton, claimed had put the town on the map. Quickly recognizing a gullible international reporter, Pendleton went on to present Blacktown's other noteworthy attributes, including the (meaningless) fact that it was, in James's words, "ideally located for travel north and south to Queensland and Victoria" (R. James, 2000, B1).

One of the best examples of international coverage of Indigenous issues was a September 17 *New York Times* editorial titled "The Other Australia," which was subsequently reprinted in the *International Herald Tribune* (Paris and Singapore). Drawing parallels between [White] Australians' and Americans' failures to apologize for past wrongs toward Indigenous peoples, the editorial pointed out that both groups of White settlers "started with the same national myth of a fearless band of Europeans claiming a new frontier for humankind." It concluded with a strongly worded critique of the Australian government's recent refusal to cooperate with UN fact-finders monitoring the treatment of Aborigines.

Commenting on the *New York Times* piece, an October 4 *Herald* article titled "Sometimes All that Glistens Isn't Olympic Gold" presented lengthy excerpts from the editorial, and criticized the *Herald*'s continued self-congratulatory posturing. Two *Herald* articles, in particular, captured the paper's attempts to frame the Olympics in general, and Freeman's role in particular, as a step toward reconciliation. Neville Roach (2000), chair of a multicultural organization (but writing in a personal capacity) claimed that Freeman "united Indigenous and non-Indigenous Australians in the most inclusive celebrations in our nation's history" and that her example should promote renewed efforts on the part of the prime minister and the Council for Aboriginal Reconciliation. For his part, the council's chair, Sir Gustav Nossal stated that the Games had done more for Aboriginal reconciliation in two weeks than months of negotiation, while Prime Minister Howard claimed that they had demonstrated that Australia was probably more "reconciled" that some people thought (Boyle, 2000).

In the second *Herald* article, Sydney Institute's executive director Gerard Henderson (2000) claimed, in a burst of wishful thinking, that "The international focus on reconciliation did not diminish the positive message from the 2000 Olympics. That's because, as in 1956 [Melbourne Olympics], individual Australians demonstrated for the world to see that they are a tolerant, good-natured people." In other words, the world didn't see the real depth of feeling, most notably anger, on the reconciliation issue—largely because of the various overt and covert state actions that restricted public protest and silenced Indigenous leaders and their supporters. As Aboriginal leader Clarrie Isaacs pointed out, "On the night that Cathy Freeman lit the flame, thousands of our people went to bed hungry and homeless, and woke up unemployed and facing trauma" (Isaacs quoted in Dreher, 2000).

The *Herald* gave Indigenous issues a prominent place in its critical post-Games coverage. An October 4 article reminded readers that, despite the "warm glow of national pride and goodwill," conditions facing Aboriginal people had not changed, and in some instances had worsened. For example, the "famous deal" between Canberra and Darwin to curtail mandatory sentencing and expand diversionary programs for juveniles had not yet been finalized, six months later (Hill, 2000). It was also reported that the Northern Territory government and the Federal Cabinet were renewing efforts to erode Aboriginal land rights, just two days after the Olympics had finished—or, as an opposition member put it, two days after Olympic visitors (and the media) had left town (Metherell, 2000b).

Although it was a minority position, a few mainstream media voices were critical of the media beat-up of the "Freeman factor." George Negus observed in the *Herald*,

> Conspiracy theorists no doubt saw the threading of indigenous performances and culture . . . —let alone the loaded symbolism of Cathy Freeman lighting the cauldron—as part of a plot to dumb-down the whole Aboriginal question. Conspiracy or not, that does appear to have been the overall effect. . . . Almost without exception, the world's media linked Freeman's gold medal to the reconciliation issues. (Negus, 2000)

He went on to point out that the international publicity Freeman attracted when she spoke out about the government's refusal to apologize was probably preempted by Howard's attack on the UN the week before the Olympics began, thereby guaranteeing that Australia's human rights record would continue to receive media attention after the Olympics had left the country.

Activists found that international media interest in nonsport stories declined dramatically as soon as the Games began. ISJA member Dan Clark described one incident during the Games when Aboriginal leader Lowitja O'Donoghue and others had tried to hold a press conference on the Stolen Generation in a SOCOG briefing room, and had to relocate it in "emergency and less salubrious surrounds in a car park." Meanwhile, in the Australian media, the only Indigenous story was Freeman, but, as Clark pointed out, "everyone was claiming ownership of Cathy's dedication and talent" and her contribution to reconciliation without giving her the right to speak for herself (D. Clark, 2000, 12).

CONCLUSION

The *Green Left Weekly* tackled the question "Did the Olympics help reconciliation?" in October (Boyle, 2000). Referring to a *Herald* letter to the editor that had asked, "How far has reconciliation come?"—and answered, "Four hundred meters," Boyle argued that progressive Australians—both White and Black—could have engaged in a more effective protest than simply applauding Freeman and celebrating the "symbols of reconciliation": "Being acknowledged in Olympic ceremonies is not enough to turn the racist tide in Australian government. It was not the best we could have done."

In fact, it could be argued that the term *imperialist nostalgia* captured the underlying message of the Olympic ceremonies: "Having altered or destroyed the culture of the 'other', the colonizers then appropriate it for their own gain, or even mourn its passing, while at the same time concealing their own complicity" and thereby making racial domination appear "innocent and pure" (Renato Rosaldo, cited in Birch, 1992, 238).

The Olympic industry succeeded in making many of Australia's other pressing social problems appear equally "innocent and pure," at least for the duration of the Games. The homelessness problem was largely contained, and the *public* behavior of police and security personnel was for the most part acceptable, although behind closed doors it was often problematic, as the preceding discussion has shown. There were minimal confrontations between protesters and police, and the planned mass protests failed to attract large numbers after police divide-and-rule tactics exploited the rifts that already existed among left-wing activist groups. In short, the years of proactive work on the part of community organizations produced some tangible results, Olympic organizers and NSW police and government authorities managed to keep up appearances, and Sydney 2000 went down in history (or at least for the next four years) as the "best ever Olympics."

Conclusion

—⟨ℴℴℴ⟩—

In their analysis of the ways in which Olympic corporate sponsors socialized children to consume their brand and the "Olympic product," Schimmel and Chandler (1998, 12) suggested, "Perhaps the Olympics *are* more capable of naturalizing, even mystifying, capitalist relations than are other forms of collective consumption" (emphasis in original). An example from the University of NSW (UNSW) journal *Show Cause* will demonstrate how this message is readily absorbed by adults as well as children. Responding to an earlier article by Angela Burroughs (1999), a reader took issue with her characterization of the Olympics as "an Andrew Lloyd Webber style production." He went on to defend the "sheer joy" that nineteen billion viewers (allegedly) feel when they watch the Games: "The joy we feel is pure. It has nothing to do with politics or economics, but it does uplift the human spirit, and provides a rare shared experience with our fellow human beings no matter who or where they are" (Vaughan, 2000, 18).

These words perfectly capture the naturalizing and mystifying dimensions that the Olympic industry creates and exploits. The almost universal appeal of the Olympics cannot be denied, and this letter illustrates the human desire to suspend critical judgment in the face of an awe-inspiring spectacle. However, to liken the Olympics to a Broadway show, in Burroughs's apt analogy, was to suggest that "the (Olympic) emperor had no clothes"—and hence to tarnish the spectacle's transcendent image. Even independent media center activists in Sydney and Melbourne admitted the difficulties of being anti-Olympic; as Sydney IMC member Hugh Trevelyan explained, "Trying to be critical of sport, even if it's corporatized, was not a big popular issue—but it was enough to get us up and running. . . ." (Trevelyan quoted in Karvelas, 2001).

Just as Sydney 2000's public relations machine generated the amnesia and euphoria described in chapter 9, it also depoliticized an inherently political enterprise. In the real world—in the streets, low-income neighborhoods, homeless refuges, and Indigenous communities—there was indisputable evidence that the staging of the Olympics served the interest of global capitalism first and foremost while exacerbating existing social problems. From this perspective, the *best ever* label was clearly misplaced.

A NEW APPROACH TO EVALUATING THE GAMES

In March 1998, the Toronto Bread Not Circuses Coalition developed a set of guidelines titled "Towards a Socially Responsible Olympics Games." These provide a valuable and timely framework by which to evaluate the successes and failures of the so-called best ever Olympics. In the following discussion, these guidelines have been adapted to the Australian context.

Public Participation and Full Democratic Accountability

- Full public disclosure of all aspects of Olympic preparations
- Public meetings and consultations, and neighborhood meetings, particularly in areas near venues
- Intervenor funding to allow independent community groups to conduct their own social/environmental impact studies
- An ongoing independent watchdog to monitor all SOCOG/OCA activities of the organizing committee
- SOCOG and all other Olympic structures to be fully and democratically accountable to the residents and voters of Sydney and NSW

Some of the most serious shortcomings of Sydney 2000 were in the areas of public participation and democratic decision making. Transparency and accountability were lacking in virtually every aspect of Olympic organizing and preparations. The dual roles of Michael Knight as Olympic minister and head of SOCOG, together with the pressure on all parties in the NSW Parliament to work in a nonpartisan manner in order to fast-track Olympic decision making (particularly financial decisions), had the effect of disenfranchising NSW citizens, while their elected representatives, with very few exceptions, jumped on the Olympic bandwagon.

Financial Guarantees

- firm financial commitments from government and private sector
- all public funds to be recovered
- all direct and indirect costs to be fully and publicly accounted for
- independent financial assessment, including cost/benefit analysis

- no tax increases

- corporate sponsors to share the financial and social risks

- IOC and AOC to share financial risks

- functional rather than extravagant Games

In typical Olympic accounting style, significant indirect costs were not included in the Sydney 2000 budget, while indirect benefits were. There was minimal sharing of financial risks, except with taxpayers, whose contribution was about half of the total cost. And in the numerous budget blowouts in the lead-up to Sydney 2000, Olympic organizers made repeated demands on government for extra funding to put the "finishing touches" on the Olympic extravaganza.

Social Equity

- Olympic committees to be representative of the gender, racial, and crosscultural makeup of the city/state/country

- Olympic housing to be 100 percent affordable and 60 percent social housing

- rent protection

- housing for the homeless

- new and upgraded affordable recreational facilities

- affordable tickets to all events; free or low-cost tickets for low-income people

- full social impact assessment

- Olympic revenues to be put in a social investment fund, controlled by the community, for socially useful projects

- nonharassment measures for street homeless people

- measures to protect civil liberties, including freedom of peaceful assembly

Sydney 2000 organizers and the NSW government performed very poorly in virtually all of these areas, most notably in their failure to institute any form of rent control or to protect disadvantaged social groups: low-income tenants, boarders, and homeless people. The proposed social investment fund for local projects, which was suggested by social service leaders in Sydney, is unlikely to materialize in any Olympic host city in the near future.

Sexual Equality and Equal Opportunity

- sexual parity on all committees, staffing, and so forth
- correcting the gender imbalance in Olympic sports
- employment equity in hiring
- accessible Games

Olympic venues were accessible to people with disabilities. However, on the other equity issues, the glib labeling of the Sydney Olympics as the *Dames' Games* was not borne out at all levels. Women were underrepresented on most Olympic boards and committees, and the Olympic legacy did not include the free or affordable recreational facilities and programs that would have benefited low-income women, particularly sole-support mothers.

Environment

- full environmental assessment and strategies at bid stage
- detailed plans for air/water quality protection and improvement
- detailed waste disposal plans
- environmental assessment of traffic and transport plans
- green construction materials
- recycling/reusing strategies

There were many genuine successes in this area, but the ongoing problem of secrecy and lack of accountability regarding environmental issues on the part of Olympic organizers from the early days of the bid to the present remains a serious concern. The Bankstown cycling track, the Bondi Beach stadium, and the incomplete remediation of Homebush Bay constitute three major environmental failures.

Employment

- no job loss
- award wage policy
- no volunteers replacing paid workers
- no loss of volunteers to existing charities

With some exceptions, unionized workers succeeded in obtaining satisfactory industrial awards for Olympic work. However, benefits were not distributed equitably throughout the Olympic workforce, many jobs were short-term, job churning was in evidence, and the use of volunteers remained problematic.

Lasting Standards

- Olympic standards should be in effect throughout the bid, preparation, and staging of the Games.

- Financial, social, and environmental impact assessments should cover at least a five-year term from the end of the Games.

Throughout the 1990s, there was extensive evidence of secrecy and obfuscation on the part of Olympic and government officials. In the absence of thorough and accurate financial, social, and environmental impact assessments—and in the general euphoria surrounding the "best ever Olympics"—they are unlikely to engage in any serious post-Games initiatives that will benefit all NSW residents. Overall, as protesters claimed, the Sydney Olympics made the world safe for global capital, while the poor disproportionately bore the burden. This pattern will not change until the Olympic industry is dismantled, and international sporting practices are transformed.

Appendix

———*ᘏᘏᘏ*———

NOTES ON METHODOLOGY

As noted in the introduction, I was born and raised in Sydney, and remain Australian in terms of citizenship and identity; hence, I have both an "insider" and an "outsider" perspective on Australian social and political issues. Since 1990, I have visited Sydney at least once per year, including an eighteen-week stay during my 1996 study leave from the Ontario Institute for Studies in Education, University of Toronto, and a second of the same duration in 2000. In 1996, I had the status of visiting scholar at the Department of Adult and Language Education, the University of Technology Sydney (UTS) (Haymarket Campus) and in 2000, at the University of NSW Center for Olympic Studies (Cliffbrook Campus). Overall, I spent more than twenty months in Sydney in the period between 1990 and 2000.

As noted in the acknowledgments, Prof. Richard Cashman, head of the UNSW Center for Olympic Studies, and Anthony Hughes, its coordinator, were gracious hosts and supportive colleagues, and I am grateful for the numerous benefits that I received while I was a visiting scholar at the center. However, since I have already been criticized, both publicly and privately, for including critiques of UNSW and the Center for Olympic Studies in recent publications and presentations, I would like to reiterate here that my understanding of academic freedom does not preclude a critical examination of either one's home university or a university at which one has the status of visiting scholar (see chapter 6). In the UNSW case, both Richard Cashman and Anthony Hughes were very supportive of my work, which they clearly understood to be critical of the Olympic industry and its associated activities; indeed, they held the view that it was important for the center to promote a range of research perspectives, including critical ones such as mine.

In terms of consultation with other Australian academics who were teaching courses and/or conducting research on Olympic-related topics, I made contact by email, telephone or in person with approximately thirty colleagues at UTS, UNSW, the University of Sydney, and several other Australian universities, many of whom responded by meeting with me and/or sending published or unpublished papers, course outlines, and other relevant materials and information.

Data Collection

On annual visits between 1990 and 1996, I obtained materials from the Sydney bid committee office, compiled files of relevant newspaper clippings (primarily from the *Sydney Morning Herald*), and observed advertising campaigns promoting the bid and the preliminary Olympic preparations. Between 1997 and 2000, my annual trips also included tours around the Homebush Bay Olympic site and Visitor Center with my colleague Judi New, then with the Moore Park Trust, and a guided tour of Olympic environmental initiatives organized by the Royal Australian Institute of Parks and Recreation in April 1998. Thanks to UNSW professor Richard Cashman and UTS professor Kristine Toohey, I gained access to the Sydney Organizing Committee for the Olympic Games (SOCOG) library in 1998 and 1999, and to the libraries of the UNSW Center for Olympic Studies, UNSW, and UTS in 1999 and 2000. I also used public libraries in Sydney, including the NSW State Government reference library. Print materials collected on these visits were supplemented with information provided on government, university, and community organizations' web sites, and I monitored international newspapers, wire services, and radio and television transcripts through the Internet. As noted in chapter 1, the major newspaper on which I relied was the *Sydney Morning Herald*. <www.smh.com.au>. Because I live in Toronto, a city that has mounted two (unsuccessful) Olympic bid campaigns since 1989, I have included Toronto media coverage of Sydney's Olympic preparations and the Games, as well as coverage in other sources such as the *Guardian* (U.K.) and the *New York Times*.

Official Olympic sources that I consulted in the course of this research included the documents, reports, and communications provided by the IOC, the Sydney bid committee, SOCOG, OCA, and the NSW and Commonwealth governments, either in hardcopy or electronic versions; these institutions' websites have been providing comprehensive information on Sydney 2000 preparations for several years. Following the approach that I took for *Inside the Olympic Industry: Power, Politics, and Activism*, although I examined a wide range of official documentary sources generated by various Olympic organizations, I did not conduct consultations with individuals associated with them. In doing so, I made a deliberate decision to focus on the concerns of disadvantaged people whose voices might not otherwise be heard, rather than on Olympic industry personnel who had ready access to public relations machinery and the mainstream media. However, I did have informal discussions with some SOCOG and OCA members in the course of public presentations and similar contexts, and in May 2000 I attended an OCA meeting as an observer (see chapter 7).

In April and May 1999, I met with members of Greenpeace, Green Games Watch 2000, Rentwatchers, and Shelter NSW, and attended a meeting of the Non-government Task Force on the Homeless, in my capacity as a member of the Toronto Bread Not Circuses steering committee. Also in April, 1999, I participated in the Bondi Olympic Watch protest meeting, and had consultations with Darryl Luscombe (Greenpeace), Brett Hoare (GGW 2000), Will Roden and Rob Plant (Shelter NSW), Beth Jewell (Rentwatchers), Darren Godwell (Aboriginal activist, research fellow, Northern Territory University), and Murray Hogarth (then *Sydney Morning Herald* environment editor).

Between February and June, 2000, I met again with members of Greenpeace, GGW 2000, Rentwatchers, and Shelter NSW, and I became an active member of a new community organization called the "Olympic Impact Coalition" (OIC), which later became the Anti-Olympic Alliance (AOA). I served on the coalition's planning committee for a one-day strategy workshop held on May 14, at which I presented an overview of international Olympic resistance based on the research for *Inside the Olympic Industry*. I attended more than ten community meetings and seminars on Olympic social impacts, including those organized by the OIC, Socialist Alternatives, PISSOFF (People Ingeniously Subverting the Olympic Farce Forever), Youth Action Policy Association, Rentwatchers, Newtown Neighborhood Center, Politics in the Pub, and the University of Sydney Institute of Criminology.

In 2000, consultations were held again with Darren Godwell, Beth Jewell, and Rob Plant, as well as with the following community, student, and media representatives: Louise Boon Kuo, coordinator, University of Technology Sydney Community Law and Legal Research Center; Amanda Cornwall, senior policy officer, Public Interest Advocacy Center; Ryan Heath, president, and Vicki Sentas, research officer, University of Technology Sydney Students' Association; the Reverend Harry Herbert, executive director, NSW Uniting Church's Board for Social Responsibility; Lenny Kovner, Bondi Olympic Watch; Gary Moore, director, NSW Council for Social Services; Jenny Munro, chair, Metropolitan Aboriginal Lands Council; Blair Palese and Corrin Millais, Greenpeace Olympic campaign coordinators; Matthew Moore, *Sydney Morning Herald* Olympic editor; and Bob Symington, coordinator, Green Games Watch. I also had extensive e-mail communication with Ray Jackson, of the Indigenous Social Justice Association, and subscribed to the group's newsletter during 2000 and

2001. As is evident throughout the book, I have relied extensively on research reports and other publications generated by these community-based organizations, most notably Greenpeace, Green Games Watch 2000, Public Interest Advocacy Center (PIAC), Rentwatchers, Shelter NSW and UTS Community Law and Legal Research Center. Such sources should not be dismissed as "unscholarly"; many of the reports were prepared by researchers with significant scholarly credentials. There is, of course, one difference: Community-based participatory research makes its political stance explicit, while mainstream academic research, including Olympic research, rarely does.

Following my return to Toronto at the end of June, 2000, I maintained regular communication with Sydney-based activists and student and community organizations through e-mail, for purposes of fact-checking, obtaining recent reports, and requesting feedback on my preliminary analyses. For similar reasons, I joined the Olympic-link and the Sydney Independent Media Center e-mail lists, and I regularly monitored the relevant web sites, including those of the Sydney and Melbourne Independent Media Centres, the Anti-Olympic Alliance, Greenpeace, and Green Games Watch 2000.

In relation to items posted to independent media center sites, on the few occasions when a news story (as opposed to an opinion piece) seemed questionable, I cross-checked with other sources; for example, I e-mailed the Melbourne IMC to ascertain whether a video substantiating an account of alleged police violence in Sydney during the Olympics had ever been posted to the site; it had not, and so I did not cite the original story.

The cutoff point for data collection was February 2001. Hence, as noted in chapter 2, statements regarding international terrorism were accurate at the time of writing.

References

―――ぺ〜〜―――

Aboriginal Tent Embassy (2000a). Media release, *IMC* (July 25)
―――. (2000b). Media release, *IMC* (September 13).
Albany Consulting Group (1997). *Social Capital in the Olympic City.* Sydney: GGW2000.
Alcorn, G. (1999). Tickets fiasco just a "small scandal." *Herald* (December 17).
Alinsky, S. (1971). *Rules for Radicals.* New York: Vintage.
Allard, T. and Peatling, S. (2000). Jobless told to chase Olympic dole. *Herald* (July 18).
Allen, L. (1996). Fears for Olympic deadlines. *Weekend Australian,* July 13–14, 1996, p. 3 Business section.
An Australian Olympic flame (2000). Editorial. *Herald* (June 7).
Anderson, T. (2000). Presentation to seminar on Olympic legislation, Institute for Criminology, University of Sydney (June 13).
Anderson, T., Campbell, S., and Turner, S. (1999). *Youth Street Rights: A Policy and Legislation Review.* Sydney: UTS Community Law and Legal Research Center and the Youth Justice Coalition (March).
Andrews, D. (1998). Feminizing Olympic reality: preliminary dispatches from Baudrillard's Atlanta. *International Review for the Sociology of Sport* 33, 5–18.
Armstrong, S. (2000). Olympia's secret. *Chatelaine* (September), 85–92.
ASIO (2000). Annual Report to Parliament, 1999–2000.
A tale of two cities (1998). *Rentwatchers Report* 1:2, 4.
ATSIC (1995). Recognition Rights and Reform: Sport and recreation. <www.atsic.gov.au.library.recognit/45.htm>.
―――. (1999). ATSIC issues: mandatory sentencing.
―――. (2000). ATSIC issues: stolen generation.
Attorney General and Minister for Defence (2000). Media release (March 16). <www.minister.defence.gov.au/2000.05100.html>.
Auf der Maur, N. (1976). *The Billion-Dollar Games.* Toronto: Lorimer.
Australia's media giants (2000). (Table based on Productivity Commission, *Business Review Weekly*). *Green Left Weekly* (April 5), 16.
Australian Bureau of Statistics (2000). Olympic Games medal tally table.
Australian Federal Police (2000). Media release: Olympic planning.

Australian Greens (2000). Media release: New "When to Shoot to Kill" manual should be released—Brown (August 29).

Australian Institute of Health and Welfare (2000). *Australia's Health 2000*. Canberra: AIHW.

Australian Tourism Commission (2000). Tourism to capitalize on Olympics success. <www.atc.net.au/news/olympics/olympic2.htm>.

Bacon, W. (2000). Police equate silence with violence. *Herald* (March 4).

Baird, J. (2000). Basic skills test forces 200,000 students to play Games. *Herald* (August 3).

Baker, M. (2000). . . . Divided we'll fall. *IMC* (September 24).

Banham, C. (1999). Stopping the Olympic juggernaut. *City Hub* (May 6), 11.

Barkham, P. (2000a). Green light for a cleaner Olympics. *Guardian Weekly* (September 14–20), 25.

———. (2000b). Special report: the Sydney Olympics. *Guardian* (September 25).

Barrett, B. (2000). Beating up: a report on police batons and the news media at the World Economic Forum, September 2000. <www.vicnet.net.au/~gcforum/BarrettReport.htm>.

Beach volleyball row turns Coates (1999). *Herald* (April 30).

Beale, B (1996). Green groups lash non-solar Olympic design. *Herald* (May 10).

Beder, S. (1994). Sydney's toxic Green Olympics. *Current Affairs Bulletin* 70:6, 12–18.

———. (1999). Media self-censorship in Australia's Olympic bid. *PR Watch* 6:2, 7–8.

Bernoth, A. (2000). Inside Sydney's new global village. *Herald* (April 11).

Birch, T. (1992). "Nothing has changed": the making and unmaking of Koori culture. *Meanjin* 51:2, 229–246.

Bita, N. (2000). Games officials pay $5460 for a dorm. *Sun-Herald* (May 7).

Blunden, H. (2000). *The Impact of the Olympics on Housing in Sydney*. Draft report, Redfern Legal Center and Rentwatchers (October).

Boarding houses (1998). *Rentwatchers Report* #2 (December), 6–7.

Boccabella, D. (1999). Open letter from Ryde Pool Action Group to Peter Winkler, Bondi Olympic Watch (April 17).

Bondi brush-off (1999). *Herald* (April 9).

Bondi—latest victim (1999). *Bondi Guardian* 1 (April 18), 1.

Bondi residents object to Olympic volleyball stadium (1999). *ABC News* (May 14).

Boon-Kuo, L. (1998). Police powers and technology, and the Sydney 2000 Olympic Games. Research project, Faculty of Law, UTS (Autumn).

———. (2000). Presentation on Olympic legislation to Socialist Alternatives meeting, UNSW (March 1).

Booth, D. (2000a). Review of *Inside the Olympic Industry*. *Olympika* 9, 122–126.

———. (2000b). Gifts of corruption? ambiguities of obligation in the Olympic Movement. *Olympika* 9, 43–68.

Booth, D. and Tatz, C. (1994). Sydney 2000: the Games people play. *Current Affairs Bulletin* 70:7, 4–11.

Borcila, A. (2000). Nationalizing the Olympics around and away from "vulnerable" bodies of women. *Journal of Sport and Social Issues* 24:2, 118–147.

Bourne, V. (2000). Second Reading Speech, Defence Legislation Amendment (Aid to Civil Authorities) Bill (August 28).

Boycott threats will cause anger (1997). AP (November 15).

Boyle, P. (2000). Did the Olympics help reconciliation? *Green Left Weekly* (October 18)

Bread Not Circuses Coalition (1990). *The Anti-Bid Book*. Toronto.

————. (1998). *Towards a Socially Responsible Olympics Games:* The Bread Not Circuses Standards for the Toronto Olympic Bid (April 21).

Brennan, A. (2000). You scratch my back. *Vertigo* 8 (September), 9.

Brohm, J-M. (1978). *Sport: A Prison of Measured Time* (translated by I. Fraser). London: Ink Links.

Brown, M. (2000). Have a nice riot. *Herald* (May 27).

Bryson, B. (2000). Sydney: on top of the world down under. *National Geographic* (August), 7–25.

Bullimore, K. (2000). AOA and the Aboriginal Tent Embassy. *Olympic-link* (September 16).

Burning issue keeps Oils in the spotlight (2000). *Herald* (October 3).

Burroughs, A. (1999). The case against the Games. *Show Cause* (December), 16–18.

Burstyn, V. (1999). *The Rites of Men*. Toronto: University of Toronto Press.

Buzzacott, K. (2000). Statement to Australia and the world. *IMC* (September 29).

Byrne. A. (1996). Games vision "boring mediocrity." *Herald* (March 15).

Callan, P. (2000). G'day my little possums. *International Express* (August 22), 19–20.

Campbell, M. (2000). G'day world from Sydney. *Globe and Mail* (September 16), O3.

Carr, B. (1999). Letter to Keith Suter, International Commission of Jurists (November 30).

Cashman, G. and Cashman, R., eds. (2000). *Red, Black and Gold: Aboriginal People and the Olympics*. Sydney: Center for Olympic Studies, UNSW.

Cashman, R. and Hughes, A., eds. (1998). *The Green Games: A Golden Opportunity*. Sydney: Center for Olympic Studies, UNSW.

Cashman, R. and Hughes, A., eds. (1999). *Staging the Olympics*. Sydney: UNSW.

Cass, D. (2000). Olympics bring Third World wages to Sydney. *IMC* (September 1).

Caution: thieves at work (1999). *Bondi Guardian* 1 (April 18), 1.

Cernetig, M. (2000). Surfboard guerrillas fight Olympic hoopla. *Globe and Mail* (September 15), A1.

Chalip, L. (2000). Leveraging the Sydney Olympics for tourism. Autonomous University of Barcelona Center for Olympic Studies. <www.blues.uab.es/olympics.studies/papers/chalip00-3.html>.

Challenge for SOCOG (1999). Editorial. *Herald* (November 23).

Chomsky, N. (1989). *Necessary Illusions*. Toronto: CBC Massey Lectures.

Chubb Security (1999). Security Guidelines. In *Business as Usual*. Sydney: NSW Chamber of Commerce.

Cilauro, S., Gleisner, T, Kennedy, J., and Sitch, R. (1995). Preface. *Frontline: the story behind the story . . . behind the stories*. Sydney: Viking.

Clark, D. (2000). The Olympic foxtrot. *Djadi-Dugarang* 2:14 (October/November), 9–12.

Clark, P. (1996). A sign of the times that they won't let you see at the Atlanta Games. *Herald* (May 24).

———. (1999). Slippery Olympics: why we're in the dark. *Herald* (March 8).

Clayton Utz and Deloitte Touche Tohmatsu (1999). Independent Review of SOCOG's Ticketing Processes: an extract (November 22). <www.Herald. com.au/olympics/news/19991122/A58756–1999Nov22.html>.

Clennell, A. (1999). Second council "police force" hired. *Herald* (May 20).

———. (2000). Anarchist protest plan revealed. *Herald* (August 7).

Coady, T. (ed.) (1999). *Why Universities Matter*. Sydney: Allen and Unwin.

Cockburn, M. (2000). Sydney 2000 Olympic Games or media games? *Show Cause* (May), 20–21.

Cockerill, M. (1998). Volleyball wants more exposure. *Herald* (April 24).

Cohen, I. (2000). *Sydney Harbor Foreshore Authority Act*: Disallowance motion. *Hansard* (May 4).

Cole, C. and Hribar, A. (1995). Celebrity feminism: Nike style post-Fordism, transcendence, and consumer power. *Sociology of Sport Journal* 12, 347–369.

Connolly, E. (2000). Protest groups prepare to head for Sydney, via Melbourne and Seattle. *Herald* (July 31).

Connolly, E. and Kennedy, L. (2000). Real damage all part of fake attack. *Herald* (May 25).

Connolly, F. (2000). Sand storm. *Daily Telegraph* (May 8), 1, 4.

Connor, A. (2000a). Council's true colors. *IMC* (September 2).

———. (2000b). Nike too busy to discuss human rights. *IMC* (September 4).

Copwatch (1998). Capsicum spray—coming to a picket line, protest or prison near you! *Framed* 35, 9–13.

Corruption: join the yachts (2000). *Vertigo* 2 (April), 6.

Costello, L. and Dunn, K. (1993). Resident action groups in Sydney: people power or rat-bags? *Australian Geographer* 25:1, 61–76.

Coultan, M. and Evans, M. (1999). Olympic torch is not news: Knight. *Herald* (March 9).

Cox, G. (1998). Faster, higher, stronger... but what about our rights? *Impact Assessment and Project Appraisal* 16:3, 175–184.

———. (1999). *Ready... Set... Go... One Year to Go*. Sydney: Shelter NSW.

Cox, G., Darcy, M., and Bounds, M. (1994). *The Olympics and Housing*. Sydney: Shelter NSW.

Crackdown on jobless revealed (2000). *Herald* (June 28).

Crimes Legislation (Police and Public Safety) Act 1998.

Critical Mass Sydney (2000). Olympians join Harbor Bridge Bike Ride. *IMC* (September 28).

Crunch time for boarding houses (1999). *Rentwatchers Report #5* (December), 3–4.

Cuneen, C. (1999). *Zero Tolerance Policing: Implications for Indigenous People*. Research paper, ATSIC (February).

Darby, A. (1996). Hands up and be counted. *Herald* (July 18).

Darcy, D. and Mason, R. (2000). Police not so predacious. *IMC* (September 25).

Dates of dignity and despair (1996). *Herald* (July 17).

Davidson, B. (1999). Olympic opportunities for local communities. In R. Cashman and A. Hughes, eds., *Auburn Council: Home of the 2000 Olympics*. Sydney: UNSW Center for Olympic Studies, 16–19.

Defence Legislation Amendment (Aid to Civilian Authorities) Act 2000

deMause, N. (2000). Gold medals, iron fist. *Village Voice* (September 13–19).

Dennis, A. (1999). G'day sport. *Herald* (May 8).

———. (2000). How the world will view us. *Herald* (January 24).

Dennis, J. (1999). Graduates outraged. *Illawarra Mercury* (May 11).

Department of Foreign Affairs and Trade (1999a). Australia to launch virtual media center website (leaflet). Commonwealth Government Olympic press kit.

——— (1999b). Fact sheets on Indigenous Australians. <www.dfat.gov.au/aboriginal_facts/>.

Department of Housing encouraged public tenants to work at the Olympics (1999). *Rentwatchers Report #5*, 7.

Derwent, G. (2000). To serve and protect. *Vertigo* 8 (September), 28.

DiManno, R. (2000a). Aboriginals seek Games victories. *Toronto Star* (September 11).

———. (2000b). No medal for wild synchro routine. *Toronto Star* (September 26).

DiMarco, (2000). Letter to the editor. *University of Toronto Bulletin* (September 25).

Dixon, D., ed. (1999). *A Culture of Corruption*. Leichhardt NSW: Hawkins Press.

Djerrkura, G. (1999). Speech to UN Working Group on Indigenous Populations, Geneva (July 17). <www.atsic.gov.au//media/speeches_transcripts/display/asp?id=23>1.

Dodson, S. and Barkham, P. (2000). Protesters limber up for the Olympics: cyber threat to opening of Sydney Games. *Guardian* (July 19), 15.

Doherty, L. (2000). Retired police game for Games. *Herald* (June 7).

Dreher, T. (2000). Indigenous rights: which way forward now? *IMC* (September 22).

Dunn, K. (1999). Auburn under the Olympics: lesson from globalization. In R. Cashman and A. Hughes, eds., *Auburn Council: Home of the 2000 Olympics*. Sydney: UNSW, Center for Olympic Studies, 20–29.

Dunn, K. and McGuirk, P. (1999). Hallmark events. In R. Cashman and A. Hughes, eds., *Staging the Olympics*. Sydney: UNSW, 18–32.

Dusk and John (2000). Sit in solidarity with Prague. *IMC* (September 27).

Dwyer, C. (2000). Who ordered the baton charges? *IMC* (September 13).

Earth First! (2000). Media threatened over pictures of police assaulting Olympic torch bearers. AOA website (July 31). <www.cat.org.au/aoa/documents/earthfirst.html>.

Editorial (1993). *Reportage* (September), 3–4.

Editorial (1999). *Bondi Guardian* (April), 1.

Eitzen, D. S. (1996). Classism in sport: the powerless bear the burden. *Journal of Sport and Social Issues* 20:1, 95–105.

Encel, S. and Nelson, P. (1996). *Volunteering and Older People*. Sydney: Consultative Committee on Ageing.

Engel, M. (2000). Through a glass darkly in praise of Fatso the Wombat. *Guardian* (September 25).

Enker, D. (2000). Art imitates strife. *Herald* TV Guide (June 12–18), 4–5.

Evans, L. (1998). Sun, sex appeal and ticket sales. *Herald* (October 22).

———. (1999). Catching the Olympic wave. *Herald* (July 12).

———. (2000). Freeman runs into a sorry mess. *Herald* (June 22).

Evans, M. (1999a). 50 Greek nationals lend a hand. *Herald* (April 2).

———. (1999b). Outrage over Bondi stands. *Herald* (April 8).

———. (1999c). Top events, top prices. *Herald* (May 14).

———. (1999d). Volunteers offered training by TAFE. *Herald* (July 16).

———. (1999e). Beach stadium cut down to size. *Herald* (August 6).

———. (1999f). Ex-Olympians told not to scalp. *Herald* (October 20).

———. (2000a). Olympic club members disappointed by benefits. *Herald* (March 6).

———. (2000b). How the Olympic faithful were left with slim pickings. *Herald* (March 6).

———. (2000c). Ticket to Ryde worth it for water polo teams. *Herald* (April 28).

———. (2000d). Pier pressure for the Bondi diggers. *Herald* (May 23).

———. (2000e). Opportunity cost dogs organisers. *Herald* (June 27).

———. (2000f). Games media ban draws US fire. *Herald* (June 29).

Evans, M., Peatling, S., and Jacobsen, G. (2000). Confusion over Games ticket sales. *Herald* (April 15).

Fairwear (2000a). Fairwear. <www.vic.uca.org.au/fairwear/info/htm>.

———. (2000b). Fairwear Code of Practice. <www.vic.uca.org.au/fairwear/cop.htm>.

Foley, G. (1998). The power of whiteness. *Gary Foley's Koori History Website* <www.oliv.com.au/foley>.

———. (1999). Cathy and the Olympics. <www.oliv.com.au/foley.news/story3.html>.

Fraser, M. (1999). The body in question. In I. Coady, ed. *Why Universities Matter*. Sydney: Allen and Unwin, 235–249.

Freire, P. (1973). *Education for Critical Consciousness*. New York: Seabury.

Gallacher, M. (2000). *Olympic Arrangements Bill*, second reading, *Hansard* (April 14).

Games dollars blowin' in the wind (1996). *Herald* (March 29).

Games time (1999). Editorial, *Herald* (May 4).

Gargalianos, D. (1999). The "Professional Practice" subject in a post graduate sport management degree. UTS website <www.greeks-for-the-games.org>.

GGW2000 (1998a). Media release: Locals and Greens join to oppose park sale for Olympic water polo venue (April 23).

———. (1998b). Media release: McDonalds recalcitrance against spirit of Green Games (April 23).

———. (1998c). Media release: Global vs. local: local communities feel Olympic onslaught (April 27).

———. (1999). Media release: Green Games Watch 2000 called for Olympic dust/health link study (September 29).

———. (2000a). Media release: OCA starts new millennium by destroying western suburbs forest (January 27).

———. (2000b). Media release: Olympic watchdogs demand OCA come clean (March 2).

Gittens, R. (2000). Sporting policies set to mine gold. *Herald* (June 7).

Global Learning Resources (1998). List of corporate universities. <www.glresources.com>

Godwell, D. (1999a). Consultation re Aboriginal issues (April 26).

———. (1999b). Olympic branding of Aborigines: the 2000 Olympics and Australia's indigenous peoples. In K. Schaffer and S. Smith, eds. *The Olympics at the Millennium: Power, Politics and the Games*. New Brunswick, NJ: Rutgers University Press.

———. (1999c). Sporting symbolism on an international stage: the right to appeal to humanity. Unpublished paper, Sydney (September).

Gosper, K. with Korporaal, G. (2000). *An Olympic Life*. St. Leonards: Allen and Unwin.

Gould, K. (2000). Sydney man jailed for Olympic disinterest. *IMC* (September 14).

Government renews push for Olympic jobs (2000). *Herald* (August 3).

Goward, P. (2000). (Commonwealth spokesperson for the Sydney 2000 Games). Speech to the National Press Club, Canberra (April 12).

Gratton, M. and Jopson, D. (2000). Black fury explodes over stolen children. *Herald* (April 3).

Gratton, M., Jopson, D., and Metherell, M. (2000). Freeman reignites the anger. *Herald* (July 18).

Gratton, M., Metherell, M., and Seccombe, M. (2000). Black backlash grows. *Herald* (April 4).

Greenpeace (1999). *A Greenpeace Briefing on Refrigeration & Air Conditioning*. Sydney: Greenpeace Australia.

———. (2000a). *The Environmental Record of the OCA*. Greenpeace Olympics campaign briefing (February 16).

———. (2000b). *Green Olympics, Dirty Sponsors*. Sydney: Greenpeace Australia.

———. (2000c). Media release: Chromosomal damage in Homebush residents (August 1).

Greens bill defeated (1999). *Rentwatchers Report #5* (December), 5.

Greens want Bondi Olympic compo (1998). *ABC News (December 13)*.

Greiner, N. (1994). Inside running on Olympic bid. *Australian* (19 October).

Grennan, H. (2000). In the red. *Herald Domain* (February 24–March 1), 22.

Half a million to leave Sydney over Olympics (2000). *Herald* (July 25).

Hall, C. M. (1989). The politics of hallmark events. In G. Syme, B. Shaw, M. Fenton and W. Mueller, eds., *The Planning and Evaluation of Hallmark Events*. Brookfield, VT: Avebury, 219–241.

———. (1994). *Tourism and Politics*. New York: Wiley.

———. (1998). Imaging, tourism and sports event fever. Paper presented to the Sport in the City Conference, Sheffield (July 2–4).

Hall, R. (1998). *Black Armband Days*. Sydney: Vintage.

Ham, P. (2000). Trouble brewing: police fear a repeat of London's J18 riots could disrupt Olympic events. *Sunday Times* (London) (August 6).

Hanna, M. (1999). *Reconciliation in Olympism: Indigenous Culture in the Sydney Olympiad*. Sydney: Walla Walla Press.

Hansson, M. and Ans, K. (2000). Homelessness—greed and the Olympics. *Guardian* (Australia) (June 28).

Head, M. (2000). Olympic security. *Alternative Law Journal* 25:3 (June), 75–80.

Headon, D. (2000). Peaks, troughs and snouts: shades of the Olympic ideal. *Sporting Traditions* 16:2, 103–115.

Healy, S. (2000). Monopolizing the "marketplace of ideas." *Green Left Weekly* (April 5), 16–17.

Heath, R. (2000a). Presentation to Rentwatchers and Newtown Neighborhood Center meeting (March 29).

———. (2000b) Consultation re student housing, University of Technology Sydney (April 13).

Henderson, G. (2000). How far will Howard take the baton? *Herald* (October 3).

Henschke, R. (2000). Olympic impact. *Vertigo* 2 (April), 26.

Herbert, H. (1999). The homeless Olympics? In C. James, R. Plant, J. South, B. Beeston, and D. Long, eds., *Homelessness: The Unfinished Agenda*. Sydney: University of Sydney, 60–62.

———. (2000a). How well are we managing the social impacts of the Olympics? *NCOSS News* (February), 8–9.

———. (2000b). Consultation re social impacts of the Olympics (March 17).

———. (2000c). Presentation to workshop on Young People and the Olympics. Youth Action Policy Association (April 5).

Herman, D. and Chomsky, N. (1988). *Manufacturing Consent: The Political Economy of the Mass Media*. New York: Pantheon.

Hill and Knowlton (2000, September). World Economic Forum, Melbourne, Australia September 2000 "S11" Protest Brief. Melbourne: Hill and Knowlton. <crosswinds.net~leeked.hillandknowlton_s11.htm>.

Hill, K. (2000). Now that the flame has gone, will racial justice see the light? *Herald* (October 5).

Hill, K. and Morris, L. (2000). Word on the street: hide the homeless. *Herald* (August 30).

Hinds, R. (2000). We are still on the wrong side of the Olympic stick. *Herald* (June 10).

Hoare, B. (1999). Consultation re Bondi Olympic Watch (April 29).

Hogan, K. and Norton, K. (2000). The "price" of Olympic gold. *Journal of Science and Medicine in Sport* (June).

Hogarth, M. (1998). Media Panel. In Cashman, R. and Hughes, A., eds., *The Green Games: A Golden Opportunity*. Sydney: Center for Olympic Studies, UNSW, 101–102.

———. (1999). Consultation re Sydney 2000 and the environment (April 22).

Hollywell, N. (2000). Juicy Reclaim the Streets story. *IMC* (September 11).

Holmes, D. (1997). Conference report: Sporting Traditions 11 conference. *ASSH Bulletin* 27, 29–32.

Horan, M. (2000). Olympic tickets up and running. *Daily Telegraph* (May 7).

Hornery, A. (1999). Games warning over T-shirts. *Herald* (October 7).

How to reduce ticket trauma (1999). *Herald* (June 4).

Human Rights and Equal Opportunity Commission (1997). Aboriginal and Torres Strait Islander Social Justice. <www.hreoc.gov.au/social_justice.statistics/index.html>.

Humphries, D. (1996a). Public funds for Games up by $400m. *Herald* (May 21).
———. (1996b). Going down: Games costs. *Herald* (July 15).
Humphries, D. and Jacobsen, G. (1999). Knight keeps mum on "special deal" packages. *Herald* (October 20).
Humphrys, E. (2000). Letter from Elizabeth Humphrys, Education Research Officer, Students' Representative Council, University of Sydney, to Rentwatchers, Vicki Sentas (UTS), James Campbell, Brigid Boman, and SRC Executive Committee (April 6).
Hutcheon, S. (1996). China's drug record blasted. *Herald*. (May 18).
Hutton, D., ed. (1987). *Green Politics in Australia*. Sydney: Angus & Robertson.
Hutton, D. and Connors, L. (1999). *A History of the Australian Environment Movement*. Melbourne: Cambridge University Press.
Inclosed Lands Protection Act 1901.
Intoxicated Persons Act 2000 No. 34.
Intoxicated Persons Amendment Bill, Second Reading (August 6, 2000)
IOC (1997). *Olympic Charter* (September 3).
———. (2000a). Media release: IOC, USOC, and SLOC jointly file groundbreaking lawsuit against cybersquatters (July 13).
———. (2000b). Media release: Sydney Olympic Games projected to set global broadcast records. <www.olympic.org/ioc/e/news/pressreleases/press_311_e.html> (August 3).
It was politics, but some don't believe it was sporting (2000). *Herald* (October 3).
Jackson, K. (2000). We'll be back to Bondi, predicts volleyball chief. *Herald* (September 26).
Jackson, R. (2000a). SOCOG follies. *Djadi-Dugarang* 2:12 (May), 7–10.
———. (2000b). Letter to South Sydney Council (August 21).
———. (2000c). SOCOG follies part two. *Djadi-Dugarang* 2:13 (September), 1–3.
———. (2001). SOCOG 3: and you're out. *Djadi-Dugarang* 3:2 (April), 1–6.
Jacobsen, G. (1998). Uni volunteers pitch in. *Herald* (October 2).
———. (2000). Rural search for 1,000 security staff. *Herald* (May 15).
James, C., Plant, R., South, J., Beeston, B., and Long, D., eds. (1999), *Homelessness: The Unfinished Agenda*. Sydney: University of Sydney.
James, P. (1998). *State of the Olympic Catchment: An Environmental and Social Profile*. Sydney: Green Games Watch 2000 and NCOSS.
James, R. (2000). Diamonds in the rough: how a suburb won at Games. *Toronto Star* (September 27), B1.
Jamieson, T. (1999). Court blow to Olympic water polo plan. *Herald* (April 27).
Jefferson-Lenskyj, N. (2000). Letter to the editor. *NOW Magazine* (September 6).
Jenkins, P. (1996). The final test. *Weekend Australian* Olympic Guide (July 13–14), 6.
Jennings, A. (1996). *The New Lords of the Rings*. London: Simon & Shuster.
———. (2000). *The Great Olympic Swindle*. London: Simon & Shuster.
Jewell, B. (2000a). Presentation to Politics in the Pub, Gaelic Club, Surry Hills (June 2).
———. (2000b). Anti-Olympic International Community Forum, organized by Bread Not Circuses Coalition, Toronto (September 13).
Jocelyn (2000). Police stamp out protest negotiations. *IMC* (September 8).

Johnston, C. (1994). The pearl in the oyster: social impacts and Sydney's Olympics. Sydney: PIAC.

Jones, B. (1999). How academe has all but lost its voice. *Herald* (June 2).

Jones, C. (2000). Blue Rodeo performs while Oils protest. *NOW Magazine* (October 5–11).

Jopson, D. (1999). Aborigines to push Games of shame. *Herald* (August 9).

———. (2000a). Protesters told: say what you like, but don't say it on Olympic grounds. *Herald* (March 28).

———. (2000b). In harmony they lament: why is sorry so hard? *Herald* (May 27).

———. (2000c). Council pegs back Aboriginal tent embassy. *Herald* (July 26).

———. (2000d). Enough is enough. *Herald* (August 7).

Jopson, D. and Martin, L. (1999). Blacks put Games threat to UN. *Herald* (July 30).

Karvelas, P. (2001). Balancing act. *Australian* (January 4).

Keating, F. (2000). My armchair Olympics. *Tablet* (October 7), 1329.

Kennedy, L. and Connolly, E. (2000). Bins banned to foil Olympic bombers. *Herald* (February 10).

Kerr, J. (2000). McMeanies has SOCOG nod to pay workers less. *IMC* (July 29).

Kesterton, (2000). Olympics vignettes. *Globe and Mail* (September 18).

Keys Young (1995). Preliminary Social Impact Assessment of the Sydney 2000 Olympics and Paralympic Games (January).

Kidd, B. (1992). The Toronto Olympic commitment: towards a social contract for the Olympic Games. *Olympika* 1, 154–167.

———. (1994). Comments on "Swimming with the big boys?" *Sporting Traditions* 11:1, 25–30.

———. (2000). Letter to the editor. *University of Toronto Bulletin* (September 25).

King, M. (1998). Problems in reporting the build up to the Sydney 2000 Olympics. *Media Report,* ABC Radio National (April 23).

Klein, N. (2000). *No Logo.* Toronto: Knopf.

Knight, M. (2000). Introduction to second reading, *Olympic Arrangements Bill. Hansard* (April 5).

Knox, M. (2000). Bad sports—the winning losers. *Herald* (October 2).

Korporaal, G. (1996a). Spoils to the victor of the money games. *Herald* (March 23).

———. (1996b). AOC is the big winner. *Herald* (April 12).

———. (1996c). Games fund-raisers go for gold. *Herald* (April 20).

———. (1996d). State's stadium bill may be kept to $150m. *Herald* (July 18).

———. (1998). Knives out since 1992. *Herald* (November 25).

Korporaal, G. and Evans, M. (1999). IOC to study Murdoch's exclusive deal. *Herald* (March 10).

Korporaal, G. and Vass, N. (1996). Olympic spoils: Carr told to back off. *Herald* (March 21).

Kovner, L. (2000). Consultation re Bondi Olympic Watch (May 27).

Kuiper, G. (2000a). UnAustralian. *IMC* (September 14).

———. (2000b). Bigger than the Olympics. *IMC* (September 15).

Laanela, M. (1999). Bulldozed. *City Hub* (May 6), 12–15.

Lague, D. (2001). Revealed: top troops spied on Olympic crowds. Herald (February 8).

Latham, H. (2000). Sport vs. Bushland. *Green Games Watch 2000* 11 (Spring), 3–5.

Law Report (2000). Protesting Legalities. *ABC Radio National* (October 24).

Lenskyj, H. J. (1992). Good sports: Feminists organizing on sport issues in the 1970s and 1980s. *Resources for Feminist Research* 20(3), 130–136.

———. (1994). Girl friendly sport and female values. *Women in Sport and Physical Activity Journal,* 3(1), 35–46.

———. (1996). When winners are losers: Toronto and Sydney bids for the Summer Olympics. *Journal of Sport and Social Issues* 20:4, 392–410.

———. (1998). Inside sport or on the margins? Women in Australian sport media. *International Review for the Sociology of Sport* 33:1, 19–32.

———. (1999). Sydney 2000, Olympic sport and the Australian media. *Journal of Australian Studies 56.*

———. (2000). *Inside the Olympic Industry: Power, Politics, and Activism.* Albany: State University of New York Press.

Lenthen, G. (1998). Tourism demands counter attack. *Herald* (June 19).

Level 7 (2000). *Vertigo* 8 (September), 7.

Lewis, S. (2000). Brilliant. *IMC* (September 16).

Lewis tells Freeman to ignore boycott call (1997). *AP* (November 22).

LHMU. (1999). Press release: gold for Olympic workers (March 12).

———. (2000a). Press release: Accor hotels make "cheeky" Olympic offer (July 28).

———. (2000b). Press release: things go better with a $100 a day extra (August 7).

———. (2000c). Press release: Samaranch hotel uses Indonesian workers during Sydney Olympics (August 28).

Local knowledge (2000). *Herald* (April 11).

Love, R. (2000). President's monthly report, University of Toronto Faculty Association (August 4).

Lumby, C. (2000). The end is nigh, and other stories. *Bulletin* (February 22), 34–38.

Luscombe, D. (1999). Consultation re Greenpeace Australia (April 23).

Lye, J. (2000). The Olympics: where have all the boarding houses gone. *Alternative Law Journal* 25:1. <www.austlii.edu.au/au/journals/AltLJ/2000/1.html>.

MacAloon, J. (2001). IOC reform, then and now: an insider's view. Presentation to Faculty of Physical Education and Health, University of Toronto (February 5).

Macey, R. (1999). $58m to cater for media. *Herald* (February 13).

Mackinnon, J. (2000). The usual suspects. *This Magazine* (July/August), 27–29.

MacNeill, M. (2000). Contested nationalisms: Canadian athlete-media-sponsor relations and preparations for the Sydney Olympic Games. Paper presented to the Fifth International Symposium for Olympic Research, "Bridging Three Centuries: Intellectual Crossroads and the Modern Olympic Movement," Sydney (September 8–10).

Magdalinksi, T. (1999). The Olympics in the Next Millennium Conference: two views. *Australian Society for Sport History Bulletin* 31, 27–28.

Magdalinksi, T. and Nauright, J. (1998). Selling the "Spirit of the Dream": Olympologies and the corporate invasion of the classroom. Paper presented to the 11th Conference of the International Society for Comparative Physical Education and Sport, Leuven, Belgium (July).

Magnay, J. (1996a). Coaches challenge FINA. *Herald* (May 7).

———. (1996b). New Games track a blow for athletes. *Herald* (May 16).

———. (1996c). Move over Nicole. *Herald* (July 15).

———. (1996d). Nervous Riley finds press not too scary. *Herald* (July 15).

———. (1997). Sold, sold, sold! *Good Weekend* (June 21).

———. (1999). Big Brother will have his eye on the Games. *Herald* (July 30).

Magnay, J. and Blake, M. (1996). Team warned on talking. *Herald* (July 18).

Magnay, J. and Evans, M. (1999). But wait, there's more. *Herald* (October 26).

———. (2000). Olympic ticketing budget in trouble. *Herald* (June 16).

Magnay, J. and Ho, C. (2000). It's bulldozers versus the beach battalion. *Herald* (March 28).

Magnay, J. and Hornery, A. (2000). Nike's "sorry" ad labeled offensive. *Herald* (June 21).

Magnay, J. and Moore, M. (1999). Murdoch gives the order on Olympics. *Herald* (May 3).

Maguire, A. (2000). A word from our sponsors. *Vertigo* 8 (September), 31.

Make Syd-e-nee a winner (2000). *Herald* TV Guide (June 12–18), 5.

Manne, R. (2000a). Bitter Olympic ironies. *Age* (September 18).

———. (2000b). Cultural cringe pushed to the fringe. *Herald* (October 2).

Marr, D. (2000). A walk across Black Australia. *Herald* (May 27).

Martin, C. (2000). $720,000 rent for city unit during Olympics. *Sun-Herald* (May 14).

Martin, L. (1999). Australia faces UN race inquiry over Wik laws. Herald (August 18).

McDougall, B. (1999). Residents to disrupt Bondi Olympic site. *Daily Telegraph* (April 19).

McGeoch, R. with Korporaal, G. (1994). *The Bid*. Melbourne: Heinemann.

McGillion, C. (2000). The brightest torch. *Tablet* (October 7), 1328–1329.

McGuire, R. (2000). Making the most of the Games. *Uniken* (May), 2.

McKay, J. (1995). 'Just do it': corporate sports slogans and the political economy of 'enlightened racism'. *Discourse* 16, 191–201.

McKay, J, Hutchins, B., and Mikosza, J. (2000). 'Shame and scandal in the family': Australian media narratives of the IOC/SOCOG scandal matrix. Keynote address, Fifth International Symposium for Olympic Research, "Bridging Three Centuries: Intellectual Crossroads and the Modern Olympic Movement," Sydney (September 8–10).

McLoughlin, T. (1999). Speech to Waverley Council (September 21). <www.voyeurmagic.com.au/olympic1.htm>.

Media, Entertainment and Arts Alliance (2000). Australian Journalists' Association Code of Ethics. <www.alliance.org.au/hot.ethicscode.htm>.

Metherill, M. (2000a). Indigenous health a century behind. *Herald* (June 23).

———. (2000b). Post-Games land rights collision. *Herald* (October 3).

Millais, C. and Palese, B. (2000). Consultation re environmental issues (April 18).

Miranda, C. (1999). The criminal-free Olympics. *Daily Telegraph* (June 18).

Mitchell, B. (1997). Jail deaths must end, warn black leaders. *Age* (February 18).

Molloy, F. (2000). Homeless kicked out to make Games pretty. *Vertigo* 8 (September), 28.

Moore, G. (2000a). Consultation re social impacts of the Olympics (March 14).

———. (2000b). Presentation to Rentwatchers and Newtown Neighborhood Center meeting (March 29).

————. (2000c). Presentation to workshop on Young People and the Olympics. Youth Action Policy Association (April 5).

————. (2000d). Letter to inaugural meeting of Anti-Olympic Alliance (May 14).

Moore, J. (2000). Letter from Minister for Defence re Defence Legislation Amendment (October 31).

Moore, M. (1997). Benighted minister faces Rentwatchers and wins embrace. *Herald* (November 15).

————. (1998a). Problems in reporting the build up to the Sydney 2000 Olympics. *The Media Report,* ABC Radio National (April 23).

————. (1998b). The secret Games. *Herald* (November 21).

————. (1999a). Games secrecy excessive, says auditor. *Herald* (January 15).

————. (1999b). Life's a beach. *Herald* (April 20).

————. (1999c). Bondi Beach may lose volleyball. *Herald* (April 26).

————. (1999d). SOCOG offers packages to select few. *Herald* (May 4).

————. (1999e). Official advice on cheap tickets squeezes out poor. *Herald* (June 3).

————. (1999f). Games tickets out of reach of majority. *Herald* (June 8).

————. (1999g). SOCOG refuses to open its deliberations to the public. *Herald* (October 22).

————. (1999h). Olympics and the print media. *Sports Factor,* ABC Radio National (November 16).

————. (2000a). When push comes to shove, it's news that is the priority. *Herald* (February 29).

————. (2000b). Mandarins call for public servants to start serving the Games. *Herald* (March 14).

————. (2000c). Princely price of breakfast at Kings. *Herald* (April 1).

————. (2000d). Consultation re mass media (May 16).

————. (2000e). SOCOG offers more incentives to reassure jittery volunteers. *Herald* (August 10).

————. (2000f). Magic words bring the house down: best ever. *Herald* (October 2).

————. (2001). Boost for ailing Games sites. *Herald* (May 30).

Moore, M. and Evans, M. (2000). Social advisor blasts SOCOG on tickets. *Herald* (February 7).

Moore, M. and AAP (1999). Revealed: rich-list Olympics. *Herald* (October 16).

Moore, M. and Aylmer, S. (1998). Members wanted. *Herald* (May 8).

Moore, M. and Korporaal, G. (1999). Mayor changes tune on volleyball. *Herald* (April 29).

Moore, M. and Magnay, J. (1999). Fans are back in the running. *Herald* (November 12).

Morris, L. (2000a). Hospitality hordes on the march to feed and house visitors. *Herald* (April 24).

————. (2000b). Public servants answer the call. *Herald* (April 24).

————. (2000c). Crisis for tenants as boarding houses shut down. *Herald* (June 20).

————. (2000d). Now rent rises hit the more affluent. *Herald* (June 24).

Morris, L. and Dent, J. (1999). Bondi may seek volleyball deal. *Herald* (April 27).

Munro, J. (2000). Consultation re Indigenous issues and protests (May 26).

Nash, C. (2000). Paying the price. *Introduction to Housing Crisis in Olympic City.* Sydney: Australian Center for Independent Journalism. <www/138.25.138.13. journalism/reportage/features/Homelessness/paying.html>.

NCOSS (1998a). Media release: Crunch time for Olympics low income tickets (June 24).

———. (1998b). Media release: Olympic ticket policy: fair, but not fair enough (August 26).

———. (1998c). Media release: Will the Olympic volunteer policy pass the acid test? (October 7).

Negus, G. (2000). Two messages for the world. *Herald* (October 13).

Newington News (Autumn 1999). (Mirvac/Lend Lease promotional material).

Nike (n.d. 1992?). *Nike Code of Conduct.*

Niland, J. (1998). The challenge of building world class universities in the Asian region. Public lecture to the National University of Singapore (June 25). <www.vc.unsw.edu.au/Speeches/98_2506_singapore.shtml>.

———. (2000). Message from the Vice-Chancellor. *Olympic Impact* 2 (March), 2.

Nile, F. (2000). *Olympic Arrangements Bill,* second reading. *Hansard* (April 12).

Nimbyism (1999). Editorial. *Herald* (April 9).

Nixon, S. (2000). Volunteering has a new appeal. *Herald* (October 5).

No fans here (2000). *Toronto Star* (September 8).

North, S. (1993a). Aid for African athletes may help Olympic bid. *Herald* (August 25).

———. (1993b). Olympic support hits record high. *Herald* (September 10)

———. (1993c). Sydney's odds on, and deservedly so. *Herald* (June 23).

Nougher, R. (1999). The politics of the Olympics. *University of Sydney News* (September 23).

O'Gorman, K. (2000). Speech at "No Olympic Police State" Rally, Sydney Town Hall (June 10).

Olds, K. (1998). Urban mega-events, eviction, and housing rights: the Canadian case. Unpublished paper, Department of Geography, University of Singapore.

Olympic Arrangements Bill, Second Reading (April 12, 2000).

Olympic Coordination Authority (1999). Waverley New Update (April).

———. (2000). Update on treatment of chemical waste. *Parramatta Advertiser* (May 3).

Olympic Coordination Authority Staff (State) Consolidated Award 1997.

Olympic Countdown: 100 Days to Go (2000). *Herald* supplement to *USA Today* (June 7).

Olympic Security Command Center (2000). *Police Olympic Games Handbook.* Sydney: NSW Police Service.

Olympics, developers win gold (1998). *Guardian* (Sydney) (June 24).

Only dealing in fax (2000). *Herald* (May 9).

Oquist, B. (2000). "Environment theme day" hit by protests. *SAMC* (September 16).

O'Rourke, J. (2000). Five secrets of our Games. *Herald* (April 13).

Ozone Showdown (1999). *Greenpeace Olympic Report* 15 (May 4), 1–2.

Pannu, R., Schugurensky, D., and Plumb, D. (1994). From the autonomous to the reactive university. In L. Erwin and D. MacLennan, eds. *Sociology of Education in Canada.* Toronto: Copp Clark Longman, 499–526.

Parker, J. (2000). Presentation to Politics in the Pub, Gaelic Club, Sydney (June 2).

Patience, A. (1999/2000). Silencing the academy? Reflecting on a dispute in a corporatizing university. *Australian Universities Review* 42/43, 64–71.

Pearce, P. (1998a). Media release, Mayor's office (April 22).

———. (1998b). Olympic update: report to Waverley Council (October 27).

———. (1999a). Mayor's column, Waverley Council (February 24).

———. (1999b). No nimbyism. Letter to the Editor. *Herald* (April 16).

———. (1999c). Public meeting, Bondi Pavilion (April 18).

———. (1999d). Media release, Mayor's office (April 20).

———. (1999e). Media release, Mayor's office (May 11).

———. (1999f). Mayor's column, Waverley Council (May 19).

———. (2000). Media release, Mayor's office (May 19).

Peatling, S. (2000a). Freedom of information. *Herald* (March 28).

———. (2000b). Visa stripped of its grip on Games tickets. *Herald* (April 13).

———. (2000c). Sand flies as protesters dig in for Olympic stand-off. *Herald* (May 5).

Performance Audit Review: The Sydney 2000 Olympics and Paralympic Games (1999). <www.audit.nsw.gov.au/olympics99/>.

Phibbs, P. (1999). The impact of an urban Olympic Games on the private rental market. Paper presented at the 41st ACSP Conference, Chicago (October).

———. (2000). The impact of an urban Olympic Games on the private rental market, Part 2. Unpublished paper, Urban and Regional Planning Program, University of Sydney.

Pilger, J. (1999). *Welcome to Australia.* <www.carlton.co.uk/data/pilger>.

Plant, R. and Roden, W. (1999). Consultation re Shelter NSW (April 22).

Politics and the Olympics (1998). Editorial. *Herald* (April 24).

Porter, M. (1999). Playing Games at our cost. *Daily Telegraph* (May 12).

Potter, B. (2000). Instant anarchy. *Australian Financial Review* (August 29).

Poynting, S. (2000). Ethnicizing criminality and criminalizing ethnicity. In J. Collins and S. Poynting, eds., *The Other Sydney: Communities, Identities, and Inequalities in Western Sydney.* Melbourne: Common Ground Publishing, 63–78.

Pratt, G. and Poole, D. (1999/2000). Global corporations "R" us? the impacts of globalization on Australian universities. *Australian Universities Review* 42/43, 16–23.

Predator (2000). Homelessness: another fine product of the adversarial legal system. *IMC* (September 10).

Protesters greet torch with jeers and fruit throwing (2000). *Herald* (September 14).

Protesters shake Olympic celebrations (1999). *Tenant News* 65 (December), 3.

Public Interest Advocacy Center (1994). Sydney 2000: "The Human Rights Games." Submission to NSW government preliminary social impact assessment (October 17).

———. (2000a). Olympics liberty and security issues: a briefing paper (February).

———. (2000b). Liberty in the Olympic City: A briefing paper (August).

Public Service Association (2000). School staff ban Olympic ticketing (March 27).

Quinlan, H. (1999a). Funding beaches' "gender-perfect" sport. *Herald* (January 8).

———. (1999b). Bondi ban wipes out medal hopes. *Herald* (May 8).

———. (1999c). Tourists spiked by Bondi ban. *Herald* (November 25).

Ranald, P. (2000). Olympics: Sydneysiders told to "change habits." *Green Left Weekly* (May 10), 7.

"Ratbags" could cause a backlash (2000). *Sun-Herald* (February 13).

Ray White Real Estate (1999). Ray White Residential Accommodation Program—Home owners. <www.raywhite.com.au/olympics/owners/>.

Real Estate Institute of NSW (1999). Residential prices are likely to keep rising. *Herald* (January 9).

Rentwatchers (2000). *We Can't Share the Spirit if We Can't Afford the Rent: Rentwatchers Information Kit.* Sydney: Rentwatchers.

Rentwatchers Report #1 (1998).

Rhiannon, L. (2000a). *Olympic Arrangements Bill,* second reading. *Hansard* (April 14).

———. (2000b). S11 and the World Economic Forum. *Earthbeat,* ABC Radio National (September 2).

Ridgway, A. (2000). Aboriginal deaths in custody: a matter of public interest. *Djadi-Dugarang* 2:14 (October/November), 3–6.

Risky routine gets noticed (2000). *CBC Sport Online* (September 26).

Ritchie, B. and Hall, C.M. (2000). Mega Events and Human Rights. Unpublished paper, University of Canberra and University of Otago.

Roach, N. (2000). Reconciliation is a race all Australians must run. *Herald* (October 2).

Roberts, R. (1999). Foreword to M. Hanna, *Reconciliation in Olympism.* Sydney: Walla Walla Press, 9–14.

Robinson, M. (2000). US athlete condemns Nike. *SAMC* (August 31).

Roden, W. and Plant, R. (1998). *The Homeless Olympics?* Sydney: Shelter NSW (June).

Rowe, D. and Lawrence, G. (1986). Saluting the state: nationalism and the Olympics. In D. Rowe and G. Lawrence, eds., *Power Play.* Sydney: Hale and Ironmonger.

Russell, S. (1994). The Sydney 2000 Olympics and the game of political repression: an insider's account. *Canadian Law and Society Association Bulletin* 18, (Fall), 9–12.

———. (1996). IOC creates specter of "terrorism" at Olympics. *Green Left Weekly* (October 30), 14.

Rutheiser, D. (1996). *Imagineering Atlanta.* New York: Verso.

Ryde Pool Action Group Inc. vs. Ryde City Council (1999). NSW Land and Environment Court (April 22). <www.austlii.edu.au.au.cases/nsw/NSWLEC/1999.96.html>.

Ryle, G. and Hughes, G. (1999). Breaking China: how Sydney stole the Games. *Herald* (March 6).

Sadleir, D. (1996). The role of intelligence. In A. Thompson, ed., *Terrorism and the 2000 Olympics.* Canberra ACT: Australian Defence Studies Center, 113–119.

Sage, G. (1999). Justice do it! The Nike transnational advocacy network: organization, collective actions, and outcomes. *Sociology of Sport Journal* 16, 206–235.

Schafer, S. (2000). Coca-Cola pays $192m to settle black workers' lawsuit. *Guardian Weekly* (November 23–29), 32.

Schimmel, K. and Chandler, T. (1998). Olympism in the classroom: partnership-sponsored education materials and the shaping of the school curriculum. Paper presented to the Eleventh Conference of the International Society for Comparative Physical Education and Sport. Leuven, Belgium (July).

Schmetzer, U. (2000). World Trade targeted down under. *Chicago Tribune* (September 13).

Scully, J. (2000). SOCOG steals students beds. *Vertigo* 8 (September), 32.

Senate Legal and Constitutional References Committee (1995). *Cashing in on the Sydney Olympics: Protecting the Sydney Olympic Games from Ambush Marketing.* Canberra ACT: (March).

Sentas, V. (1998). NSW: Police state 2000. *Framed* 35 (June), 1–5 <www. justiceaction . . . au/Framed/Iss31_40/Frmd_35/Fr25_Txt1.html>.

———. (2000). Jobless harassment. *Olympic-link* (June 28).

Sharma, S. and O'Brien, E. (2000). Slave labor! SOCOG revs up the recruitment drive. *Vertigo* 8 (September), 14.

Shaw, J. (2000). *Intoxicated Persons Amendment Bill,* second reading. *Hansard* (August 6).

Short, A. and Cowell, P. (1999, April 19). *Impact of Bondi Beach Olympic Beach Volleyball Stadium.* Coastal Studies Unit, University of Sydney. <www.waverley. nsw.gov.au/info/olympic/usyd/summary.htm>.

Short, K. (1996). *Management of Contaminated Sites for the Sydney Olympics 2000.* Prepared for Green Games Watch 2000, 1996.

Simson, V. and Jennings A. (1992). *The Lord of the Rings.* Toronto: Stoddart.

Sinclair, J. (2000). More than an old flame: national symbolism and the media in the torch relay ceremony of the Olympics. *Media International Australia* 97 (November), 35–46.

Skive (2000). S26 victory at Broadway squats. *IMC* (September 26).

Smith, C. (2001). Toronto is blunting its creative edge. *Star* (January 27).

Smith, P. (1996). This time, Capo, you weep alone. *Herald* (July 17).

So this is Australia? (2000). *Real Games.* <www.realgames.org/>.

SOCOG: time for an inquiry (1999). Editorial. *Herald* (November 26)

———. (1999a). Media Volunteer Program: Sydney 2000 Olympic Games.

———. (1999b). Media release: Games organizers praised for employees' award (January 29).

———. (1999c). Media release: SOCOG Board approves release of the host city contract. (February 10).

Sometimes all that glistens isn't Olympic gold (2000). *Herald* (October 4).

South Sydney Council vs. Coe (2000). NSW Land and Environment Court (August 17). <www.austlii.edu.au.au.cases/nsw/NSWLEC/2000.186.html>

Squatters living free and easy on Broadway (2000). *Daily Telegraph* (October 17).

State Environmental Planning Policy No. 10: Retention of Low-Cost Rental Accommodation (January 2000).

State Environment Planning Policy No. 38: Olympic Games and Related Projects 1995.

Sullivan, Gavin (2000). Sharing the spirit. *Realgames* website. <www.realgames.org/newsmedia/st_0003_share_spirit.html>.

Susskind, A. (1996a). Architects strike gold—by design. *Herald* (March 15).

———. (1996b). Olympic designs "limited by price." *Herald* (April 1).

Sydney Harbor Foreshore Authority Regulation (1999).

Sydney Housing Action Collective (2000a). *SHAC Handbook.* <www.squat.net/shac>.

———. (2000b). Sample letter. <www.squat.net/shac>.

Sydney IMC—about us (2000). *IMC* home page.

Sydney Olympic and Paralympic Games 2000 (State) Award (1999).

Sydney Olympics 2000 Bid Committee Ltd. (1992). *Fact Sheets* (June 24).

Sykes, R. (1989). *Black Majority.* Hawthorn, VIC: Hudson.

Symington, B.(2000). Protesters warned against camping on Bressington or Mason Parks. *IMC* (September 15).

Szentkuti, N. (2000). Peace Walk update. <www.lakeeyre.green.net.au/camped-botany-bay-2.html>.

Tatz, C. (1995a). The dark side of Australian sport. *Inside Sport* (March), 19–24.

———. (1995b). *The Obstacle Race.* Sydney: UNSW Press.

Tatz, C. and Booth, D. (1994) "Swimming with the big boys?": the politics of Sydney's 2000 Olympic bid. *Sporting Traditions* 11:1, 3–23.

Taylor, J. (2000). Grand stand. *Herald* Domain (April 8).

Teenager tries to steal torch. *Globe and Mail* (August 26).

Temple, W. (2000). Confessions of an Olympic "ratbag." *Daily Telegraph* (March 28).

Testing (1996). Editorial. *Herald* (July 18).

The factions (1999). *Herald* (August 9).

The Games (1998). (ABC television series).

The media and the Olympic Bid (1993). Editorial. *Herald* (July 15).

The other Australia (2000). Editorial. *New York Times* (September 17).

Things go better with $100 a day extra. *Miscellaneous Workers Union News* (August 28). <www.lhmu.org.au/union/193.html>.

Thompson, A., ed. (1996). *Terrorism and the 2000 Olympics.* Canberra: Australian Defence Studies Center.

———. (1997). Dangerous Games: terrorism and the 2000 Olympics. *ABC National* (June 1).

Thorne, R. and Munro-Clark, M. (1989). Hallmark events as an excuse for autocracy in urban planning: a case study. In G. Syme, B. Shaw, M. Fenton, and W. Mueller, eds., *The Planning and Evaluation of Hallmark Events.* Brookfield, VT: Avebury, 154–171.

Throwing sand in our faces (1999). Editorial. *Daily Telegraph* (April 19).

Time/CBC Viewer's Guide (2000). *Toronto Star* advertising feature (September 9).

To the rich, the Olympic race (2000). *Economist* (September 23), 92.

Tonkin, L. (2000). Presentation to Public Forum on the Social Impact of the Olympic Games on Young People, Surry Hills (April 5).

Turner, G. and Cunningham, S. (1997). *The Media in Australia Today.* Sydney: Allen and Unwin.

Turner, M. (1996). Atlanta's team goes for broke. *Herald* (March 23).

21 arrested at Bondi (2000). *Eastern Suburbs Messenger* (May 11), 9.

2000 Games Media Unit (2000). Media release: The Australian Government and the Sydney 2000 Games.

Uni's suite deal (1999). *Daily Telegraph* (May 12).

Unolympics.com (2000). IOC backs away from legal action. *IMC* (September 29).

UNSW (1998). Media release: Olympian and tv network join UNSW Olympic Studies Center (August 28).

———. (1999). Media release: UNSW's corporate suite an investment (May 12).

UNSW Branch, National Tertiary Education Union (1999). Minutes of meetings (May 26). <www.nteu.org.au/unsw/index.html>.

UNSW Center for Olympic Studies (1999). Annual Report.

UTS Community Law and Research Center and Youth Justice Coalition (1998). *Youth Street Rights* (pamphlet).

———. (2000). *Activists' Rights Guide* (pamphlet). <www.cat.org.au.our-rights>.

UTS Olympic Projects (2000). <www.uts.edu.au/oth/olympic.projects.html>.

UTS Students' Association (2000). How they're sharing the spirit in three easy steps (2000). *Orientation Handbook,* 38–39.

Vass, N. (1995). Privacy fear on Games crime check. *Herald* (July 29), 11.

Vaughan, G. (2000). Olympic joy. *Show Cause* (May), 18.

Verco, N. (2000). Letter from Natasha Verco, SRC President, University of Sydney, to Professor Gavin Brown, Vice-Chancellor (May 4).

Verghis, S. (1999). 1,000 angry voices cry foul over Bondi. *Herald* (June 21).

Vincent, P. (2000). Games plan. *Herald* (March 4).

Vinson, T. (2000). *Counting the Street Homeless.* Sydney: Shelter NSW.

Wade, (1999). "We're staying": Bondi battlers for tenancy justice. *Rentwatchers Report* #4 (September), 2.

Wainwright, R. (1999). Station rethink to delay Bondi trains. *Herald* (April 20).

Wamsley, K. and Heine, M. (1996). Tradition, modernity, and the construction of civic identity: the Calgary Olympics. *Olympika* 5, 81–91.

Warren, N. (2000). Presentation to Rentwatchers and Newtown Neighborhood meeting (March 29).

Waverley Council Master Agreement (2000). OCA and Waverley Council (May 11)

Wells, J. (1996). Capo falls to the white man's burden. *Herald* (July 7).

What price gold? (2000). *The Sports Factor,* ABC Radio National (June 2).

Whiddett, A. (1996). Terrorism and 2000 Olympics. In Thompson, A., ed., *Terrorism and the 2000 Olympics.* Canberra: Australian Defence Studies Center, 103–112.

Whitson, D. and Macintosh, D. (1996). The global circus: international sport, tourism, and the marketing of cities. *Journal of Sport and Social Issues* 23, 278–295.

Wilkinson, J. (1999). Bondi a "unique" Games venue. *Southern Courier* (April 13).

Wong, P. (2000). *Olympic Arrangements Bill,* second reading. *Hansard* (April 12).

Woolsey, G. (2000). IOC pulling the plug on website messages. *Toronto Star* (August 31).

Work the Dream (2000). Official guide to Games jobs. *Sun-Herald* (March 12).

Wright, G. (1996). Mix-up hits private sector involvement. *Herald* (May 24).

WYkanak, D. (2000). Letter to Mary Robinson, United Nations High Commissioner for Human Rights (June 2).

WYkanak vs. OCA (2000). Land and Environment Court.

Young, C. (2000). Summer Games so far: no worries mate. *Toronto Star* (September 22).

Young, K. (2000). Why I'm not game for the Olympics. *Vancouver Sun* (September 28).

Young, P. (2000a). Greenpeace downgrades Olympic record. *Globe and Mail* (August 19) S1, S12.

———. (2000b). Eric the Eel, the splash of Sydney. *Globe and Mail* (September 29), 7.

Index

⟞⟨ଓ/ଓ/ଓ⟩⟝